Windows® 8 Five Minutes at a Time

Lance Whitney

WILEY

John Wiley & Sons, Inc.

Windows® 8 Five Minutes at a Time

Published by
John Wiley & Sons, Inc.
10475 Crosspoint Blvd.
Indianapolis, IN 46256
www.wiley.com

WILEY

Credits

Acquisitions Editor
Aaron Black

Project Editor
Kristin Vorce

Technical Editor
Vince Averello

Senior Copy Editor
Kim Heusel

Editorial Director
Robyn Siesky

Business Manager
Amy Knies

Senior Marketing Manager
Sandy Smith

Vice President and Executive Group Publisher
Richard Swadley

Vice President and Executive Publisher
Barry Pruett

Project Coordinator
Patrick Redmond

Graphics and Production Specialists
Jennifer Henry
Jennifer Mayberry

Quality Control Technician
Lauren Mandelbaum

Proofreading and Indexing
Wordsmith Editorial
Estalita Slivoskey

About the Author

Lance Whitney is a freelance writer and reporter in the New York City area. For the past 20 years, he has written articles, columns, and reviews for a variety of technology publications and websites. He currently freelances for CNET as a news and technology reporter and writes a monthly utility column for *Microsoft TechNet* magazine.

Throughout his varied career, Lance has worked as a writer and editor in advertising, marketing, and publishing. He also spent ten years in the IT department at an international company where he handled everything from local technical support to global software projects.

He and his wife share their home with two cats — Mr. Putter and Miss Kitty — both of whom insisted on appearing in this book.

You can follow Lance on Twitter at @lancewhit.

Acknowledgments

I would like to thank my acquisitions editor at Wiley, Aaron Black, for giving me the assignment to write this book and having faith in this first-time book author. I'd also like to thank my project editor, Kristin Vorce, for guiding me through the process whenever I had questions or concerns. And I'd like to thank my technical editor, Vince Averello, for the many hours he put in testing all of the tasks and steps detailed here.

To my wife Cely and to my parents.

Table of Contents

Beat the Clock 228

Introduction

Windows 8 represents the most radical change to Microsoft's operating system since Windows 95 was released 17 years ago. With its new Start screen and interface, the latest version of Windows is an attempt to create a single operating system designed to run on both traditional PCs and tablets.

But no one likes change. People used to the familiar Start menu and features of Windows 7, Vista, and XP may find Windows 8 challenging and frustrating, at least until they learn all the tips and tricks for navigating and using the new operating system.

This book is designed to share many of those tips and tricks so that you can move beyond the challenges and frustrations to take full advantage of the new flavor of Windows.

People new to Windows 8 should find this book helpful, though it's also geared toward those who've already dabbled with the new version. Even users who have been working and playing with Windows 8 might still find themselves in uncertain territory. You may be confused or discouraged by certain aspects of the new version. You may be uncertain where to find or how to use certain features. Or you may already feel comfortable with Windows 8 but simply want to discover more of the hidden shortcuts and other surprises lurking about.

Though Windows 8 is aimed toward both PCs and tablets, this book is directed strictly toward PC users. Tablet owners can tap and swipe their way throughout the Start screen and Windows 8 apps. But PC users can just as easily navigate and work with apps via traditional mouse and keyboard, a topic covered by several tasks throughout this book.

The book is divided into four sections. The first three sections — The Basics, Be Imaginative, and Beat the Clock — are task-oriented. All three sections contain a series of unique tasks, each with individual steps. By following the steps and completing each task, you should gain a greater understanding of Windows 8 and its various applications and features.

As the title promises, each task is designed to be completed in five minutes or less. But don't worry, there's no stopwatch. You can take as much or as little time as you want with each individual task. The goal is to learn from the task so you can use that knowledge to more easily and effectively work with Windows 8.

Most of the tasks are designed to be self-contained, so you can pick any task anywhere in the book, rather than having to go from start to finish. Some tasks refer to other tasks as prerequisites, but those are noted in the book.

The fourth section — Inquiring Minds — is a Q&A that answers common questions that you may have about Windows 8.

As with anything new and different, Windows 8 can present obstacles to people accustomed to the traditional look and feel of previous versions of Windows. But the information in this book should give you greater control of the new environment so that you can more easily feel at home.

What Is New in Windows 8?

The most dramatic change in Windows 8 is the one that stares you in the face just after you log in — the Start screen.

Replacing the traditional Start menu familiar to longtime Windows users, the new Start screen is based on tiles. Instead of clicking a Start button to open a cascading menu of folders and shortcuts for your applications, a Start screen appears where you click on tiles to launch your apps and features.

People used to launching their software programs through the Start menu may at first be thrown off by the Start screen. It is a totally new and different way of organizing and opening your applications.

The Start screen does lack some of the benefits of the Start menu. For example, you can organize your Start screen tiles into groups, but you cannot organize them into folders, as you can your Start menu shortcuts.

But the Start screen offers some advantages. It can display live tiles with updated information and let you pin specific types of information directly on the screen. As such, the Start screen serves not only as a launching pad to open your apps but as a way to view new information, notifications, and other items of interest all in one place.

The familiar desktop still exists as well, only now it is set up as another app. Click on the Desktop tile on the Start screen, and the same screen and environment found in past versions of Windows appear.

You can customize and personalize the desktop by setting up shortcuts so that you can quickly access your favorite programs. The desktop environment itself has been beefed up with a revamped Task Manager and File Explorer, and new tools such as File History, Storage Spaces, and Hyper-V.

Those who choose not to use the Start screen can still easily use the desktop as their primary working area.

Windows 8 Editions

For Windows 8, Microsoft trimmed down the number of editions available compared with previous versions of Windows.

Individual PC users have a choice of Windows 8 (standard) or Windows 8 Pro. Windows 8 Pro offers several advanced features not found in the standard edition; otherwise the two are virtually the same.

Windows 8 Enterprise is available for businesses that have enterprise licensing agreements with Microsoft. So this version would not be available to individual users unless deployed by their organization's IT department.

The differences between Windows 8 (standard) and Windows 8 Pro are described on the following page.

Feature Comparison: Windows 8 versus Windows 8 Pro

Table A.1 lists the features in both Windows 8 and Windows 8 Pro.

Table A.1 Windows 8 versus Windows 8 Pro

Feature	Windows 8	Windows 8 Pro
Upgrade from Windows 7 Starter, Home Basic, or Home Premium	x	x
Upgrade from Windows 7 Professional or Ultimate		x
Start screen	x	x
Semantic Zoom	x	x
Live Tiles	x	x
Windows Store	x	x
Apps (Mail, Calendar, People, Messaging, Photos, SkyDrive, Reader, Music, Video)	x	x
Connected standby	x	x
Microsoft account	x	x
Desktop	x	x
Installation of desktop applications	x	x
Updated File Explorer (previously called Windows Explorer)	x	x
Windows Defender	x	x
SmartScreen	x	x
Windows Update	x	x
Enhanced Task Manager	x	x
Switch languages on the fly (language packs)	x	x

Feature	Windows 8	Windows 8 Pro
Multiple monitor support	x	x
Storage Spaces	x	x
Windows Media Player	x	x
Exchange ActiveSync	x	x
File history	x	x
ISO/VHD mounting	x	x
Mobile broadband support	x	x
Picture password	x	x
Remote Desktop (client)	x	x
Reset and refresh your PC	x	x
Snap	x	x
Touch and Thumb keyboard	x	x
Trusted boot	x	x
VPN client	x	x
BitLocker and BitLocker To Go		x
Boot from VHD		x
Client Hyper-V		x
Domain Join		x
Encrypting File System		x
Group Policy		x
Remote Desktop (host)		x

Windows 8 Requirements

The requirements listed by Microsoft include the following:

1 GHz or faster processor

1GB RAM (32-bit) or 2GB RAM (64-bit)

16GB available hard drive space (32-bit) or 20GB (64-bit)

DirectX 9 graphics device with WDDM 1.0 or higher driver

1024 × 768-pixel screen resolution to run Windows 8 apps

1366 × 768-pixel screen resolution to snap Windows 8 apps

Start

Mail

Tile

People

Photos

RUSSELL 2
825.12 ▲ +1.05%
8/21/2012 11:23 AM

Messaging

Wi-Fi indicator

Battery Level
indicator

12:05 Tuesday
August 21

Account name

Charms bar

Search charm

Lance
Whitney

21
Tuesday

Maps

SkyDrive

Boston Herald - Yankees can't hold off
Chicago rallies in 9-6 loss

U.N.: World needs drought
policies

74°
New York City
Sunny (Clear)
84°/66°

1 Weather

Search

Share charm

Share

Start charm

Start

Devices charm

Devices

Settings charm

Settings

Live tile

The Basics

Learn how to navigate and customize your Windows 8 environment to work more effectively.

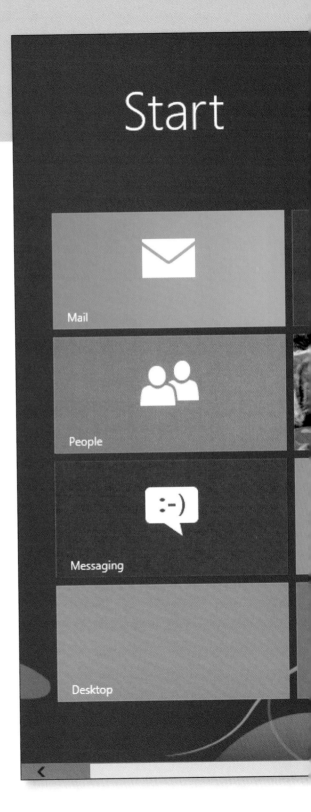

Lance
Whitney

22
Wednesday

Train derailments fuel debate
over transporting coal

Store

Music

AQ
-0.29% (-8.95)
:15 PM EDT

Boston Herald - Olympic champ picks
up New England endorsement deal

Video

69°
New York City
Clear
83°/67°

Internet Explorer

Maps

Camera

SkyDrive

Navigating the Windows 8 Start Screen

Y ou can easily find an application's Start screen tile if you only have a small number of tiles on the screen. But the more apps you install, the wider your Start screen becomes, which forces you to move around the screen to find the apps you need. Windows 8 tablet users can quickly navigate the Start screen by swiping their fingers left and right. But traditional PC users can also move around the Start screen using a desktop with an external keyboard and mouse, or a laptop with its built-in keyboard and trackpad. This task explores the different ways you can navigate the Start screen using your trusty keyboard and mouse.

1 Use a laptop trackpad: Swipe your fingers up and down the trackpad, and you will move left and right on the Start screen. If horizontal scrolling is enabled on your trackpad, you can also swipe your fingers right and left to move right and left on the screen.

2 Use an external mouse: Move your mouse sideways to reach the left or right edges of the Start screen.

3 Use a mouse scroll wheel: Move the scroll wheel on your mouse up and down to move left and right on the Start screen.

4 Use right- and left-arrow keys: Press the right- and left-arrow keys to move right and left one column at a time on the Start screen.

tip Moving left and right on the Start screen works only if you have more column tiles than can be seen on the screen at one time.

5 Use up- and down-arrow keys: Press the down- and up-arrow keys on your keyboard to move down and up one tile at a time on the Start screen.

6 Use Home and End: Press Home to move to the first tile on the Start screen. Press End to move to the last tile on the Start screen.

7 Use Tab: Press Tab to move between the Start screen tiles and your profile name and picture in the upper-right corner of the screen.

tip You can use many of these same mouse and keyboard movements to navigate certain other screens, such as the Apps screen.

Quick Fix

Accessing the Login Screen

At the initial Windows Lock screen, drag the screen up with your mouse or press any key to get to the login screen.

Pinning an Application to the Start Screen

Start screen tiles are already set up for all the apps that come with Windows 8, such as Mail, Music, People, Photos, and Calendar. Tiles are also automatically created for every application that you install in both Windows 8 apps and desktop apps. But you will probably want to create tiles for your most commonly used applications so you can quickly launch them from the Start screen. This process is known as pinning an app to the Start screen. The Apps screen displays all the apps installed on your computer, so this is a good place to look for apps to pin to the Start screen. This task shows you how to pin and unpin an app on the Start screen.

1 Open the app bar: Right-click any empty area in the Start screen to display the app bar at the bottom of the screen.

2 Open the Apps screen: Click the All Apps button on the app bar.

3 Choose your app: Right-click the app that you want to add to the Start screen.

4 Pin to the Start screen: Click the Pin to Start button on the app bar.

5 Return to the Start screen: Click the Start screen thumbnail in the lower-left hot corner or press the Windows key to return to the Start screen.

6 View the new tile: Scroll to the far right side of the Start screen, and you will see a tile for the app you selected.

tip *You can right-click multiple tiles on the Start screen and unpin them all in one shot.*

7 Unpin an app: Right-click a tile in the Start screen to display the app bar. Click Unpin from Start to remove it from the Start screen.

Quick Fix

Switching between the Start Screen and Desktop

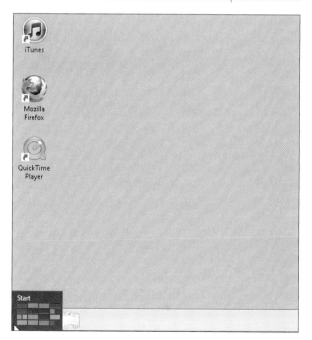

From the Start screen, click the Desktop tile to move to the desktop. From the desktop, move your mouse to the lower-left hot corner and click on the thumbnail for the Start screen.

Creating and Naming Groups of Apps

The Start screen can easily become cluttered with dozens of tiles for all the applications you run in Windows 8. For every application you install — Windows 8 apps and desktop apps — one or sometimes several tiles are populated in the Start screen. The more apps that you install, the more cluttered your Start screen becomes, and the more difficult it becomes to find the tiles for specific apps. You cannot change the behavior of the Start screen. But you can organize all of your tiles into groups and give each group a name. This task covers how to organize and name your group tiles.

1 Drag first tile: Drag a tile to the right or left of its current group until you see a transparent vertical bar. Drop the tile, and you will see a space between it and its former group.

2 Drag more tiles: Select additional tiles that you want to add to your new group. Drag and drop them next to the original tile.

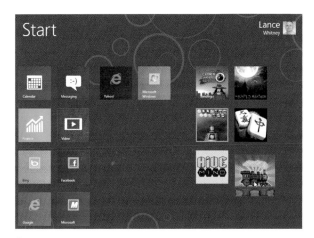

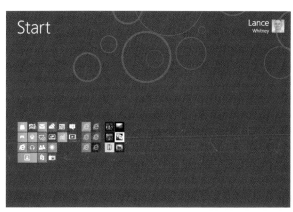

3 Drag tiles into other groups: Drag and drop other tiles into their own separate groups using the same process. For example, you can organize tiles for websites into one group and tiles for games into another group.

4 Zoom out: Click the Semantic Zoom button in the lower-right corner of your screen to zoom out of the Start screen.

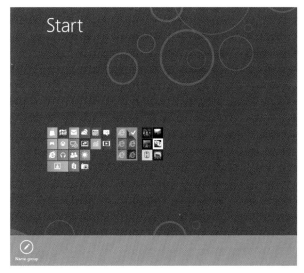

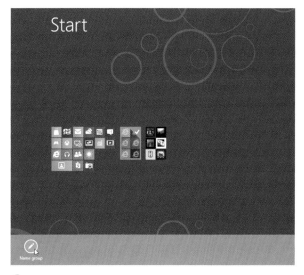

5 Right-click group: Right-click a group of tiles that you want to name.

6 Name group: Click the Name group button at the bottom of the screen.

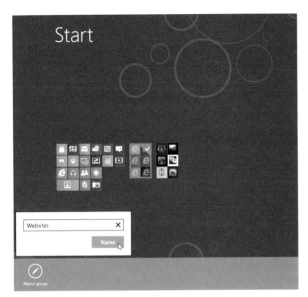

7 Click Name: Type a name for that tile group and then click Name.

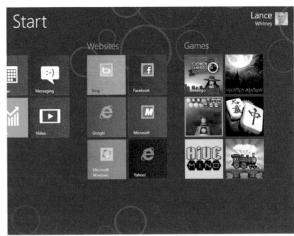

8 Zoom in: Click any empty area of the Start screen to zoom in. The new name appears above the tile group. Repeat that process for the other tile groups.

tip You can also resize a Start screen tile to change the overall layout, a task covered in the next section.

Quick Fix

Turning Off Live Tiles for Certain Tiles

Certain tiles, such as Mail, Calendar, People, and Weather, are set up as live tiles to deliver updated information. You can turn off a live tile if do not need to see the updated information. Right-click the tile. Click the Turn live tile off button from the app bar.

Resizing a Start Screen Tile

As you view the Start screen, you will see that tiles appear either as small squares or as large rectangles. You can change the size of certain tiles to make them small or large. Increasing the size of a tile for an app that you frequently use gives it more prominence. Decreasing the size of a tile allows you to squeeze more tiles into the same amount of space, saving room on the Start screen. Not all tiles can be resized this way — for example, tiles for the Camera app, Maps app, and Windows Store app cannot be resized. But many of the apps that come with Windows can be resized. Tiles for certain third-party apps can also be resized. This task explains how to resize a Start screen app.

1 Look for Resize option: Right-click the tile for an app on the Start screen. If the tile can be resized, a button appears on the app bar that says Larger or Smaller.

2 Increase or decrease the tile size: If the app is small, click Larger to resize it into a large rectangle. If the app is large, click Smaller to resize it into a small square.

tip You can change the tile size for certain Windows 8 apps but not for desktop apps.

3 View new tile: The tile resizes and the surrounding tiles move to fill the increased or decreased space.

Quick Fix

Uninstalling a Windows 8 App

You can uninstall certain Windows 8 apps. Right-click a Windows 8 app, such as Mail, Maps, Calendar, or Weather. Right-click the app's tile. Click Uninstall from the app bar.

Searching for Apps, Settings, and Files

W indows 8 provides a search feature that lets you track down applications, settings, files, and other items. The search feature can find specific Windows software programs installed on your PC; it can find key Windows settings and options; and it can find documents, photos, songs, videos, and other types of files. It can also search for content within specific applications, such as Mail, People, Music, and Photos. You can access the search feature from the Charms bar or by pressing the first letter of your search term anywhere in the new Windows 8 environment. This task shows you how to search for apps, settings, files, and other items.

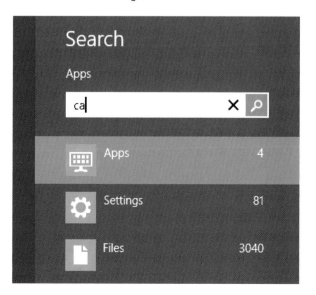

1 Type the first few letters: From the Start screen or Apps screen, type the first few letters of the app, file, or setting that you want to find.

tip Launch a search by moving your mouse to the lower-right hot corner and clicking the Search icon at the top of the Charms bar.

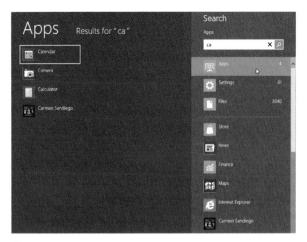

2 View results: The search bar displays a list of the items found that start with the letters you typed. By default, the results display only apps that start with the letters. The number next to the word Apps reveals how many apps were found.

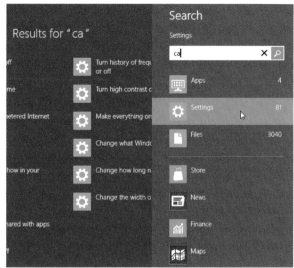

3 Search settings: If you are looking for a Windows setting instead of an app, click the Settings option at the top of the right sidebar. The number next to the word Settings tells you how many settings were found.

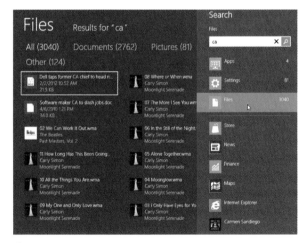

4 Search files: If you are looking for a file, click the Files option at the top of the sidebar.

tip You can start typing the name of an app as soon as you launch Windows to search for and launch that app.

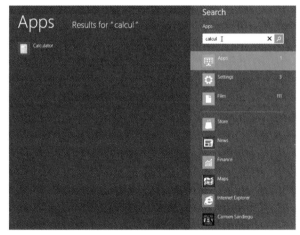

5 Narrow results: You can narrow the results by typing additional letters in the search bar's search field.

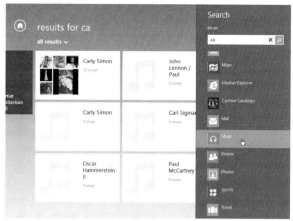

6 Launch the item: From the list of apps, settings, or files on the left, click the item you want to open.

tip Launch a search by holding down the Windows key and pressing Q.

7 Search for other items: If the item you want to find is related to or part of a specific category or application, click that category or application from the list below Apps, Settings, and Files. For example, if are looking for information on a particular song or artist, click the Music app. The Music app opens to display information on the name you typed in the search field.

Searching for Apps in the Windows Store

Store

Spotlight

kindle

Kindle
Free ★ ★ ★ ★

All stars

The winners of the First Apps Contest
8 great apps for Consumer Preview

Autodesk
SketchBook

msnbc.com

Got apps?
Yes, yes you do.

Top free

SketchBook Express
Free ★ ★ ★ ★

msnbc.com
Free ★ ★ ★ ★

New
releases

The Windows Store offers a variety of Windows 8 apps that you can download, some free and some paid. It also offers links to desktop apps where you can learn more about the apps and download them through their external websites. The Windows Store spotlights certain apps, pointing you to categories such as All stars, Top free, New releases, and Picks for you. You can browse the store by category or search for specific apps by name. As with other Windows features, the Windows Store uses the built-in Windows search feature. This task explores how to search for apps in the Windows Store.

1 Enter the Windows Store: Launch the Windows Store app by clicking its Start screen tile.

tip You do not need to launch the Windows Store first. Instead, launch the Search feature and then select Store from the search categories.

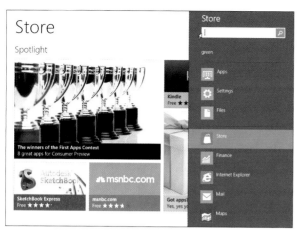

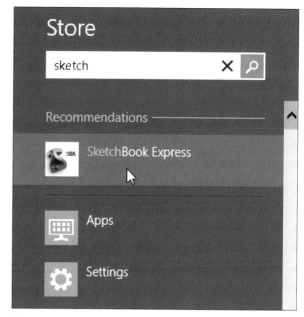

2 Launch the Search feature: Hold down the Windows key and press Q to display the search tool.

tip You can write a review of an app in the Windows Store.

3 Type the first few characters: Type the first few characters of the app that you want to find in the search field in the upper right of the Search sidebar. Windows displays the names of any recommended apps that match your search term.

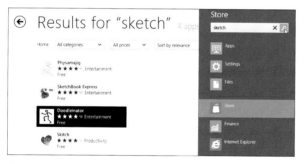

4 Search for all apps: Click the search icon to the right of the search field to display all apps that match your search term.

5 Click an app: The results appear on the left side of the screen. Click an app to view its dedicated app page. Here you can read an overview, details, and reviews about the app.

Downloading Apps from the Windows Store

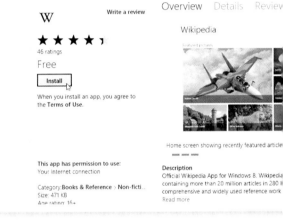

The Windows Store offers a variety of apps that you can download, some free and some paid. The Windows Store spotlights certain apps, pointing you to such categories as All stars, Top free, New releases, and Picks for you. The store organizes apps into general categories, including Games, Social, Entertainment, Photos, Music & Video, Sports, Books & Reference, News & Weather, and Productivity. You can browse the store by category or search for specific apps by name. Clicking an app brings you to a detailed description page where you can learn more about the app and install it. Finally, the store provides links to standard desktop applications that you can download and install from the software vendor's website. This task explores how to download apps in the Windows Store.

1 Enter the Windows Store: Launch the Windows Store app by clicking its Start screen tile.

2 View the Windows Store: You can scroll through the Store to view the various categories of apps, including Games, Social, Entertainment, Shopping, and Education.

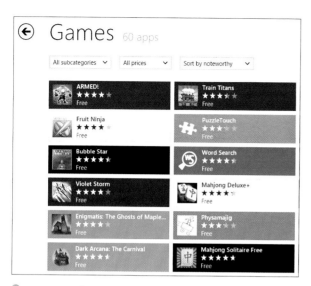

3 Browse for apps: Click the name of a specific category, such as Games, to view its apps.

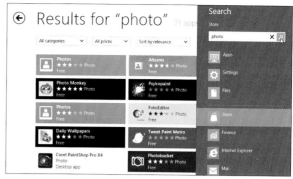

4 Search for apps: You can also search for any app in the store by name or description. Hold down the Windows key and press Q to open the Search bar. In the search field, type the name or description of an app, such as Photo. Windows displays suggested apps with that name or description. You can also click the Search icon to see a full list of apps that match your search term.

tip You can browse the Windows Store or open an existing app while any new apps are installing.

5 Select an app: From the search results, click an app to display its full page description.

6 View the app's description: In the app's description page, click Overview to read information about the app. Click Details to see product specifications and requirements. Click Reviews to read reviews from other users.

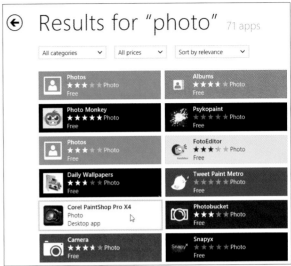

7 Install the app: Click Install to download a free app. A message that the app is installing appears at the top. Another message appears after the app has been installed.

8 Select a desktop app: A desktop app displays the description Desktop app under its name. Click a desktop app that you want to view in order to display its description page.

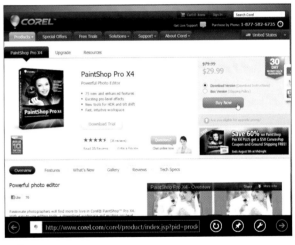

10 View the app's description: Internet Explorer opens to display the app's product page. You can download a free app or purchase and then download a paid app.

9 View the desktop app's description: The desktop app's description page opens where you can see an overview and details. To view more information and potentially install the app, click the Go to developer's website link.

Working with Multiple Windows 8 Apps

Y ou can launch multiple Windows apps one after the other from the Start screen or Apps screen. Unless you close it, each Windows 8 app that you launch stays open, albeit in an idle state. You can display thumbnails for all open Windows 8 apps and switch from one to another. You can view two Windows 8 apps at a time, one taking up a third of the screen and the second taking up the other two-thirds of the screen. You can also manually close an open Windows 8 app. This task explains how to display and work with multiple Windows 8 apps.

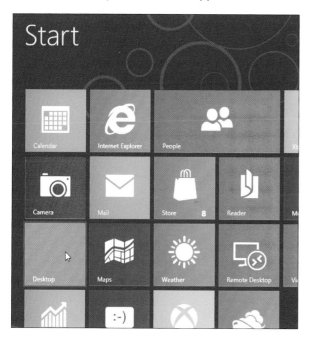

1 Open Windows 8 apps: Open your first Windows 8 app from the Start screen. Return to the Start screen by pressing the Windows key or clicking on the thumbnail for the Start screen in the lower-left hot corner. Open a second Windows 8 app. Return to the Start screen. Open a third Windows 8 app. Return to the Start screen.

2 Viewing last open app: From the Start screen, move your mouse to the upper-left hot corner. You see a thumbnail for the last Windows 8 app that you opened.

tip Hold down Alt or the Windows key and press Tab to cycle through open apps. Release the key when the app you want to open is highlighted.

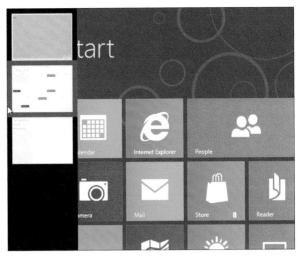

3 View all open apps: Move your mouse down the screen, making sure you keep the cursor as close as possible to the left border of the screen. As you move your mouse down, you see additional thumbnails for each open app.

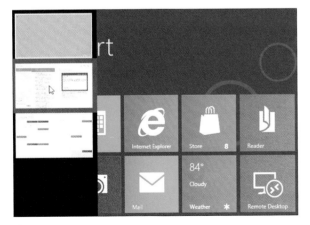

4 Switch to an open app: Click on the thumbnail of the app that you want to open.

5 Snap a second app: From your current app, move your mouse to the upper-left hot corner. Then move your mouse to the thumbnail of the second app you want to view. Right-click on the thumbnail and select Snap left or Snap right.

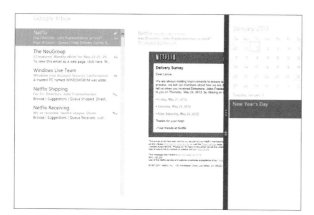

6 View two apps side by side: The second app displays on the left or right side of the screen depending on the option you selected, taking up one-third of the screen. The first app takes up the other two-thirds of the screen.

7 Resize an open app: Move your mouse to the vertical scroll bar separating the two apps until your cursor turns into a small vertical line with two arrows. Double-click or drag the scroll bar to increase or decrease the size of the window. To make a window full screen, click and drag the scroll bar all the way to the left or right.

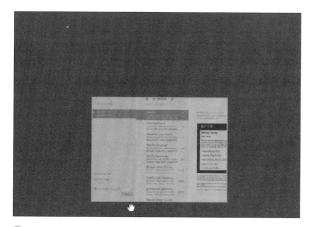

8 Close your current app: Move your mouse to the top of the app's screen until your cursor turns into a folded hand. Click and drag the window all the way to the bottom of the screen until the app disappears.

9 Close any open app: Return to the Start screen. Move your mouse to the upper-left hot corner. Move your mouse down to the thumbnail of the app you want to close. Right-click on the thumbnail and click Close.

tip Snapping a Windows 8 app and displaying two apps side by side requires a screen resolution of at least 1366 X 768 pixels.

warning Desktop apps do not appear in their own individual thumbnails but rather in one single thumbnail representing the entire desktop.

Shutting Down or Restarting Windows

W indows 8 does not provide the traditional desktop Start menu, so there is no Shut Down or Restart command accessible from the Start button. But Windows 8 does offer you a variety of other ways to shut down or restart your computer. You can shut it down or restart it from the Charms bar, from the Sign out screen, or from the desktop. You can also shut it down by pressing the Power button or closing the lid if you are using a laptop. This task shows you the different ways to shut down or restart Windows 8.

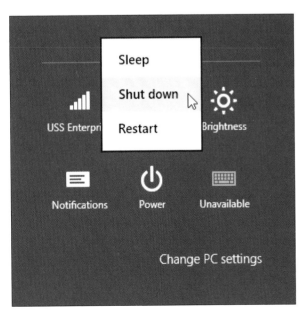

1 Shut down or restart from Charms bar: From the Start screen, hover your mouse over the Semantic Zoom button in the lower-right hot corner until you see the five charms for the Charms bar. Move your mouse up the bar and click the Settings icon. From the Start sidebar, click the Power icon at the bottom. You should see a pop-up menu with at least three commands: Sleep, Shut down, and Restart. Click Shut down to power off your PC; click Restart to reboot it.

tip Hold down the Windows key and press I to access the Start sidebar.

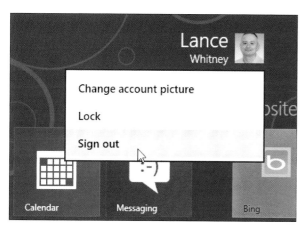

3 Shut down or restart from the desktop: From the desktop, press Alt+F4 to access the Shut Down Windows dialog box. From the box's drop-down menu, choose Shut down or Restart.

2 Shut down or restart from Sign out screen: From the Start screen, click your account name and picture in the upper-right corner, or press Ctrl+Alt+Delete. Click Sign out. From the Lock screen, press any key to access the login screen. Click the icon in the lower-right corner. From the pop-up menu, choose the Shut down or Restart command.

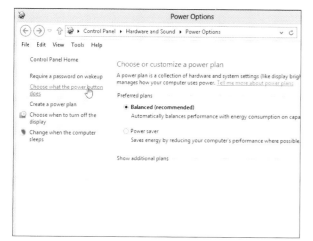

4 Define Power buttons: From the desktop, hover your mouse in the lower-right hot corner to display the Charms bar. Click the Settings charm. Click Control Panel at the top of the desktop sidebar. Click the Hardware and Sound category and then click the Power Options subcategory. From Power Options, click the Choose what the power button does setting on the left sidebar.

5 Press Power button on a desktop PC: On a desktop computer, select the Shut down option in the When I press the power button drop-down menu. Click Save changes.

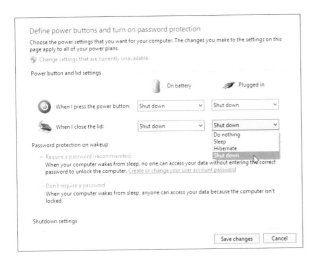

6 Press Power button or close the lid on a laptop: On a laptop, select the Shut down option in the When I press the power button drop-down menu. You can also select the Shut down option in the When I close the lid drop-down menu. You can set these options for either On battery or Plugged in, or both.

Uninstalling a Desktop Application

You can uninstall a desktop application through its Start screen or Apps screen tile. Right-click the app's tile. Click Uninstall from the app bar. Windows opens the Programs and Features window in the desktop where you can uninstall the application.

Putting Windows to Sleep

You can use most of the same settings and options to put Windows 8 into sleep mode as you do to shut it down or restart it. Putting Windows to sleep keeps all the applications, files, and other contents in memory active so that you can easily and quickly return to your work when the computer wakes up. Sleep mode is a good option if you intend to leave your laptop for an hour or two and want to keep it running but preserve power if it is operating off the battery. This task explains how to put Windows into sleep mode.

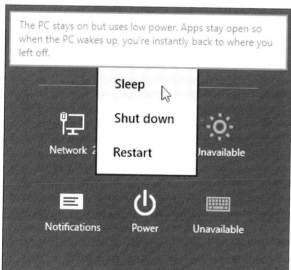

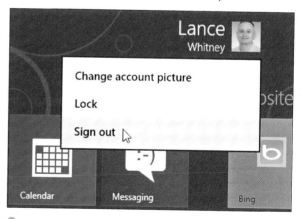

1 Sleep from the Charms bar: From the Start screen, hover your mouse over the Semantic Zoom button in the lower-right corner until you see the five icons for the Charms bar. Move your mouse up the bar and click the Settings icon. From the Start sidebar, click the Power icon at the bottom. A pop-up menu appears with several options, including Sleep. Click Sleep.

2 Sleep from Sign out screen: From the Start screen, click your account name and picture in the upper-right corner, or press Ctrl+Alt+Del. Click Sign out. From the Lock screen, press any key to access the login screen. Click the icon in the lower-right corner. From the pop-up menu, choose Sleep.

3 Sleep from the desktop: From the desktop, press Alt+F4 to access the Shut Down Windows dialog box. From the box's drop-down menu, choose Sleep.

tip You can put a desktop PC into sleep mode to lower its power consumption, but it is most beneficial for a laptop running off battery power.

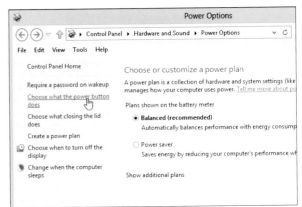

4 Define the Power buttons: From the desktop, hover your mouse in the lower-right hot corner to display the Charms bar. Click the Settings charm. Click Control Panel at the top of the desktop sidebar. Click the Hardware and Sound category and then click the Power Options subcategory. From Power Options, click the Choose what the power button does setting on the left sidebar.

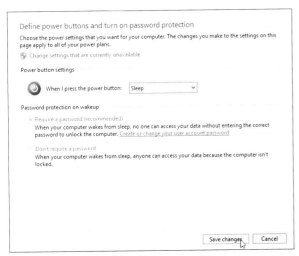

5 Press the Power button on a desktop PC: On a desktop computer, select the Sleep option in the When I press the power button drop-down menu. Click Save changes.

6 Press the Power button or close the lid on a laptop: On a laptop, select the Sleep option in the When I press the power button drop-down menu. You can also select the Sleep option in the When I close the lid drop-down menu. You can set these options for either On battery or Plugged in, or both.

Hibernating Windows

Y ou can use most of the same settings and options to put Windows 8 into hibernate mode as you do to shut it down, restart it, or put it to sleep. Putting Windows into hibernate mode moves all of your current applications, documents, and data from memory onto the hard drive to preserve your current state. When the PC comes out of hibernate mode, everything that was saved is then restored into memory so you can pick up exactly where you left off. Resuming your work after Windows comes out of hibernate mode takes a bit longer than if it is coming out of sleep mode. This task explains how to hibernate your PC.

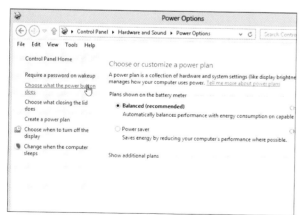

1 Access the Shut down settings: From the desktop, hover your mouse in the lower-right hot corner to display the Charms bar. Click the Settings charm. Click Control Panel at the top of the desktop sidebar. Click the Hardware and Sound category and then click the Power Options subcategory. From Power Options, click the Choose what the power button does setting on the left sidebar.

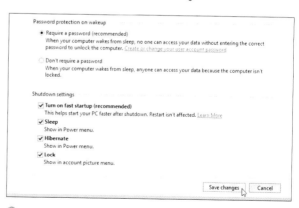

2 Display the Hibernate command: In the Define power buttons and turn on password protection section, click the Change settings that are currently unavailable option. Scroll down to the bottom of the screen to the Shut down settings area and select the Hibernate check box. Click Save changes.

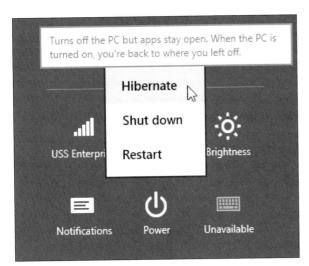

3 Hibernate from the Charms bar: From the Start screen, hover your mouse over the Semantic Zoom button in the lower-right corner until you see the five icons for the Charms bar. Move your mouse up the bar and click the Settings icon. From the Start sidebar, click the Power icon at the bottom. A pop-up menu appears with several options, including Hibernate. Click Hibernate.

4 Hibernate from Sign out screen: From the Start screen, click your account name and picture in the upper-right corner, or press Ctrl+Alt+Delete. Click Sign out. From the Lock screen, press any key to access the login screen. Click the icon in the lower-right corner. From the pop-up menu, choose Hibernate.

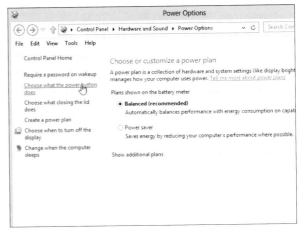

5 Hibernate from the desktop:

From the desktop, press Alt+F4 to display the Shut Down Windows dialog box. From the box's drop-down menu, choose Hibernate.

tip You can put a desktop PC into hibernate mode to cut off its power consumption, but it is most beneficial for a laptop running off battery power.

6 Define the Power buttons: From the desktop, hover your mouse over the lower-right hot corner to display the Charms bar. Click the Settings charm. Click Control Panel at the top of the desktop sidebar. Click the Hardware and Sound category and then click the Power Options subcategory. From Power Options, click the Choose what the power button does setting on the left sidebar.

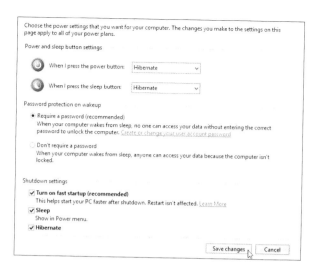

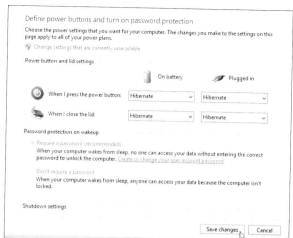

7 Press the Power button on a desktop PC: On a desktop computer, select the Hibernate option in the When I press the power button drop-down menu. If an option appears for When I press the sleep button, you can also change that to Hibernate. Click Save changes.

8 Press the Power button or close the lid on a laptop: On a laptop, select the Hibernate option in the When I press the power button drop-down menu. You can also select the Hibernate option in the When I close the lid drop-down menu. You can set these options for either On battery or Plugged in, or both. Click Save changes.

Quick Fix

Emulating Pinch and Zoom on a PC

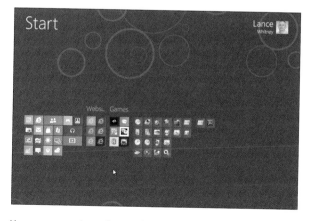

You can zoom in and out of the Start screen and other Windows 8 apps on a PC. Hold down the Ctrl key and move the scroll wheel on your mouse up and down.

Customizing the Desktop

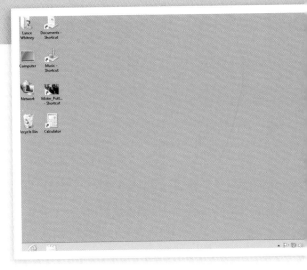

The Windows 8 desktop starts off as a virtual blank slate with just a shortcut to the Recycle Bin and no other visible shortcuts or icons. And because the Windows 8 desktop does not provide a traditional Start button or menu, it seemingly offers no clear, direct access to all the applications and features that you need. But just as you could in previous versions of Windows, you can customize the Windows 8 desktop by populating it with icons and shortcuts for the programs that you use most frequently. This task explains how to set up your desktop to access your favorite applications and features.

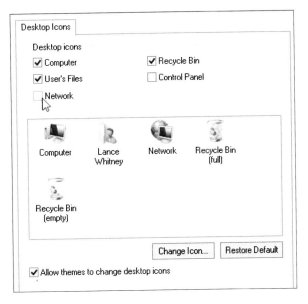

1 Add common icons to your desktop: Right-click anywhere on the desktop and choose Personalize from the pop-up menu. Click the option to change desktop icons. Select the icons you want to appear on the desktop and click OK. You can choose from among Computer, your user folder, Network, Recycle Bin, and Control Panel.

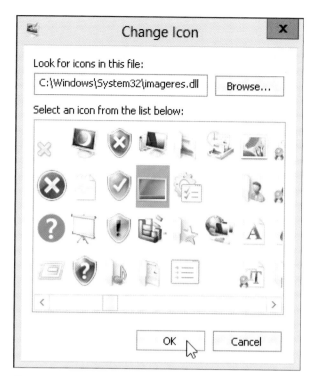

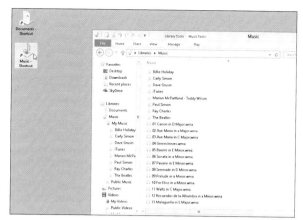

3 Add folder shortcuts from File Explorer: Open
File Explorer from the taskbar. In the Libraries section, select
the Documents folder and drag it to your desktop to create a
shortcut to that folder. A Create link in desktop message
appears. Release your mouse button. Repeat the process for
Pictures, Music, and any other folders that you want to see on
the desktop.

2 Change a desktop icon: Right-click anywhere on
the desktop and choose Personalize from the pop-up menu.
Click the option to change desktop icons. Click a specific icon
and then click Change Icon. Windows displays a range of icons
from one of its library files. Choose the icon you want to use
and click OK. You can also revert back to any icon's original
image by clicking it and clicking Restore Default.

4 Add icons for individual files: Open File Explorer.
Select an individual file, such as a document, photo, song, or
other item that you want to add to the desktop as a shortcut.
Right-click the file and drag it to the desktop with your right
mouse button. Release your mouse button. Windows asks if
you want to copy, move, or create a shortcut to the file. Select
the Create shortcut here option. You can repeat that process
for any other frequently used files.

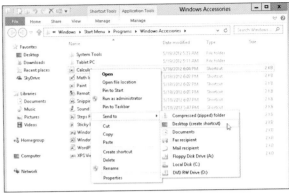

6 Send the application to the desktop: Click Open file location. Windows displays the application's shortcut in File Explorer. Right-click the shortcut, then choose Send to, and then Desktop (create shortcut).

tip You can also add apps from the Start screen to your desktop using the Open file location button.

5 Add icons from the Apps screen: Open the Apps screen in the Windows 8 environment. Right-click any desktop app that you want to add to the desktop. A desktop app displays an Open file location button on the app bar; a Windows 8 app does not display that button.

Quick Fix

Accessing the Charms Bar

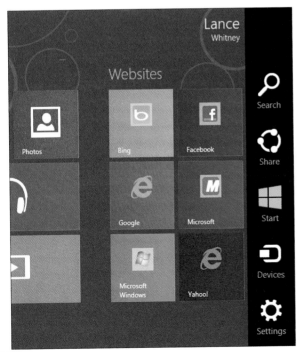

You can access the Charms bar a couple of different ways. Click the Semantic Zoom button in the lower-right corner of the screen and move your mouse up the screen, or hold down the Windows key and press C. The options in the Charms bar change depending on the application you are using.

Using the File Explorer Ribbon

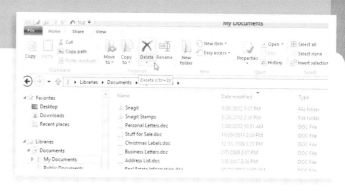

File Explorer has been redesigned for Windows 8 with a Ribbon, similar to the Ribbon that was introduced in Microsoft Office 2007 and has since appeared in other Microsoft programs. The Ribbon replaces the standard pull-down menus from Windows Explorer. But it offers access to the full array of features and commands that let you manage your folders and files. Selecting a drive letter, folder, or file in File Explorer displays a Ribbon with commands specific to each item. Selecting certain types of folders or files, such as Photos or Music, also displays a Ribbon with commands specific to those types of files. This task explains how to use the Ribbon to manage different files and other items.

1 Launch File Explorer: Open the desktop and launch File Explorer from its taskbar icon.

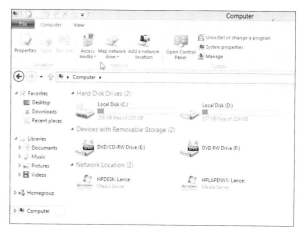

2 View Ribbon commands for Computer: Click the Computer icon in File Explorer. A Computer menu appears on the Ribbon. Click that menu. Commands appear to connect to a Media server, map a network drive, and add a network location.

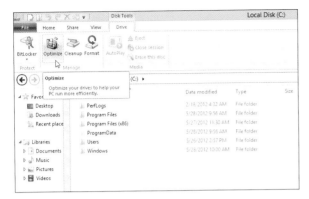

3 View Ribbon commands for C drive: Click the Local Disk icon, typically your C drive. A Share menu appears on the Ribbon. Click that menu. Commands appear to burn the drive to disc and set advanced sharing. A Drive menu also appears on the Ribbon. Click that menu. You will see commands to optimize, clean up, or format your drive.

4 View Ribbon commands for your libraries: Click the Libraries folder. A Manage library button appears on the Ribbon. Click that button. Commands appear that you can use to manage your library, set a Save location, and optimize the library for certain folders.

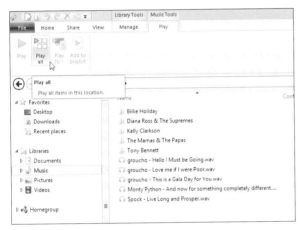

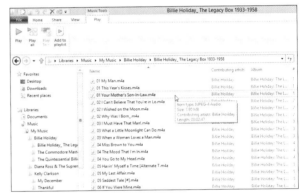

6 View Ribbon commands for a file: Drill down through your Music folder until individual tracks on the right pane of File Explorer appear. Select a track and click Play to play it. The Music app or Windows Media Player opens to play the track. Press the Stop button to stop the music. Move your mouse to the lower-left hot corner and click on the desktop thumbnail to return to the desktop.

5 View Ribbon commands for a folder: Click the Music folder under Libraries. A Play all button appears. Click that button. A command to play all your music appears.

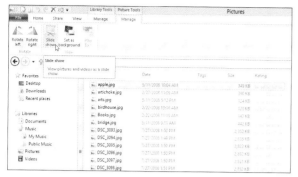

tip You can hide the Ribbon by clicking the Minimize Ribbon icon in the upper-right corner. Click the icon again to restore the Ribbon.

7 View Ribbon commands for a different file:
In File Explorer, click the Pictures folder under Libraries. Drill down until individual images appear on the right pane of File Explorer. Click an image. Click the Manage tab on the Ribbon. Commands to rotate left, rotate right, run a slide show, or set your current image as the background image appear.

Quick Fix

Setting Up a Microsoft Account

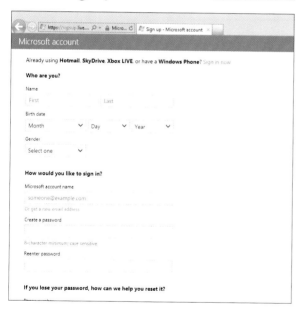

To take full advantage of Windows 8, you can set up an online Microsoft account. Logging in with this account lets you synchronize many of your settings and customizations across multiple Windows 8 PCs. Go to https://signup.live.com/signup.aspx. Type your contact information and create an e-mail address and password. Type the captcha security code. Click I accept. You now have a new Microsoft account that you can use to log in to Windows 8.

Opening Two Instances of File Explorer

You can open File Explorer by clicking its taskbar shortcut. By default, the Explorer window points to the Libraries folder. Now you want to open a second instance of File Explorer, perhaps to copy or move files from one window to another or simply to display the contents of two different folders at the same time. If you click the Explorer taskbar icon, your current instance of Explorer simply shuts down. How can you open more than one instance of File Explorer and easily work with each separate window? This task explains how to open and display two instances of File Explorer.

1 Open the first instance: Open File Explorer from its taskbar icon.

tip You can also cascade multiple windows so that one appears on top of the other.

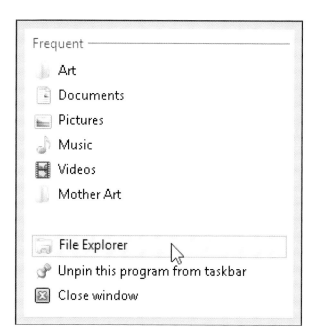

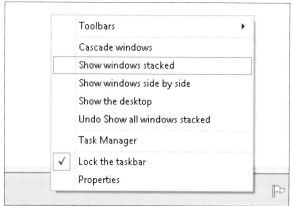

3 Display both instances stacked: Right-click the taskbar. In the pop-up menu that appears, click Show windows stacked. One window appears on top of the other.

2 Open the second instance: Right-click Explorer's taskbar icon and click File Explorer. One instance appears in the foreground; the other in the background.

tip You can undo the stacked or side-by-side option so that the windows return to a cascading position.

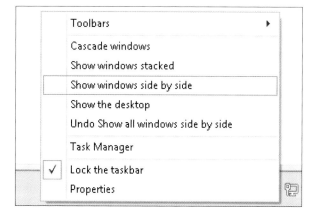

4 Display both instances side by side: Right-click the taskbar. In the pop-up menu that appears, click Show windows side by side. The two windows appear next to each other.

Copying or Moving Files

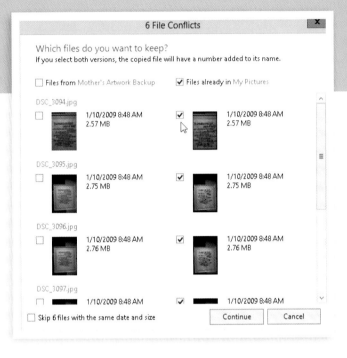

The basic process of copying and moving files in Windows 8 is the same as it was in previous versions of Windows. But Windows now offers better feedback in the dialog box that appears during a file copy or move, especially when copying or moving large files or multiple files in one shot. Windows 8 also combines the various dialog boxes that used to appear when you copy or move one group of files after another. Now just one dialog box appears for all the files being copied or moved. Windows 8 also displays an improved dialog box that appears when you try to copy or move a file that already exists in the destination. This task explores how to copy or move files in File Explorer.

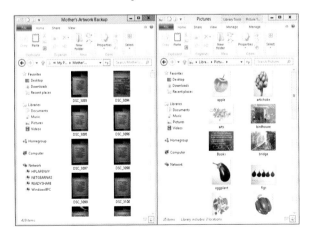

1 **Open File Explorer:** Open two instances of File Explorer and display them side by side (see previous task on how to do this). Select your source folder with files that you want to copy in one instance and your destination folder in the other instance.

2 Copy multiple files: Select multiple files to copy from the source folder. Click the Copy button on the Ribbon, or press Ctrl+C.

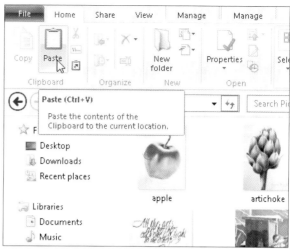

3 Paste files: Move to the destination folder in the other instance of File Explorer. Click the Paste button or press Ctrl+V.

tip The overall process and dialog boxes are the same whether you are copying or moving files.

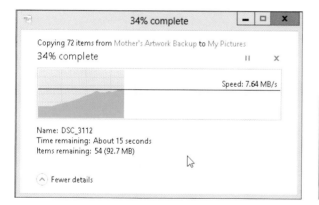

4 View the dialog box: A dialog box appears displaying the speed and status of the file copy.

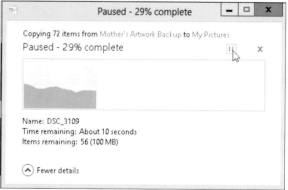

5 Pause the copy: Click the Pause button in the dialog box to pause the copy process. Click the Pause button again to resume the file copy.

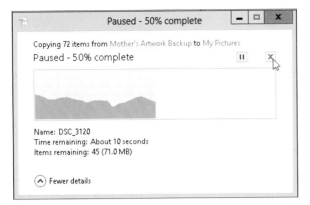

6 Cancel the copy: Click the X to cancel the file copy.

7 Copy or move files that already exist: If you try to copy or move a file that already exists in the destination folder, a new Replace or Skip Files dialog box appears to help you make the right choice. Select the same files that you copied in the earlier step in the source folder. Click the Copy button. Move to the destination folder in the other instance of File Explorer. Click the Paste button.

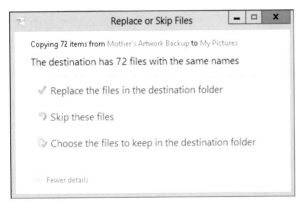

8 Replace or skip all files: The Replace or Skip Files dialog box appears that offers three choices: Replace the files in the destination folder, Skip these files, or Choose the files to keep in the destination folder. The first option replaces all the files in the destination with the source files; the second option leaves the destination files alone.

tip You can also select the check box at the bottom of the File Conflicts dialog box to skip all files with the same date and size.

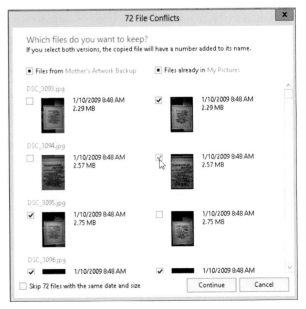

9 Replace or skip files selectively: The third option displays the source and destination files and asks which ones you want to keep. You can select all files from the source or destination by selecting the check box above the file list; or you can select the check box for each individual file. If you select both the source and destination version, Windows adds a number to the copied file.

Customizing the Taskbar

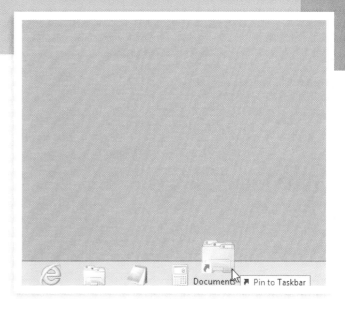

The taskbar in Windows 8 starts off displaying icons for just two programs — Internet Explorer and File Explorer. Because the Windows 8 desktop does not offer the traditional Start menu, you may want to rely more heavily on the taskbar to provide access to your most frequently used applications. Just as you could in previous versions of Windows, you can customize the Windows 8 taskbar by adding icons and shortcuts for applications and folders. You can pin applications from the Start screen or Apps screen. You can also pin applications and folders from the desktop or from File Explorer. This task explains how to pin icons to the taskbar.

1 Pin app from Apps screen to taskbar: Open the Apps screen from the Start screen by right-clicking your mouse and clicking the All Apps button on the app bar. Right-click a desktop application that you want to pin to the taskbar. Click the Pin to taskbar button on the app bar. Open the desktop by holding down the Windows key and pressing D. The application's icon appears on the taskbar.

tip If you do not see the Pin to taskbar button, then the app is a desktop app, which you cannot pin to the taskbar.

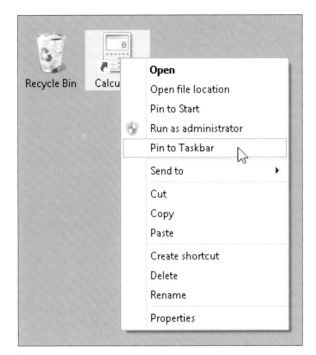

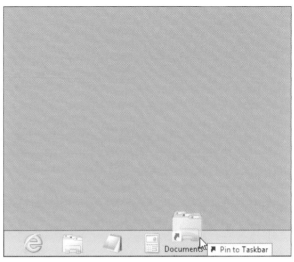

2 Pin app from desktop to taskbar: This step assumes that you have already added some shortcuts for certain desktop applications to your desktop. You can pin those desktop application shortcuts to the taskbar. Open File Explorer. Right-click a desktop shortcut and choose Pin to Taskbar from the pop-up menu. The application's icon appears on the taskbar.

3 Pin folder to taskbar: Open File Explorer. Select a folder, such as Documents, and drag it to your desktop. Right-click the folder's shortcut and choose Properties from the pop-up menu. In front of the path displayed in the target field, type the word "explorer." Click OK. Drag the folder to the taskbar until a Pin to Taskbar message appears. Release the mouse button. A copy of the folder appears on the taskbar.

tip You can right-click a taskbar icon to access its jump list of frequently used and pinned files and features.

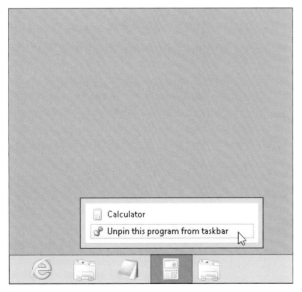

4 Unpin app from taskbar: Right-click the app's taskbar icon and choose Unpin this program from taskbar from the pop-up menu.

Adding a Taskbar Toolbar

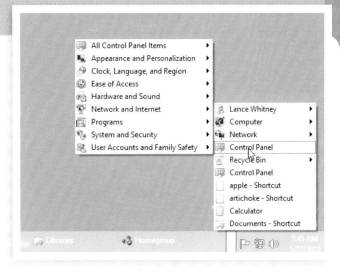

One way to set up access to different applications, folders, and files is by adding a toolbar to the Windows desktop task-bar. Windows 8 offers four toolbars that you can add — an Address toolbar, a Links toolbar, a Touch Keyboard tool-bar, and a desktop tool-bar. The Address toolbar lets you directly enter and access website addresses without having to open your web browser. The Links toolbar offers access to all of your Internet Explorer favorites. The Touch Keyboard toolbar displays an on-screen Touch Keyboard, which can be useful if you need to input characters from a different language. And the desktop toolbar offers access to all of your desktop icons as well as folders for other content. This task explains how to add a taskbar toolbar.

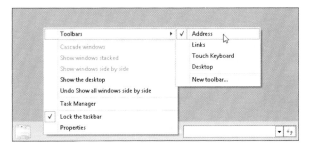

1 Add an Address toolbar: Right-click the taskbar. In the pop-up menu that appears, click Toolbars and then click Address. A new toolbar that lets you type an Internet address appears. Typing an address for a website opens the site in the desktop version of Internet Explorer.

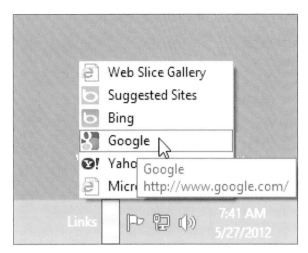

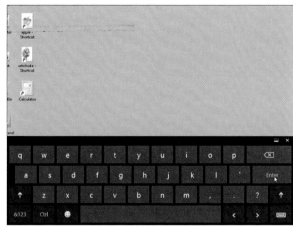

2 Add a Links toolbar: Right-click the taskbar. In the pop-up menu, click Toolbars and then Links. A new toolbar named Links appears. Click the double right arrow next to the word Links to see a list of all your Internet Explorer favorites. Unlock the taskbar. You can now also expand the Links toolbar by dragging the dotted separator bar in front of the word Links. Dragging the bar to the left displays the icons for your IE favorites.

3 Add a Touch Keyboard toolbar: Right-click the taskbar. In the pop-up menu, click Toolbars and then Touch Keyboard. A keyboard icon appears on the taskbar. Click the icon to display the keyboard on your desktop.

> *tip* You can add multiple toolbars to your taskbar and drag the dotted separator bar to control the size of each one.

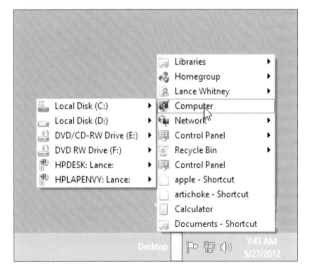

4 Add a desktop toolbar: Right-click the taskbar. In the pop-up menu, click Toolbars and then Desktop. A new desktop toolbar appears. Click the double right arrow next to the word Desktop to see a list of all desktop icons and folders. You can also expand the desktop toolbar by dragging the dotted separator bar in front of the word desktop. Dragging the bar to the left displays the icons for the individual folders.

Re-creating the Quick Launch Toolbar

Versions of Windows prior to Windows 7 offered a Quick Launch toolbar that provided access to certain applications, folders, files, and other features. The toolbar was displayed on the taskbar to enable the quick and easy launch of those features. The Windows 8 taskbar does not offer direct access to the Quick Launch toolbar. But you can re-create this toolbar and add shortcuts to the Quick Launch folder for your most frequently used applications and files. By default, the Quick Launch toolbar displays shortcuts for Internet Explorer, Show desktop, and Switch between windows, but you can add more. This task explains how to re-create the Quick Launch toolbar and add shortcuts to it by populating the Quick Launch folder.

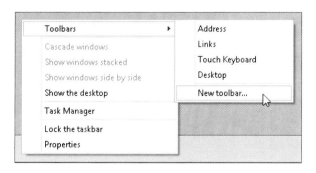

1 Right-click the taskbar: In the pop-up menu, choose Toolbars ➜ New toolbar. From the File Explorer window, type **%appdata%\Microsoft\Internet Explorer\Quick Launch** and then click Select Folder. The Quick Launch toolbar appears on the taskbar.

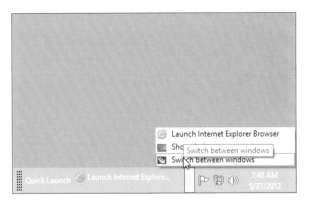

2 View the Quick Launch icons: Click the double arrow next to the Quick Launch toolbar. Shortcuts for Internet Explorer, Show desktop, and Switch between windows appear. You can also expand the toolbar by dragging the dotted separator bar in front of the words Quick Launch. Make sure the taskbar is unlocked first.

tip Dragging a folder or file with your right mouse button to its destination always displays a pop-up menu that contains options for copying, moving, or creating a shortcut to the file.

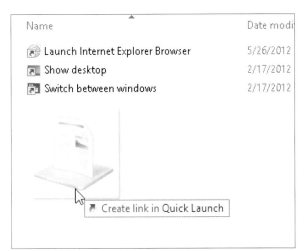

3 Add more shortcuts to Quick Launch: By populating the Quick Launch folder, you can add shortcuts to the Quick Launch toolbar for any applications or folders you want. Open File Explorer. Type **%appdata%\Microsoft\Internet Explorer\Quick Launch** in the address bar. Shortcuts for Internet Explorer, Show desktop, and Switch between windows appear. Open a second instance of File Explorer and look for any folder that you want to add to the Quick Launch folder. Drag that folder to the Quick Launch folder. When the Create link in Quick Launch message appears, release your mouse button.

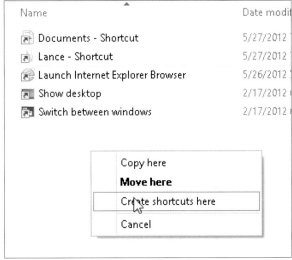

4 Add folders directly to Quick Launch: You can add other folders stored on your hard drive to the Quick Launch folder. For example, you can add your Users folder to the Quick Launch folder. Move to your hard drive in the second instance of File Explorer. Open the Users folder. You should see a folder with your name. Right-click that folder and drag it to the Quick Launch folder. Release your mouse button. In the drop-down menu that appears, click Create shortcut here.

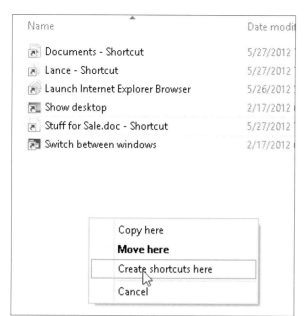

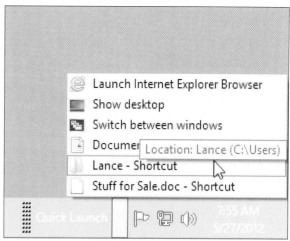

6 View Quick Launch toolbar: Click the double arrow next to the Quick Launch toolbar to view the new folders and shortcuts that you just added.

5 Add files directly to Quick Launch: You can add specific files, such as one of your documents, to the Quick Launch folder. Open the Documents folder under Libraries in the second instance of File Explorer. Right-click a specific document and drag it to the Quick Launch folder. Release your mouse button. In the pop-up menu that appears click Create shortcut here.

Quick Fix

Locking Windows

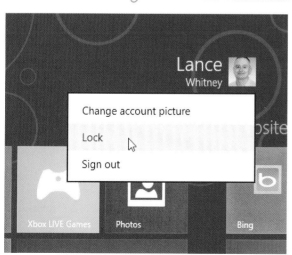

You can return to the Windows 8 Lock screen to prevent someone else from using your computer by locking it. Click your profile picture in the upper-right corner of the Start screen and select Lock from the pop-up menu, or just hold down the Windows key and press L.

Searching for Items in File Explorer

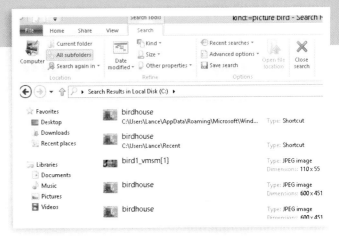

Windows 8 offers a new Search feature accessible from the Windows 8 environment, but you can still search for folders, files, and other content using the traditional desktop via File Explorer. Using File Explorer provides more options than does the Windows 8 search feature. As always, you can search for folders and files throughout your hard drive or other locations. You can search the contents of files to find specific documents. You can also set a variety of parameters to filter the search. The Windows 8 version of File Explorer offers a new Ribbon menu called Search specifically to help you find items. This task explains how to search for items in File Explorer.

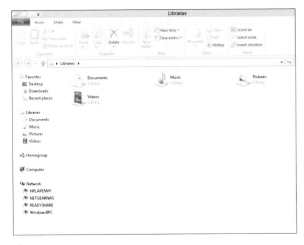

1 Launch File Explorer: Open the desktop and launch File Explorer full screen.

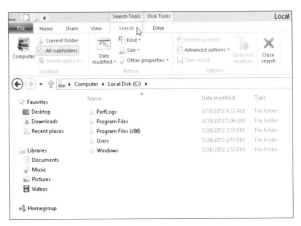

2 Access the Search menu: Double-click your hard drive. Click in the search field to the right of the address bar. A Search menu appears from the Ribbon.

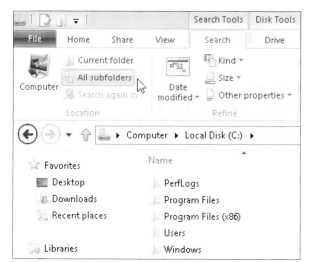

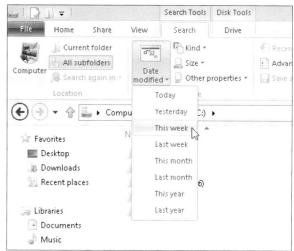

3 Choose the location: Click the Computer button on the Search toolbar if you want to search your entire computer. Click the Current folder icon on the toolbar if you want to search just your current folder. Otherwise, leave the setting at All subfolders if you want to search your current folder and all subfolders.

4 Choose the date: Click the Date modified button if you want to filter the results by a specific date range, such as today, yesterday, or this week. The results display according to the date you specify.

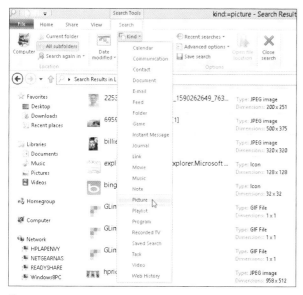

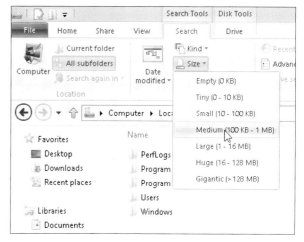

5 Choose the kind of file: Click the Kind button to specify a file type, such as document, e-mail, folder, music, picture, or video. The results display according to the kind of file you specify.

6 Choose the size: Click the Size button to specify a size for the file. The results display according to the size you specify.

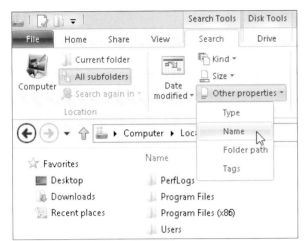

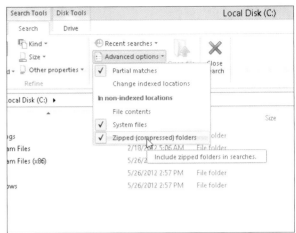

7 Choose other properties: Click the Other properties button to select a type, name, folder path, or tag for the file. The results display according to properties you specify.

8 Choose Advanced options: Click the Advanced options button to enable or disable partial matches and to change which locations on your hard drive are indexed by Windows. You can also choose to search the contents of system files and zipped files.

9 Save your search: After you have set all the parameters, you can save your search by clicking the Save search button.

10 Type your search term: Type your search term in the search field after any parameters that appear. Windows searches for that term using the parameters you specify.

tip Searching nonindexed files and contents will result in longer but more comprehensive searches.

11 Open the item: The search results appear in File Explorer. Double-click the folder or file that you want in order to open it.

Quick Fix

Creating a New Taskbar Toolbar

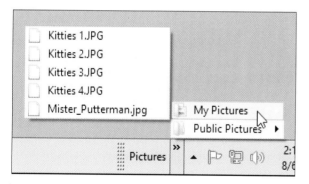

Open File Explorer. Right-click the taskbar and then click Toolbars. Select the New toolbar option. From the File Explorer window, browse to a specific folder. For example, you can choose the Documents folder, the Music folder, or the Pictures folder. Click the Select folder button. A toolbar with the name of the folder appears on the taskbar. Click the double right arrow next to the name of the folder to see all of its subfolders and files.

Customizing the Quick Access Toolbar

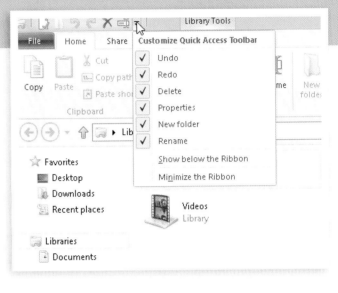

The new File Explorer in Windows 8 offers a Quick Access toolbar, the same type of toolbar found in Microsoft Office 2007 and 2010 applications, such as Word, Excel, and Outlook. This toolbar in File Explorer offers access to commonly used commands, including Undo, Redo, Delete, Properties, New folder, and Rename. You can customize this toolbar by choosing which commands to enable and disable. You can also add more commands to the toolbar from the File Explorer Ribbon, such as Cut, Copy, Paste, Email, Zip, Print, and Options. This task explains how to customize the Quick Access toolbar in File Explorer.

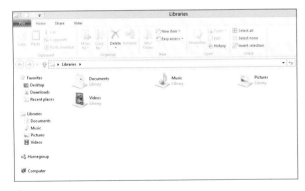

1 Open File Explorer: Open the Windows desktop and launch File Explorer from its toolbar icon.

2 Access the Quick Access toolbar: Click the down arrow next to the Quick Access toolbar on the Title bar.

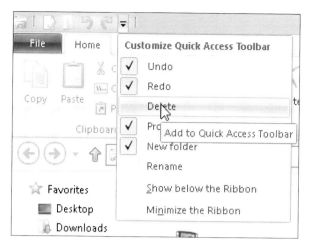

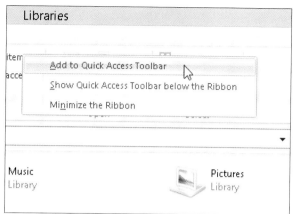

3 Add or remove items: By default, the Properties and New folder options are enabled. You can disable either of those by clicking them, and enable other commands by clicking them. Each time you enable or disable a command, the Quick Access menu shuts down, so you will need to reopen it to customize it further.

4 Add other commands to the toolbar: Right-click any command on the Ribbon. An Add to Quick Access Toolbar option appears. Click that option to add that command to the Ribbon. The Ribbon provides three menus — Home, Share, and View. You can add any command from any of those three menus to the Quick Access toolbar, even ones that are grayed out.

5 Remove a command: Right-click the Quick Access toolbar command that you want to remove and click Remove from Quick Access Toolbar.

tip You cannot sort the items in the Quick Access toolbar, so you must add them in the order in which you want them to appear.

6 Move the Quick Access toolbar: Click the down arrow next to the Quick Access toolbar. Click Show below the Ribbon to move the toolbar so it appears below the ribbon.

Managing Columns in File Explorer

The Details view in File Explorer displays columns for each folder and file with key information. By default, the columns display the name of the file, the date it was last modified, the file type, and the size. But you can add more columns with further details on specific folders and files. You can also remove columns that you do not need, and you can reorder the columns that appear, sort your folders and files alphabetically by column, and even filter your folders and files by column. This task explains how to work with columns in File Explorer.

Documents

Group by ▾
Add columns ▾

	Image file names
Sort by ▾	File name extensions	Hide selected items
	Hidden items
	Show/hide

Add columns:
- ✓ Name
- ✓ Type
- ✓ Size
- ✓ Date created
- ✓ Title
- ✓ File description
- ✓ File extension
- ✓ File version
- Folder path
- Authors
- Categories
- Tags
- Choose columns...

	Type	Size
ɔs	File folder	
:ers.doc	File folder	
.doc	DOC File	531 KB
ibels.doc	DOC File	39 KB
:ers.doc	DOC File	122 KB
doc	DOC File	478 KB
iformati	DOC File	126 KB
.gents.dc	DOC File	471 KB
ttorneys	DOC File	103 KB
	DOC File	27 KB

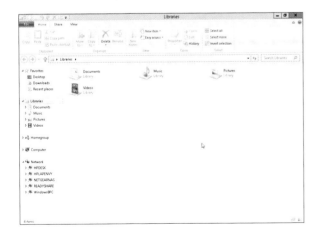

1 Launch File Explorer: Open the desktop and launch File Explorer full screen.

2 Open a folder: Open a specific folder with content, such as the Documents folder. Select the Details view from the Ribbon if not already selected.

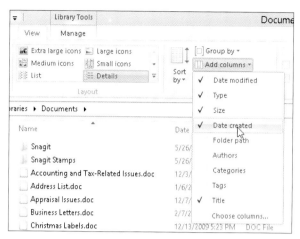

3 Add or remove columns: Click the View menu from the Ribbon. Click the Add Columns button. A list appears of all possible columns with check marks in front of the ones currently displayed. Select any columns you want to add. Deselect any columns you want to remove. After you add or remove a column, the Add Columns drop-down menu disappears, so you will have to reopen it to continue.

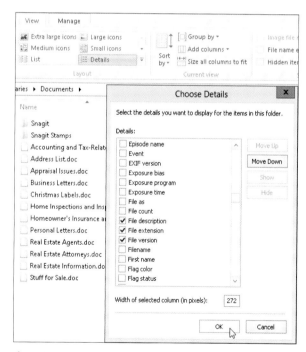

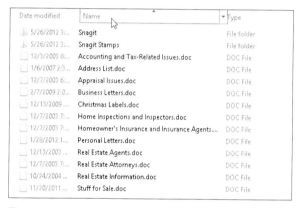

5 Change the order of columns: You can sort the order of the columns by dragging and dropping a column to a different spot. For example, you can drag the Name column to the right so that it appears after the Date modified column.

4 Add other columns: Click the Add Columns button. In the drop-down menu, click Choose columns. A long list appears with a range of details, some specific to certain types of files, such as E-mail address for Contacts, F-stop for photos, and Album artist for music. Select the columns that you want to display for your current folder. Click OK.

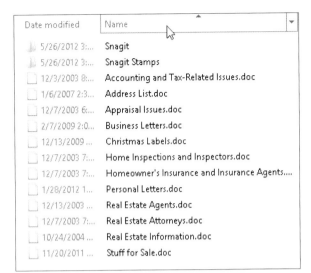

6 Sort by columns: Click the column heading that you want to sort by. For example, you can click the Name column to sort A–Z by filename. Clicking it again sorts the files Z–A by filename. You can click the Date modified column to sort by date, from earliest to most recent. Clicking the column again sorts by date, from most recent to earliest.

7 Filter columns: You can filter a column to see only certain folders or files. For example, click the drop-down arrow next to the Date modified column. Select a specific date or date range to narrow the results.

tip Columns are specific to each folder, so you can display different columns for different folders.

8 Group by columns: You can group your folders and files by certain columns, such as Date modified. Click the Group by button and then click Date modified. The folders and files are grouped by date, such as Yesterday, Earlier this year, and A long time ago.

Modifying the Windows Send to Menu

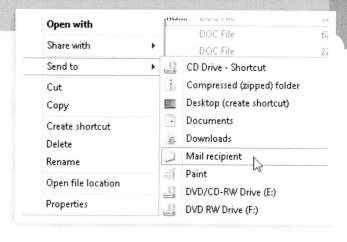

The Windows Send to menu lets you send or copy a file to different applications or folders through File Explorer, saving you the time and effort of having to open the file to perform a certain action. For example, the Send to menu lets you run such actions as copy a file to the Documents folder, zip (compress) a file, create a desktop shortcut of the file, e-mail a file, or fax a file through Windows fax software. You can access the Send to menu by right-clicking a file and clicking Send to from the pop-up menu. You can also modify the SendTo folder itself by adding or removing different applications and folders. This task explains how to modify the Send to menu.

1 Access the SendTo folder: Open the desktop and launch File Explorer. Type **%APPDATA%\Microsoft\Windows\SendTo** in the address field. You see the existing items in the Send to menu.

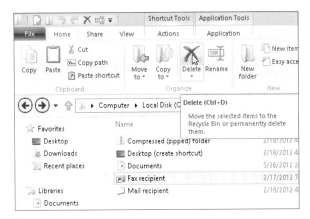

2 Remove items: Remove any item from the Send to menu that you do not need. For example, you can remove the item for Fax recipient by selecting it and clicking the Delete button from the Ribbon.

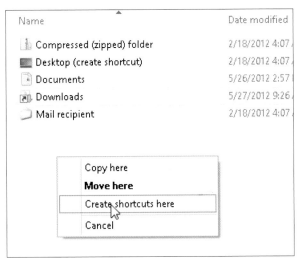

3 Add a folder: You can add a folder to the Send to menu. For this example, the Downloads folder is added. Open a second instance of File Explorer. Click the Downloads folder under Favorites. Drag the Downloads folder with your right mouse button and release it over the SendTo folder in the first instance of File Explorer. In the pop-up menu that appears, click Create shortcuts here.

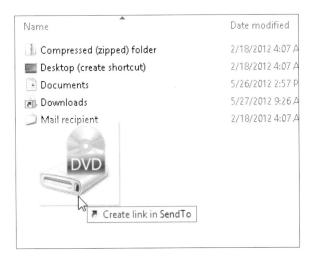

4 Add a location: You can also add a location, such a drive letter. For this example, the CD-ROM drive is used, assuming it is a recordable CD-ROM drive. Click Computer in the second instance of File Explorer. Drag the CD-ROM/DVD drive with your left mouse button onto the SendTo folder in the first instance of File Explorer. Release the mouse button when you see the Create link in SendTo message.

5 Add an application: You can add a specific application to the Send to menu. For this example, Paint is used. In the second instance of File Explorer, click your hard drive. Type Paint in the search field. From the results that appear, select one of the shortcuts for Paint. Drag the Paint shortcut with your right mouse button and release it over the SendTo folder in the first instance of File Explorer. In the pop-up menu that appears, click Copy here.

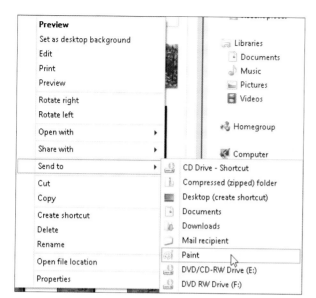

tip You can also add network drives to the SendTo folder.

6 View Send to menu: View your modified Send to menu. Right-click any file in File Explorer and access the Send to menu. You should see the new locations for your Downloads folder and your CD-ROM drive among the other selections. Selecting the Downloads folder copies the file to that folder. Selecting your CD-ROM drive prompts you to insert a recordable disc in the drive to which the file can be copied. Selecting the Paint program opens the file in Paint, but only if it is an image file that Paint can read.

Pinning Desktop Items to the Start Screen

Any desktop application that you install is automatically given a tile on the Start screen. So you do not need to manually pin it to the Start screen. However, if you unpinned a desktop application from the Start screen and want to pin it back, you can do so from the desktop. Also, you may want to pin certain desktop folders to the Start screen so that you can easily access them without having to open the desktop first. For example, you can pin your Documents folder or your Music folder to the Start screen. This task explains how to pin an application or folder to the Start screen.

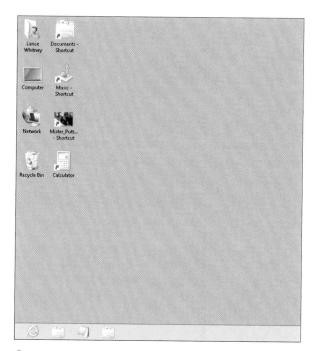

1 Open the desktop: Open the desktop by clicking the Desktop tile on the Start screen.

2 Select an application: If you already have shortcuts for certain applications on the desktop or taskbar, right-click one of those shortcuts and select Pin to Start from the pop-up menu.

3 Select a folder: Open File Explorer. Right-click a folder that you want to pin to the Start screen, such as Documents, Pictures, or Music, and select Pin to Start from the pop-up menu.

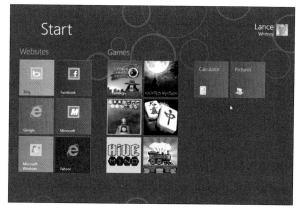

4 View the folder or the app: Launch the Start screen by pressing the Windows key. You should see tiles for the folder and application at the end of the Start screen.

tip You can also pin certain desktop icons, such as Computer, Control Panel, and Network to the Start screen.

5 View the folder or the app: In the Start screen, double-click the tile for the application or folder that you just pinned to the Start menu. Windows opens the desktop and launches the application or opens the folder.

Quick Fix

Previewing a File in File Explorer

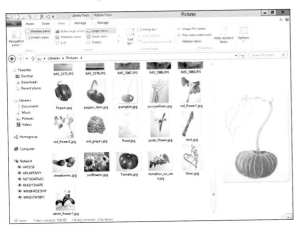

Open File Explorer. Browse to and select the file you want to view. Click the View menu to display the View Ribbon. Click the Preview Pane command on the View Ribbon. The file displays in the right pane of File Explorer. You cannot view all types of files, but you can view a wide variety, including images, HTML files, and certain types of documents.

Creating a Desktop Shortcut for All Apps

Normally, you have to open the Start or Apps screen to launch most of your apps — Windows 8 or desktop. This can be clumsy and time consuming if you are working in the desktop and need to keep going back to the Start screen to launch multiple desktop apps, one after another. Instead, you can create a desktop shortcut that points to all the apps on the Apps screen so you do not have to keep returning to the Windows 8 environment to launch an app. This task shows you how to create a desktop shortcut that lets you launch any app.

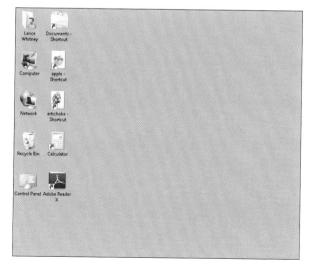

1 Open the desktop: Launch the desktop if it is not already running.

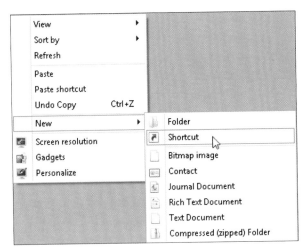

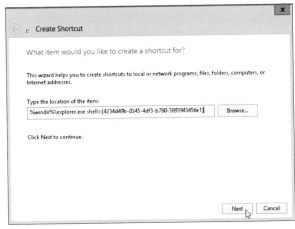

2 Create the shortcut: Right-click any empty area of the desktop. In the pop-up menu, click New and then click Shortcut.

warning Each time you close your new shortcut for Windows 8 apps, the order and display are reset back to the default.

3 Type the shortcut path: In Create Shortcut dialog box, type **%windir%\explorer.exe shell:::{4234d49b-0245-4df3-b780-3893943456e1}** in the Type the location of the item field. Click Next.

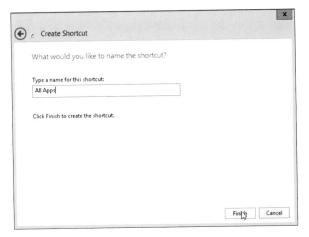

4 Name the shortcut: In the Type a name for this shortcut field, type a name for the shortcut, such as All Apps. Click Finish.

5 Open the folder: Double-click the new shortcut to view the icons for all your apps.

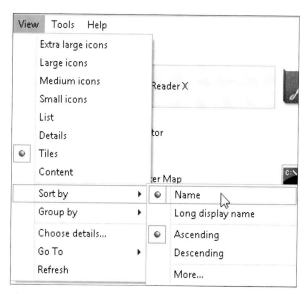

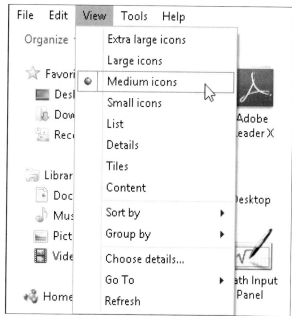

6 Sort the items: By default, the icons may not be sorted in alphabetical order. Click the Organize button at the top of the left pane. Click Layout and then Menu bar. Choose View → Sort by → Name. Make sure that Ascending is also selected.

7 Change the display: Click the View menu. Choose the view that you prefer, from Extra large icons to Content, which shows certain details such as the modified date and size.

Quick Fix

Viewing File Extensions

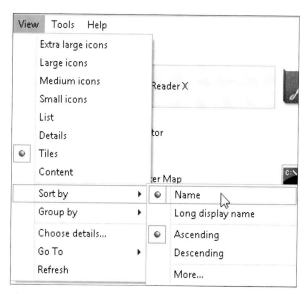

Open File Explorer. Click the View menu from the Ribbon. Select the File name extensions check box to view extensions. Deselect the check box to turn off extensions.

tip You can also change from one view to another by continually clicking the Change your view button in the upper-right corner.

Connecting to a Wi-Fi or Cellular Network

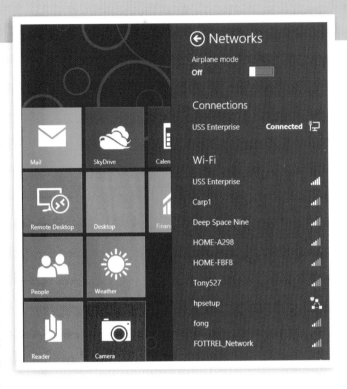

onnecting to Wi-Fi or cellular networks in previous versions of Windows could sometimes be problematic in terms of finding the right drivers and software. For Windows 8, Microsoft developed its own universal driver to help Wi-Fi and cellular hardware work in a more plug-and-play fashion. Windows 8 also offers a new panel accessible from both the Windows 8 environment and the desktop that lets you view available Wi-Fi and cellular networks. The new Networks panel lets you easily connect to any network. This task shows you how to connect to a Wi-Fi or cellular network.

1 Launch Start screen: Open the Start screen.

tip You can also access the Network sidebar by clicking the Wi-Fi icon in the system tray of the desktop.

2 Go to Settings: Hover your mouse over the Semantic Zoom button to display the Charms bar. Click the Settings charm.

3 Open the Networks panel: The icon for wireless networks displays the word Available if accessible Wi-Fi networks are in your location.

4 View available networks: The Networks panel appears as a sidebar on the right. If the computer is already plugged into a router, the Connections section displays the name of the wired network. The Wi-Fi section displays any Wi-Fi networks that are available.

5 View details on available networks: Hover your mouse over the name of any Wi-Fi network. Windows tells you what type of security is enabled for that network.

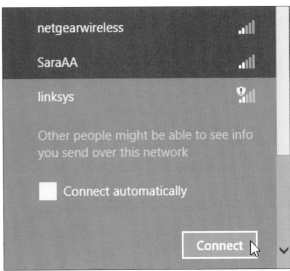

6 Click a network: Click the name of a Wi-Fi network. If it is an unsecured network, Windows warns you that other people might be able to see info you send over this network.

7 Choose your network: Click Connect to connect to your preferred Wi-Fi network. You can also select the Connect automatically check box if you want to automatically connect to this network any time it is within range of your computer.

8 Enter the network security key: If the network is secure, Windows prompts you to enter the password or network security key. Type the key. You can click and hold down the eye icon to reveal the characters of the password to ensure that you typed them correctly. Click Next.

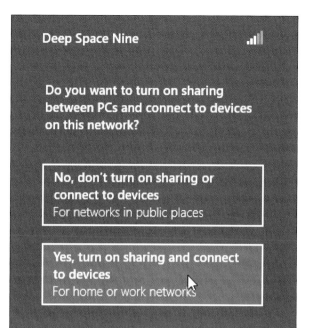

9 Turn on sharing: Windows asks if you want to turn on sharing or connect to devices. Select Yes if you are connecting to a secure home or work network; select No if you are connecting to a public network.

10 Connection made: If the connection is successful, Connected appears next to the name of the Wi-Fi network. An icon also shows the strength of the network's signal.

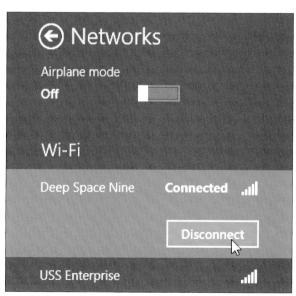

11 Disconnect from network: If you want to manually disconnect from the network, click the network name and click Disconnect.

12 Connect to a 3G/4G network: Click the connection for your 3G or 4G network. Click Connect. If the connection is successful, Connected appears next to the name of the network.

13 Access an Ethernet network: If your desktop or laptop is plugged directly into a router, then the connection should automatically be established.

14 Turn off Networks sidebar: Click any empty area in the Windows 8 environment to turn off the Networks sidebar.

Quick Fix

Unhiding Files and Folders in File Explorer

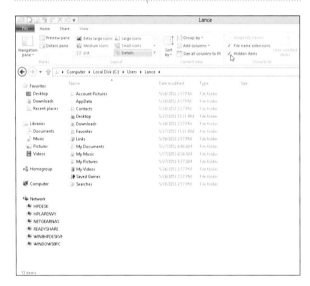

Open File Explorer. Click the View menu from the Ribbon. Select the Hidden items check box. Folders and files that are normally hidden are now visible. Deselect the check box to hide them.

Managing a Wi-Fi or Cellular Network

Windows 8 has several options for controlling and managing your Wi-Fi and cellular connections. You can view connection properties to check or change the security and encryption types and the network security key for your own network. You can set a network as a metered connection to keep track of how much data it is using, a handy option for cellular accounts with a limited number of monthly minutes. You can also display the estimated data use to see how many megabytes you have downloaded using a certain connection, another useful option for cellular accounts. This task shows you how to manage your Wi-Fi and cellular networks.

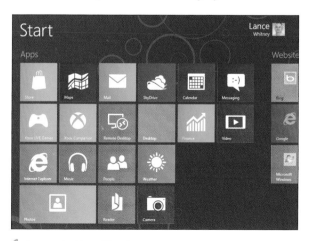

1 Launch the Start screen: Open the Start screen.

2 Go to Settings: Hover your mouse over the Semantic Zoom button to display the Charms bar. Click the Settings charm.

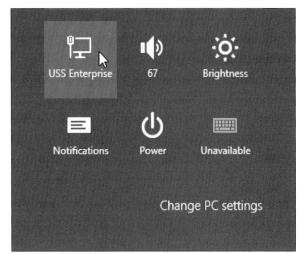

3 Open the Networks panel: The first icon for wireless networks shows that it is available if accessible networks are in your location. Click that icon.

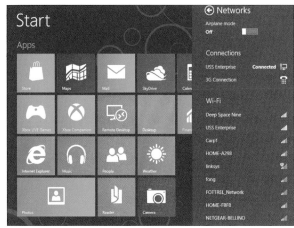

4 View available networks: The Networks panel displays as a sidebar on the right. The Connections section displays any available connected wired network and any 3G/4G connections. The Wi-Fi section displays available Wi-Fi networks.

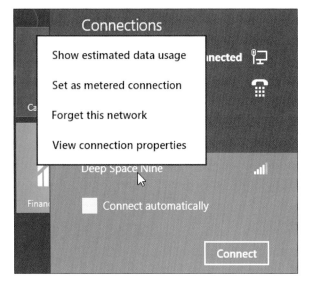

5 View options:
Right-click a network connection that you have already used in Windows 8, such as your home network. A pop-up menu with four options appears.

tip You can turn on Airplane mode to disable Wi-Fi and cellular access and save battery power on your laptop.

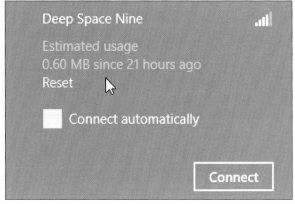

6 Show estimated data usage: Click Show estimated data usage. Estimated usage appears showing how many megabytes of data have been used over a certain period. You can click Reset to set the estimated usage counter back to zero. To hide the data usage, right-click the network again and click Hide estimated data usage.

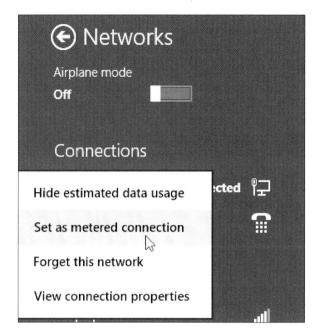

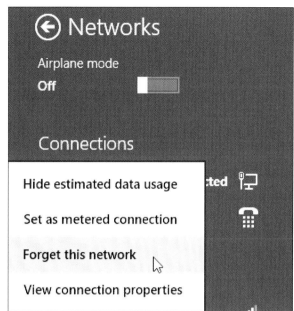

7 Set as metered connection: Click Set as metered connection if you want to limit the amount of usage on this network. This means that certain noncritical Windows updates and other software are deferred until you are on a nonmetered connection. Therefore, you may want to set your 3G or 4G connection as a metered connection to reduce the amount of data that gets downloaded. To turn off the metered connection, right-click the network and click Set as nonmetered connection.

8 Forget this network: Click Forget this network for a network that you do not need to connect to again. Forgetting the network removes the stored information for the network security key.

9 View connection properties: Click View connection properties to open the Windows desktop and display the network's security and encryption types and security key, which gives you the ability to change the security key if necessary.

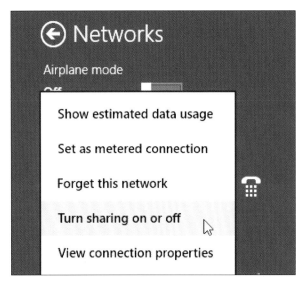

10 Turn sharing on or off: This option appears on the right-click pop-up menu for any live connections. Click Turn sharing on or off if you want to change the network's current sharing setting.

11 Turn off Networks sidebar: Click any empty area in the Start page to turn off the Networks sidebar.

tip You can access the Networks sidebar by clicking the Wi-Fi icon in the system tray of the desktop.

Quick Fix

Changing the View in File Explorer

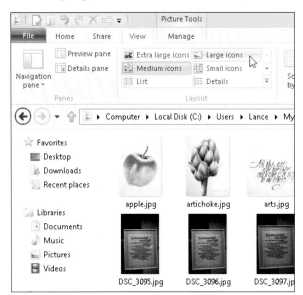

Open File Explorer. Click the View menu from the Ribbon. Hover your mouse over the different views — Extra large icons, Large icons, Medium icons, Small icons, List, Details, Tiles, and Content — to preview the different views. Click the bottom scroll arrow to see the Tiles and Content views. Click the view you want to use for your current folder.

Setting Ease of Access Features

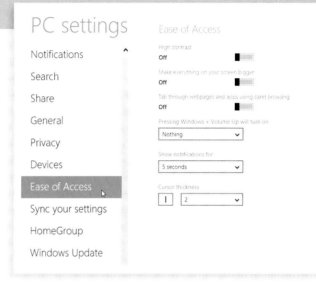

W indows 8 offers certain Ease of Access features aimed especially at people who have poor eyesight or other difficulties with their vision. These features are designed to change certain colors, enlarge the content, and enable an audio narrator. Other Ease of Access features include an on-screen keyboard and a magnifier. Sticky keys let you press one key at a time for key combinations rather than having to press both keys at the same time. And filter keys ignore additional presses of the same key. You can enable Ease of Access features at the login screen or in the PC Settings screen, though both screens show slightly different features. This task explains how to enable the Ease of Access features.

1 Enable Ease of Access at login: Boot up Windows 8. At the Lock screen, press any key on your keyboard to access the login screen. At the login screen, an Ease of Access icon appears in the lower-left corner.

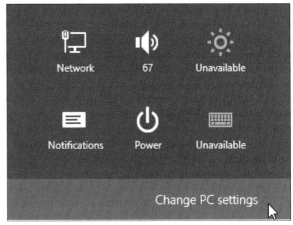

3 Enable Ease of Access through PC Settings: You can enable or disable each Ease of Access feature after you log in to Windows. At the Start screen, click the Semantic Zoom button in the lower left to display the Charms bar. Click the Settings Charm. Click the Change PC Settings link at the bottom of the sidebar.

2 Click the Ease of Access icon: A menu with the following items appears: Narrator, Magnifier, On-Screen Keyboard, High Contrast, Sticky Keys, and Filter Keys. The Narrator begins speaking to introduce you to and explain each feature. To enable the Narrator, Magnifier, or On-Screen Keyboard, click the feature. To turn on High Contrast, Sticky Keys, or Filter Keys, move the black box on the horizontal bar to the right.

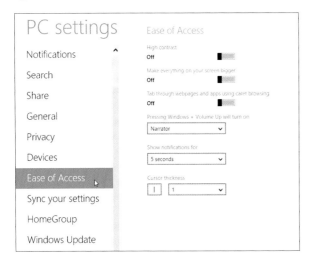

4 Click Ease of Access: In the PC Settings screen, click Ease of Access. Options appear for High contrast, Make everything on your screen bigger, and Tab through web pages and apps using caret browsing. Another option lets you control what happens when you press the Windows key and the Volume Up key. A Notifications option determines how long a notification appears on the screen, and a Cursor thickness option controls the width of the cursor.

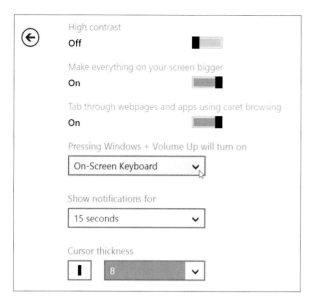

tip Caret browsing lets you use the Home, End, Page Up, Page Down, the arrow keys, and Tab to navigate many web pages.

5 Enable your settings: You can turn on any of the first three options by moving the black box on the horizontal bar to the right. You can customize the other three options by setting a specific value. After you set the appropriate options, you can close the PC Settings window by clicking any empty area of the Start screen.

Quick Fix

Disabling the File Explorer Ribbon

Open File Explorer. Click the Minimize the Ribbon icon (the up arrow to the left of the question mark icon). The Ribbon closes and remains closed so that only the Menu names are visible. Click the same icon, which is now Expand the Ribbon, to reenable the Ribbon.

Displaying Administrative Tools

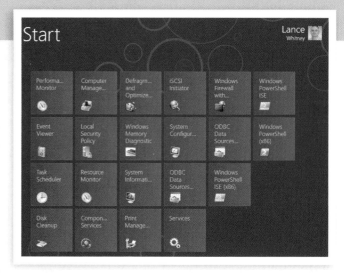

The Windows 8 Administrative Tools are a collection of system tools and features. Some of them are tools you may never use. But others can come in handy at times, especially when you need to troubleshoot problems, check on your Windows configuration, or run diagnostics. Some of the most useful tools include System Information, Disk Cleanup, System Configuration, Computer Management, and Windows Memory Diagnostic. By default, the Administrative Tools do not appear on the Windows Start screen, so they are not easily accessible. But you can quickly add them to the Start screen. This task shows you how to display the Administrative Tools on the Start screen.

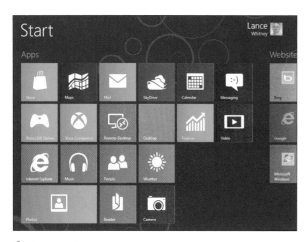

1 Access Start screen: Open the Start screen.

2 Display Charms bar: Hover your mouse over the Semantic Zoom button in the lower-right corner to display the Charms bar.

3 Open Settings: Click the Settings charm. Click the Tiles link at the top of the menu under the word Start.

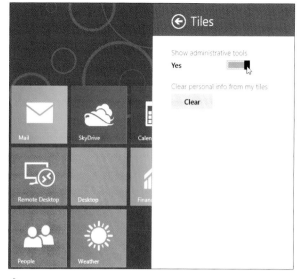

4 Turn on administrative tools: Move the white square on the bar under Show administrative tools to the right so it says Yes.

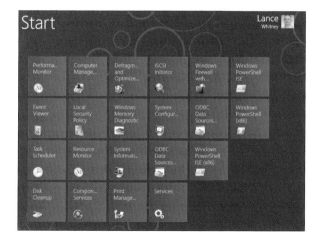

5 Return to Start screen: Click any empty area of the Start screen to turn off the sidebar. Scroll to the right on the Start screen until you see all the individual tiles for the administrative tools.

tip The Administrative Tools tiles are not organized, so you may want to create and name a separate group to better arrange them.

Dual-Booting with Another Version of Windows

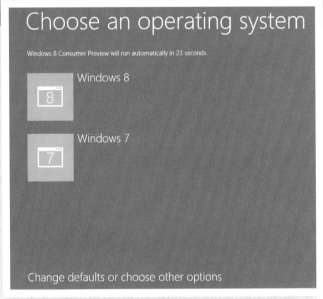

Choose an operating system

Windows 8 Consumer Preview will run automatically in 23 seconds.

Windows 8

Windows 7

Change defaults or choose other options

You can install Windows 8 on a computer without replacing your current version of Windows. This process allows you to dual-boot Windows 8 with a previous version of Windows, so you have the option of loading either one. This is a good way to test Windows 8 on an existing computer without losing access to Windows 7, Vista, or XP. When your computer boots up, Windows 8 displays a boot menu that lets you select which version of Windows to load. This task explains how to set up and dual-boot Windows 8 with another version of Windows.

1 Open Disk Management: Free up space on your hard drive to install Windows 8. For this example, Windows 7 is used. Open Control Panel. Click System and Security. In the Administrative tools section, click Create and format hard disk partitions.

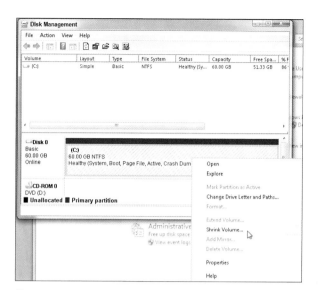

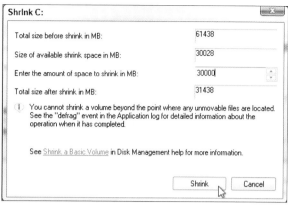

2 Select your primary partition: In the Disk Management window, right-click your primary partition, typically your main hard drive, and select Shrink Volume from the pop-up menu.

3 Create free space: Type a number in the Enter the amount of space to shrink in MB field. At least 16GB of space are needed for the 32-bit version of Windows 8 and 20GB for the 64-bit version. If you plan to install applications and add files, add more free space. Assuming you have enough space, type a number ranging from 30 to 50GB, which is 30,000 to 50,000MB, and then click Shrink.

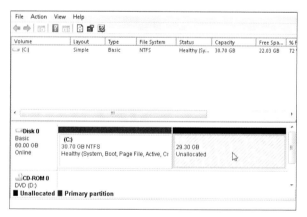

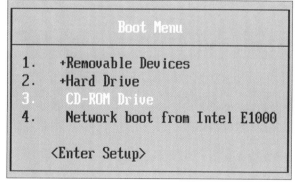

4 Check the drive: After the shrink process is complete a new partition showing the amount of free, or unallocated, space appears.

5 Reboot your computer: Insert your Windows 8 installation disc and reboot your computer. Press the appropriate key to boot off your CD-ROM/DVD drive. When you see the Boot Menu, select the CD-ROM/DVD drive option. A message appears telling you to Press any key to boot from CD or DVD. Press any key on your keyboard. The Windows 8 installation loads from the disc.

6 Install Windows 8: Select the options for language, time, and keyboard input. Click Next. Click Install now. Type the product key. Click Next. Accept the license terms. Click Next.

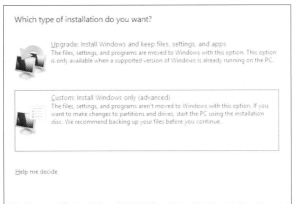

7 Choose custom install: A window appears asking which type of installation you want. Select the Custom: Install Windows only (advanced) option.

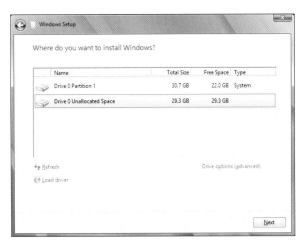

8 Choose where to install Windows 8: The next window asks where you want to install Windows 8. Select the Unallocated Space drive. Click Next. Windows 8 installs and then lets you personalize it.

tip You must choose Windows 8 as the default OS to see the Windows 8 boot menu.

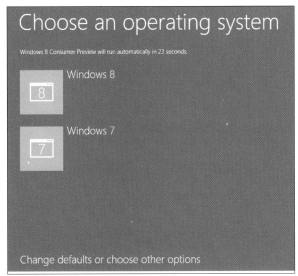

9 Choose Windows from the boot menu: Each time you boot your PC, the Windows 8 boot menu appears. The boot menu offers a choice to load Windows 8 or your previous version of Windows. Click the version of Windows that you want to load.

Setting Up Windows 8 after Installation

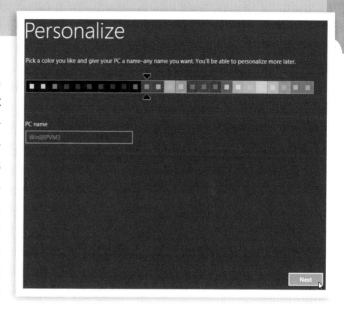

After you install Windows 8, a setup process runs that enables you to personalize your Windows environment. The setup process lets you choose a background color for Windows, a name for your PC, and a wireless network if you are using a laptop or a desktop with a wireless connection. Further, you can choose to use Express settings to set the default options for a range of settings, or you can customize each setting. Using the Express settings is a quicker option, but customizing each setting individually gives you more granular control over each one. This task explains how to set up Windows 8 after it has been installed.

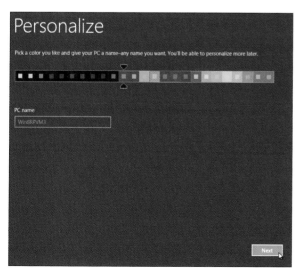

1 Chose the color and PC name: The first screen to appear is called Personalize. Choose the background color that you want to appear in Windows. Type the name that you want to assign to your PC. Click Next.

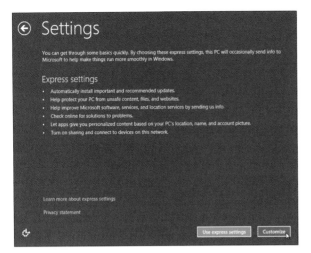

2 Configure settings: On a laptop, a Wireless screen appears asking if you want to connect to a Wi-Fi network. Click Connect and type your network password, or skip this step. After you connect, or if you skip this step, the next screen asks if you want to use Express settings to set up your PC or if you want to customize each option. If you are comfortable with Express settings, click Use express settings; otherwise click Customize.

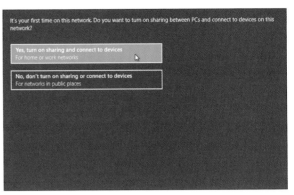

3 Turn on sharing: If you clicked Customize, the next screen asks if you want to turn on sharing and connect to devices on your home network. If this is a home network, you can click that option. Click Next. If you clicked Express settings instead of Customize, the next screen to appear asks you to Sign in to your PC, as described in Step 7.

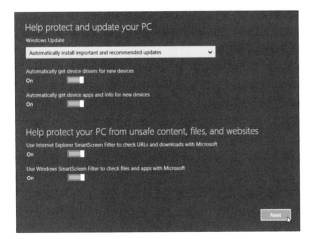

4 Enable Windows Update: The next screen asks if you want to enable Windows Update to get device drivers, apps, and info for new devices, and use Internet Explorer SmartScreen Filter. Make your choices and click Next.

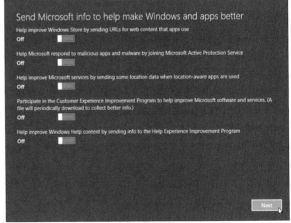

5 Send information to Microsoft: The next screen asks if you want to send information to Microsoft to help make Windows and apps better. Some people have privacy concerns over sending such information, but Microsoft does use it for legitimate reasons, so you can safely enable this option if you want. Click Next.

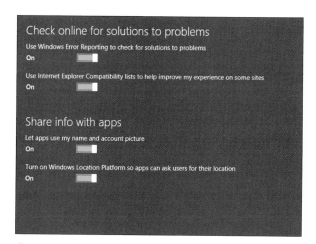

6 Check online for solutions: The next screen asks if you want to check online for solutions to problems and share info with apps. Make your choices and Click Next.

7 Sign in: The next screen asks you to sign in with your Microsoft account. If you do not have a Microsoft account, click Sign up for a new email address. A screen appears where you can set up a new account. If you want to use a local account instead, click the Sign in without a Microsoft account link. Otherwise, type the e-mail address for your Microsoft account. Click Next.

8 Type your Microsoft account password: At the next screen, type your Microsoft account password. You can click and hold down the eye icon next to the password field to reveal the characters of your password to ensure that you enter it correctly. Click Next. You eventually see the message Preparing Windows. After the preparation is complete, Windows 8 loads.

9 Add security info: At the next screen, confirm the phone number you used when creating your Microsoft account. This phone number is used by Microsoft to call or text you with a reset password code if you cannot sign in to your account.

tip You can change any setting at any time. Open the Charms bar. Click the Settings charm and then click Change PC settings.

10 Wait for your account to be set up: Windows sets up your account and then delivers you to the Start screen.

Quick Fix

Managing the Taskbar

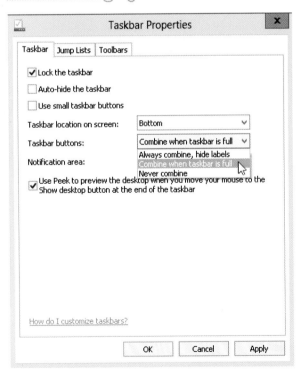

Right-click the taskbar. Click Properties and then select Auto-hide the taskbar to make it appear only when you move your mouse to the bottom of the screen. Select Lock the taskbar so it cannot be moved. Select Use small taskbar buttons to reduce the size of the icons. Click the Taskbar location on screen drop-down menu and set the location: Bottom, Left, Right, or Top. Click the Taskbar buttons drop-down menu to determine whether taskbar buttons will be combined.

Updating Windows 8

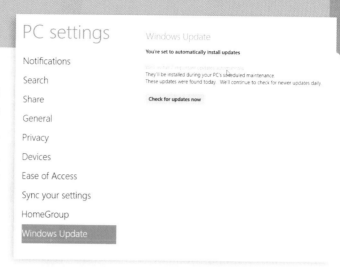

Windows 8 carries on the tradition of periodically offering security fixes, new hardware drivers, and other updates for the operating system and Microsoft software. Some of these are critical fixes that should be applied as soon as possible, while others are simply recommended or optional updates that you can install if you wish. When you first personalize Windows 8, you are asked how you want the operating system to handle updates. You can install them automatically, download them but choose whether to install them, check for updates but choose whether to download and install them, or never check for updates. You can change those settings as well as view and install available updates. This task explains how to update Windows 8.

1 Open the Windows Update screen: Open the desktop. Hover your mouse in the lower-right hot corner to display the Charms bar. Click the Settings charm. Click Control Panel at the top of the desktop sidebar. From Control Panel, click System and Security. Click the setting for Windows Update. The screen displays how many updates are available, if any.

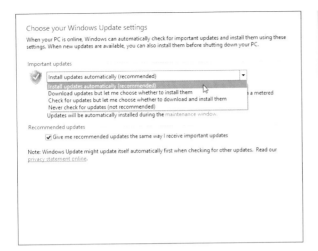

2 Change settings: Click Change settings. Click the drop-down menu under Important updates if you want to change the setting. Leave the Recommended updates check box selected if you want Windows to handle those in the same way it handles important updates. Click OK.

3 View update history: Click the link to View update history to see a list of updates that have already been installed. Click OK.

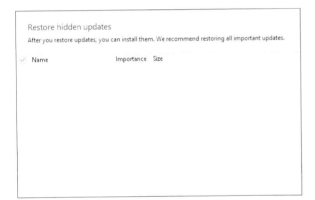

4 Restore hidden updates: Click the setting to Restore hidden updates if you previously hid any updates from view. Click Restore to restore any hidden updates, or Cancel to return to the previous screen.

5 Check for updates: Click the Check for updates setting to see if updates are available. If a notice of any updates appears, click the link to see the updates. You can then install the updates if you want.

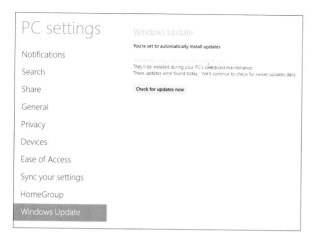

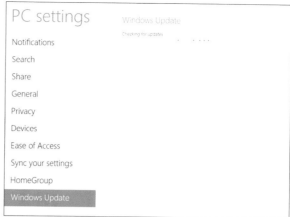

6 Open Windows Update from PC Settings 8 screen: Open any Windows 8 screen or app. Hover your mouse in the lower-right hot corner to display the Charms bar. Click the Settings charm. Click the Change PC settings link. Click the Windows Update setting at the bottom of the left sidebar. Windows displays a We'll install *X* important updates automatically link, where *X* is the number of updates.

7 Check for more updates: Click Check for updates now to see if any other updates are available. Windows checks for more updates.

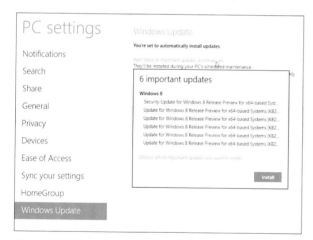

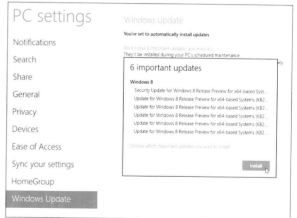

8 View all updates: You can wait for the updates to be installed automatically, or you can install them yourself. To install them yourself, click We'll install *X* important updates automatically. A list of all updates appears.

9 Install all updates: Click Install to install all the updates.

tip If you have automatic updates turned on, you do not need to manually check for or install updates unless you want to install an update immediately.

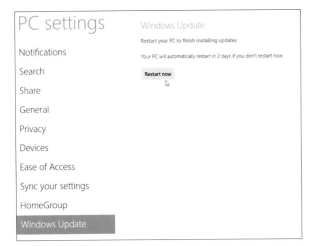

10 Restart your PC: After the updates have been installed, you may be prompted to restart your PC. You can click Restart now or wait for your PC to automatically restart.

tip You can check for and install updates from either the Control Panel or the Windows 8 PC settings screen.

Be Imaginative

Discover the features behind many of the new apps that come with Windows 8.

billie

y

Lance Whitney

Marty Whitney

>

⏻

Adding a Microsoft Account to Windows

You can add new accounts to Windows 8, either Microsoft accounts or local accounts. Through multiple accounts, you can then share your PC with family members or other people, each within their own unique environments. A Microsoft account gives you the ability to automatically log in to different online services and synchronize certain content and settings across multiple Windows 8 computers. You can either add an existing Microsoft account or create a new one by requesting a new e-mail address. You can also modify those accounts as Standard ones with limited capabilities or Administrator ones with full privileges. This task explains how to add existing and new Microsoft accounts to Windows 8.

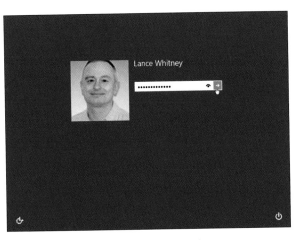

1 Log in: Log in to Windows with an Administrator account.

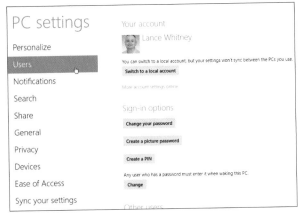

2 Access the users page: Hover your mouse in the lower-right hot corner to display the Charms bar. Click the Settings charm and then select the Change PC settings option. In the left pane of the PC settings screen, click Users.

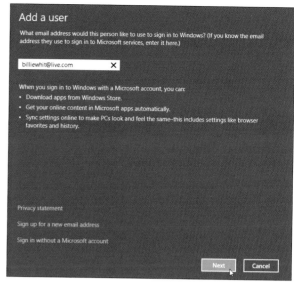

3 Add a user: In the Other users section, click the Add a user button.

4 Use an existing Microsoft account: To use an existing Microsoft account, type the account's e-mail address. Click Next.

5 View Family Safety option: At the next screen, select the Turn on Family Safety option if this will be a child's account. Otherwise, click Finish. The account is added.

6 Sign out: Open the Start screen by pressing the Windows key or clicking on the thumbnail in the lower-left hot corner. Click your account name and picture in the upper-right corner. From the menu, click Sign out.

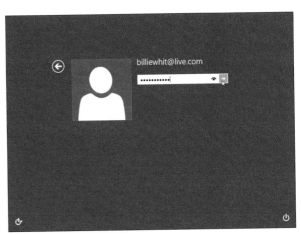

7 Log in with new account: Press any key to get past the Lock screen. Click the name and picture of the account that you just added.

8 Type the password: Type the account's password.

Your PC will be ready in just a moment

9 Wait for account setup: Windows prepares a fresh environment for the new account.

10 View Start screen: The Start screen appears for the new account.

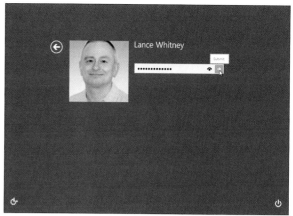

12 Log in as Administrator: Log in with your original account, the one with administrative privileges.

11 Sign out: Click the account name and picture in the upper-right corner. From the menu, click Sign out.

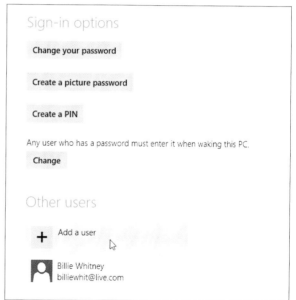

13 Access the Users page: Hover your mouse in the lower-right hot corner to display the Charms bar. Click the Settings charm and then select the Change PC settings option. In the left pane of the PC settings screen, click Users.

14 Add a new Microsoft account: In the Other users section, click the Add a user button.

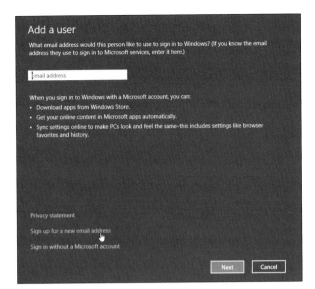

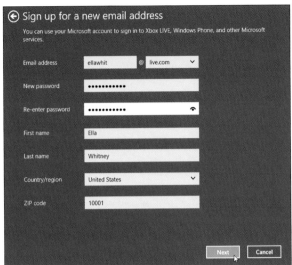

15 Request a new Microsoft account: To request a new e-mail address, click Sign up for a new email address.

16 Enter information for new address: In the Sign up for a new email address screen, choose an e-mail address using either hotmail.com or live.com as the domain name. Type a password, and then type your first name, last name, country, and ZIP code. Click Next.

17 Enter security info: At the Add security verification info screen, type your phone number, an alternate e-mail address, and a secret question and answer. Click Next.

18 Enter personal information: At the Finish up screen, type your date of birth, your gender, and the characters for the CAPTCHA security. Click Next. Windows warns you if the e-mail address you chose is already taken. If so, you need to select a different address. Choose a different address and keep clicking Next to go through the same screens again.

19 Finish: At the next screen, select the Turn on Family Safety check box if this will be a child's account. Otherwise, click Finish.

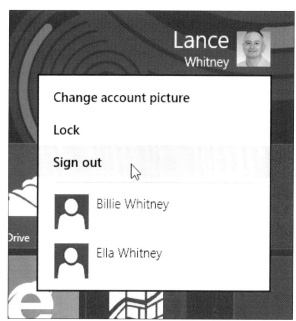

20 Sign out: Return to the Start screen by pressing the Windows key or clicking on the thumbnail in the lower-right hot corner. Click your account name and picture in the upper-right corner. From the menu, click Sign out.

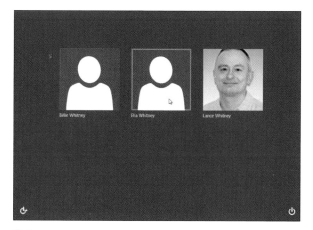

21 Log in with new account: Press any key to get past the Lock screen. Click the name and picture of the account that you just added.

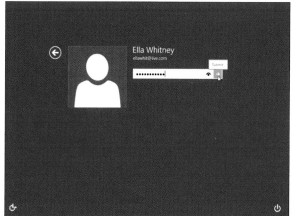

22 Type the password: Type the account's password.

Your PC will be ready in just a moment

23 Wait for account setup: Windows prepares a fresh environment for the new account.

Start

Ella Whitney

Mail   Photos   Camera   Maps   News

SkyDrive   Xbox LIVE Games   Messaging   Desktop   Sports

Music   Sunday   Weather   Travel

People   Video   Internet Explorer   Store   Finance

24 View Start screen: The Start screen appears for the new account.

tip When choosing the e-mail address for a new account, pick something unique; otherwise you will keep discovering that it is already taken.

tip You must be logged in as an Administrator to add an account.

Adding a Local Account to Windows

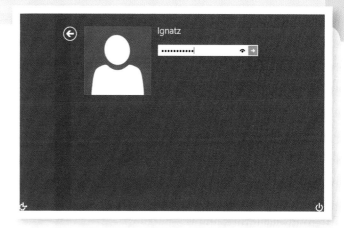

You can add a new account to Windows 8, either a local account or a Microsoft account. By using multiple accounts, you can then share your PC with family members or other people, each with their own unique environments. A local account does not require you set up access through Microsoft. If you do not plan to use online services such as SkyDrive or synchronize content across multiple Windows 8 computers, then a local account should suffice. You can also modify a local account as a Standard one with limited capabilities or an Administrator one with full privileges. This task explains how to add a local account to Windows 8.

1 Log in: Log in to Windows with an Administrator account.

2 Access the Users page: Hover your mouse in the lower-right hot corner to display the Charms bar. Click the Settings charm and then the Change PC settings option. In the left pane of the PC settings screen, click Users.

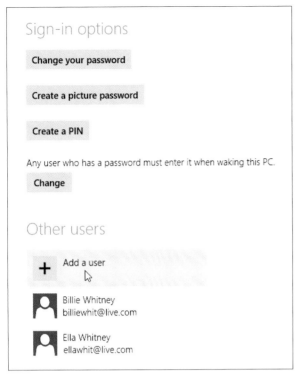

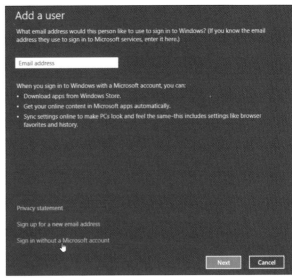

4 Use a local account: To add a local account, click Sign in without a Microsoft account.

3 Add a user: In the Other users section, click the Add a user button.

5 Choose Local account: The next screen explains the difference between using a Microsoft account and using a local account. Click Local account.

6 Enter account information: At the next screen, type the username, password, and password hint for the new account. Click Next.

7 Finish: At the next screen, select the Turn on Family Safety check box if this is a child's account. Otherwise, click Finish.

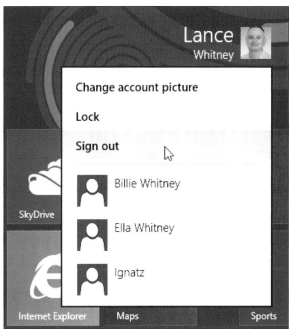

8 Sign out: Return to the Start screen by pressing the Windows key or clicking on the thumbnail in the lower-left hot corner. Click your account name and picture in the upper-right corner. From the menu, click Sign out.

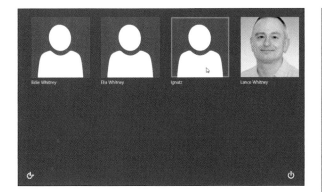

9 Sign in with new account: Press any key to get past the Lock screen. Click the name and picture of the account that you just added.

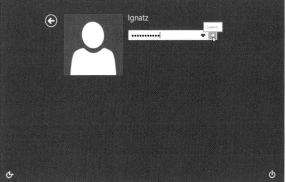

10 Type the password: Type the account's password.

Your PC will be ready in just a moment

11 Wait for account setup: Windows prepares a fresh environment for the new account.

12 View Start screen: The Start screen appears for the new account.

tip You must be logged in as an Administrator to add an account.

Changing the Time Zone

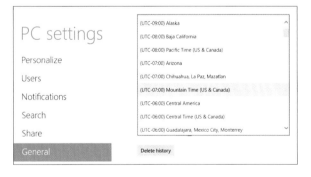

From the Start screen, type the word **time**. Click Settings. In the search results on the left pane, click the Change the time zone setting. From the Time section on the General screen, select your time zone in the drop-down menu. You can also set the option to automatically adjust for daylight saving time.

Logging in with
Different Accounts

You can set up multiple accounts on your Windows 8 computer. You may have an account for yourself and separate accounts for other family members or people who use the computer. You could even have both a local account and a Microsoft account for yourself. After you set up all of your necessary accounts, you can choose which one to use when you log in to Windows. You can also easily switch from one account to another directly from the Start screen so that both accounts are signed in, or sign out completely and then sign back in with a different account. This task explains how to log in with different accounts.

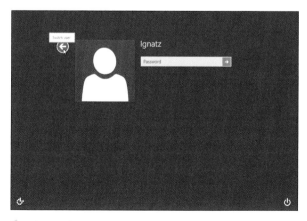

1 View all accounts: Reboot your computer. Press any key to get past the Windows 8 Lock screen. The login screen displays the last account that was used to access the computer. Click the Switch user button to the left of your account picture.

2 Choose account: From the screen showing all available accounts, click the account that you want to use.

3 Log in with account: From the login screen, type the password for the account you chose.

4 View Start screen: The account's Start screen appears.

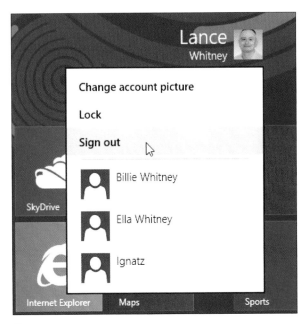

5 Log out from Windows: Click your account name and picture at the top-right corner of the screen. From the menu, click Sign out. Your account is signed out completely.

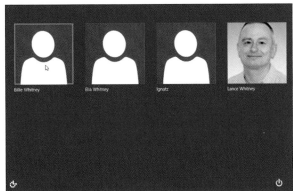

6 View all accounts: Press any key to get past the Windows 8 Lock screen. The screen shows all available accounts. Click the account you want to use.

tip Switching from one account to another rather than logging out completely ensures that the first account's apps, files, and documents remain open.

7 Log in with account: From the login screen, type the password for the account you chose.

8 View Start screen: The account's Start screen appears.

9 Switch to different account: Click your account name and picture at the top-right corner of the screen. Click the account that you want to switch to.

10 Log in with account: From the login screen, type the password for the account you chose.

11 View Start screen: The account's Start screen appears.

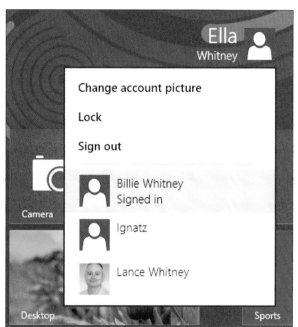

12 Switch to previous account: Click your account name and picture at the top-right corner of the screen. The previous account displays "Signed in" underneath it, indicating that the account is still signed in to Windows. Click that account.

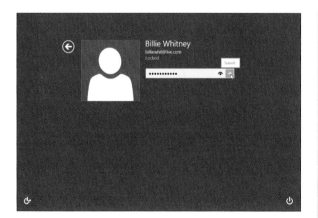

13 Log in with account: From the login screen, type the password for the account you chose.

14 View Start screen: The account's Start screen appears.

Managing Your User Accounts

A fter you set up accounts in Windows 8 for yourself and potentially for other users of the PC, you may need to change certain features of those accounts. For example, you may want to change the account name or password. You may want to change the account type to Standard or Administrator. You may want to limit the account using the Family Safety feature. Or you may simply want to delete the account if it is no longer needed. You can perform all of these tasks for all accounts from the Manage Accounts page. This task explains how to manage your user accounts.

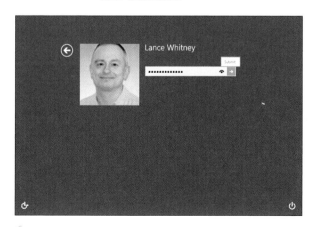

1 Log in: Log in to Windows with an Administrator account.

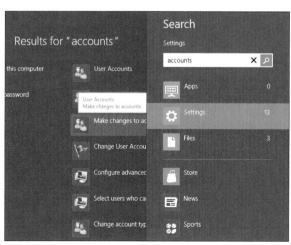

2 Open the Manage Accounts page: At the Start screen, type **accounts**. Click Settings below the search field. In the search results in the left pane, click Make changes to accounts.

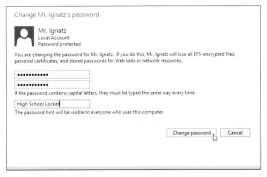

3 Choose the account: In the Manage Accounts window, select the account you want to change.

4 View options: Depending on the account type, you see different options. A local account displays options to change the account name, change the password, set up Family Safety, change the account type, and delete the account. A Microsoft account displays options to set up Family Safety, change the account type, and delete the account. For this example, it is assumed the account is local.

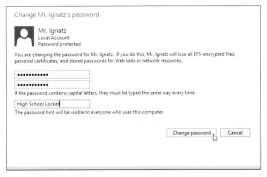

5 Change the account name: Click the option to change the account name. In the Type a new account name screen, type a new account name in the text field. Click Change Name. The name is changed, and you are returned to the Change an Account screen for that account.

6 Change the password: Click the option to change the password. In the Change password screen, type the new password and then type it again as confirmation. Type a password hint. Click Change password. The password is changed, and you are returned to the Change an Account screen for that account.

tip You must be logged in as an Administrator to change any properties of a user account.

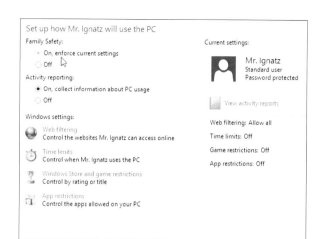

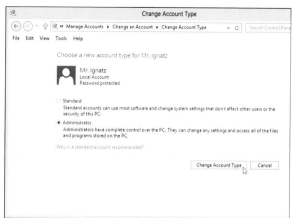

Click Set up Family Safety. Click the account to which you want to apply Family Safety. The account must be set up as a Standard user, not an Administrator. In the screen to set up how the user will use the PC, select the On, enforce current settings radio button. Make sure that under Activity reporting the On, collect information about PC usage radio button is selected. You can also set specific restrictions for web filtering, time limits, the Windows Store, games, and apps.

Click the option to manage another account and select the account you want to manage. Click the Change the account type option. From the Choose a new account type screen, select either Standard or Administrator. The screen explains the difference between the two account types. Click Change Account Type. The account type changes, and you are returned to the Change an Account screen for that account.

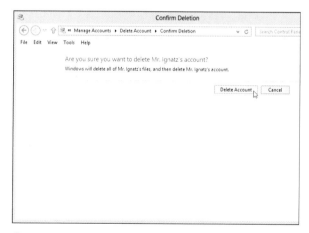

tip You may want to set up just one Administrator account to manage Windows and then set up the rest as Standard accounts.

Click the option to delete the account. Windows asks if you want to keep the user's files. Click Delete Files or Keep Files depending on your preference. At the next screen, click Delete Account. The account is deleted, and Windows returns you to the Manage Accounts screen.

tip To first add a new user, you must go to the Users section in the PC settings screen.

Changing Your Account Picture

Your account picture appears on the Windows 8 login screen and in the upper-right corner of the Start screen. If you are using a Windows account and previously set up an image for your profile, then that image appears as your account picture. If you are using a local account or a Microsoft account with no associated picture, then the picture appears as just a plain generic image. You can easily change that generic image into a photograph of yourself or some other picture that you want to represent you. You can also switch to a different image by picking one from your Windows Pictures folder or taking a new photo through your PC's webcam. This task explains how to set up and change your Windows 8 account picture.

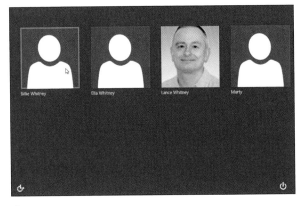

1 Log in to Windows: Log in with the account whose picture you wish to change.

2 Access your account picture: From the Start screen, click your account name and picture in the upper-right corner. From the menu, click Change account picture.

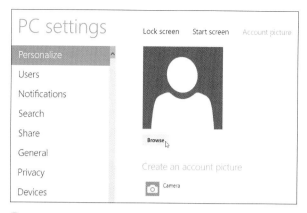

3 View pictures: The PC settings screen opens to display your current account picture. Click Browse to view other images stored in your Windows Pictures folder.

4 View local pictures: In the Windows Pictures app, you can view existing pictures stored directly in the folder.

5 Find pictures from other folders: Click the Files link in the upper-left corner. A list of other folders appears. You can choose a picture from Music, your desktop, Downloads, or anywhere else on your computer. If you have a SkyDrive account, you can also click the SkyDrive icon at the bottom of the list to choose a picture from your SkyDrive storage space.

6 Pick a picture: Click on an existing picture. From the app bar, click Choose image.

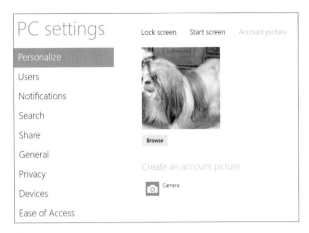

7 View new picture: The new picture replaces the older picture or generic image as your account picture.

8 Snap a picture: You can also take a new picture using the Windows Camera app. Under the Create an account picture link, click the Camera app icon. In the Camera app, click Camera options on the app bar to change the photo resolution. From there, click More to change the brightness or contrast. Click the Timer button on the app bar to set a 3-second timer. Press the spacebar or click the left mouse button to take the actual picture.

tip As you add more pictures, they display in the PC settings screen so you can easily change your account picture to a previous selection.

9 Crop or retake photo: Drag the fill handles or the sides of the picture to crop it. Move your mouse into the image and drag the cropped square to change the position. If you like the photo, click OK to make it your new account photo. If you are not happy with it, click Retake to snap another photo.

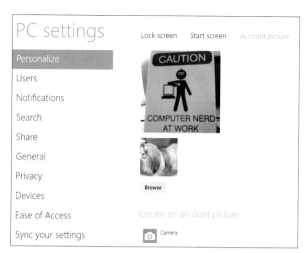

10 View new picture: The new picture replaces the older picture or generic image as your account picture.

11 Change picture: The previous picture appears below. Click on that picture to switch back to it.

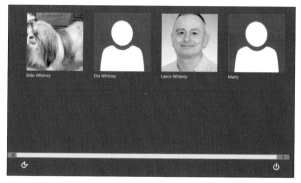

tip If you are using a Microsoft account, the new image you choose appears on your Microsoft account page as well.

12 View picture at login: Log out of Windows. Click on the Lock screen. The photo appears as the new picture for your account.

tip You first need to add images to your Windows Pictures folder in order to use them as account pictures.

Switching to a Local Account

Switch to a local account

You can use an account on this PC only, instead of signing in with your Microsoft account. Save your work now, because you'll need to sign out to do this.

First, we need to verify your current password.

Billie Whitney
billiewhit@live.com

Current password

ou can log in to Windows 8 with a Microsoft account or a local account specific to your PC. What is the difference between the two? A Microsoft account provides easy access to your online services, such as SkyDrive. It can sync key settings among your different Windows 8 PCs. And you can more quickly download Windows Store apps that you have already installed on other PCs. But if you do not need the quick online access or synchronization, you may prefer to use a local account. If you have already set up and logged in with a Microsoft account, you can easily convert that into a local account. This task explains how to switch to a local account.

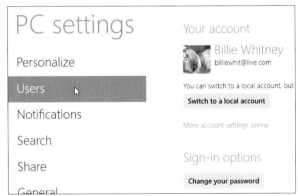

PC settings

Personalize

Users

Notifications

Search

Share

General

Your account

Billie Whitney
billiewhit@live.com

You can switch to a local account, but

Switch to a local account

More account settings online

Sign-in options

Change your password

1 Log in: Log in to Windows with your current Microsoft account.

2 Access the Users page: Hover your mouse in the lower-right hot corner to display the Charms bar. Click the Settings charm and then click Change PC settings. In the left pane of the PC settings screen, click Users.

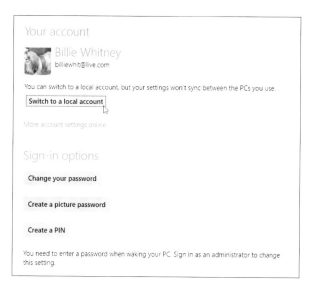

3 Choose to switch to local account: Under your current Microsoft account, click Switch to a local account.

4 Enter current password: At the Switch to a local account screen, type your current account password. Click Next.

5 Enter account information: At the next screen, type the username, password, and password hint for your new local account. Click Next.

6 Sign out: At the next screen, click Sign out and finish to log out of your current Microsoft account.

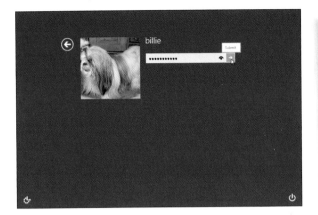

tip You can still use Mail, Photos, and other apps associated with your Microsoft account, but you need to log in individually to use them.

7 Log in with new account: Press any key to get past the Lock screen. Click your account name and picture. Type the password for your new local account.

Quick Fixes

Changing the Date or Time

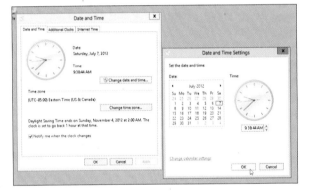

From the Start screen, type the word **time**. Click Settings. In the search results on the left pane, click the Date and Time setting. In the Date and Time window, click Change date and time. If you receive a User Account Control window, type your password and click Yes. In the Date and Time Settings window, you can now change the date and/or time. Click OK.

Setting Spell Check

From the Start screen, type the word **spell**. Click Settings. In the search results on the left pane, click the Autocorrect misspelled words setting. In the Spelling section on the General screen, you can set autocorrect misspelled words and highlight misspelled words to on or off.

Switching to a Microsoft Account

Sign in with a Microsoft account

Marty Whitney
martinwhit@live.com

You're almost done changing your account. Next time you sign in to Windows, use your Microsoft account and password.

You can log in to Windows 8 with a local account or a Microsoft account. A local account is considered by some people to be safer and more secure as it does not require the use of an online username and password. However, a local account is limited in that it does not sync settings among your different Windows PCs and does not provide quick access to SkyDrive and other online accounts and services. For those reasons and more, you may want to switch from a local account to a Microsoft account. This task explains how to switch to a Microsoft account.

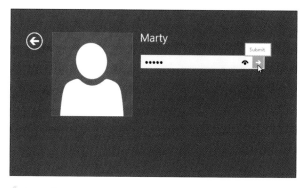

1 Log in: Log in to Windows with your local account.

2 Access the Users page: Hover your mouse in the lower-right hot corner to display the Charms bar. Click the Settings charm and then select the Change PC settings option. In the left pane of the PC settings screen, click Users.

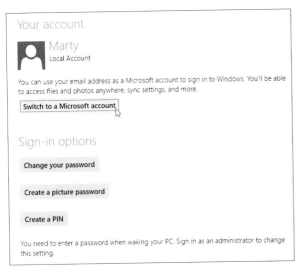

3 Choose to use Microsoft account: Under your current local account, click Switch to a Microsoft account.

4 Enter current password: At the Sign in with a Microsoft account screen, type your current local account password. Click Next.

5 Enter your account information: At the next screen, type the e-mail address for your Microsoft account. If you do not already have a Microsoft account, click Sign up for a new e-mail address and follow Steps 15 through 19 in the task "Adding a Microsoft Account to Windows." If you have a Microsoft account and have typed your e-mail address, click Next.

6 Enter your password: At the Enter your Microsoft account password screen, type the password for your Microsoft account. Click Next.

7 Enter security verification info: At the Enter security verification info screen, confirm your phone number, alternate e-mail address, and secret question if you selected one. Click Next.

8 Sign in with a Microsoft account: At the Sign in with a Microsoft account screen, click Finish to prepare your Microsoft account.

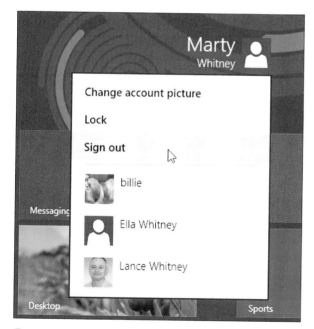

9 Sign out of current account: Open the Start screen by pressing the Windows key or clicking on the thumbnail in the lower-left hot corner. Click your account name and picture in the upper-right corner. From the menu, click Sign out.

10 Log in with new account: Press any key to get past the Lock screen. Select your account. Type the password for your new Microsoft account.

tip You can access your online Microsoft accounts and services without having to log in each time to use them.

Changing Your Password Protection

Windows 8 provides built-in security by requiring you to log in with a username and password, whether you use a local account or a Microsoft account. But you can simplify or strengthen your password security a number of ways. You can change the password for your local account or Microsoft account, making it stronger or easier to remember, or hopefully a combination of both. You can replace your password with a PIN that might be simpler to remember, though you can still use either your password or your PIN. This task explains how to change the options for your password protection.

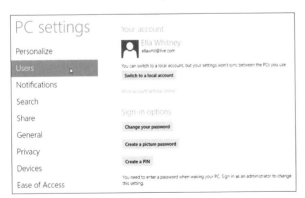

1 Access the Users page: Hover your mouse in the lower-right hot corner to display the Charms bar. Click the Settings charm and then click Change PC settings. In the left pane of the PC settings screen, click Users.

2 Change your password: Under the Sign-in options section, click Change your password. At the Change your password screen, type your current password and then type your new password once and then again to confirm it. Click Next.

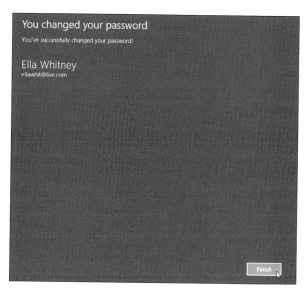

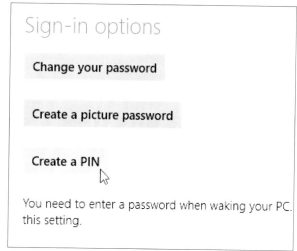

3 View confirmation of password change: A message appears that you changed your password. Click Finish. You are returned to the PC settings screen.

4 Create a PIN: Under the Sign-in options section, click Create a PIN.

5 Confirm your password: Type your current password. Click OK.

6 Enter the PIN: In the Create a PIN screen, type your PIN once and then again to confirm it. (Your PIN can be up to four numbers.) Click Finish.

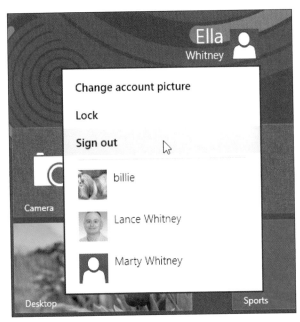

7 Sign out: Open the Start screen by pressing the Windows key or clicking on the thumbnail in the lower-left hot corner. Click your account name and picture in the upper-right corner. From the menu, click Sign out.

8 Sign in with PIN: Press any key to get past the Lock screen. Click your account name and picture. Type your new PIN to log in to Windows.

tip After you set up a PIN, Windows displays a Sign-in options link at the login screen, letting you use your password or PIN.

Quick Fix

Using Microsoft Reader to View a PDF

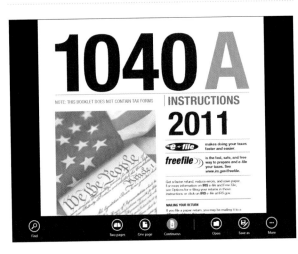

Open Internet Explorer by clicking its Start screen tile. For example, you might want to view online tax return instructions in PDF form. Browse to the IRS form site at www.irs.gov/formspubs and download a PDF. After the download completes, click Open folder. Double-click on the PDF to open it in Microsoft Reader. Right-click on the screen to open the app bar where you can change the layout, find text within the file, and access other options.

Creating a Picture Password

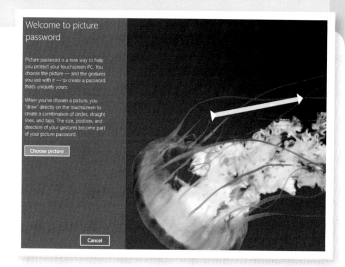

Windows 8 provides traditional security in the form of a password or a PIN, which you can set or change as explained in the previous task "Changing Your Password Protection." But new to Windows is an option to use a picture password. This option lets you use a picture of your choice, and then draw lines or circles, or tap on any area of the picture to set up your security. Logging in using a picture password requires you to enter the same gestures in the same order. Though this option is perhaps better suited for a touch-screen tablet, PC users can set up a picture password and simply use a mouse to create and recreate the gestures. This task explains how to set up a picture password.

1 Access the Users page: Log in with the account for which you want to create a picture password. Hover your mouse in the lower-right hot corner to display the Charms bar. Click the Settings charm and then the Change PC settings option. In the left pane of the PC settings screen, click Users.

2 Set up a picture password: Under the Sign-in options section, click Create a picture password.

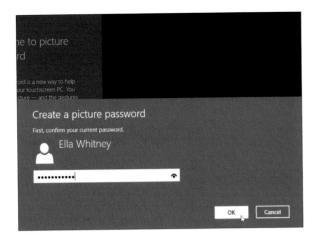

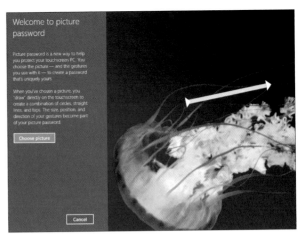

3 Enter password: At the Create a picture password screen, type your current account password. Click OK.

4 Read directions: The Welcome to picture password screen explains how the process works and displays the steps for creating gestures on a picture.

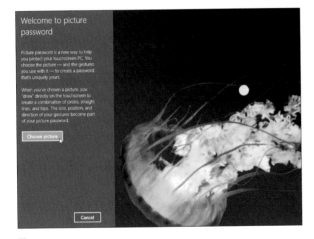

5 Choose a picture: Click Choose picture to select an image from your Pictures library.

6 Select your picture: From your Pictures library, click the picture you want to use. Click Open.

7 Set up your picture: In the How's this look? screen, drag your picture up, down, left, or right to position it.

8 Use the picture: If you want to pick a different picture, click Choose new picture. Otherwise, click Use this picture.

9 Set up gestures: At the Set up your gestures screen, follow the instructions to draw the three gestures — any combination of lines, circles, and/or taps. After each gesture, Windows displays a line, circle, or tap to confirm the gesture.

10 Confirm your gestures: At the Confirm your gestures screen, draw the three gestures again to confirm them.

11 Receive congratulations: If all goes well, you should receive a congratulations message indicating that you have successfully created your picture password. Click Finish.

tip Drawing the gestures is much easier with an external mouse than with a trackpad.

12 Sign out: Return to the Start screen by pressing the Windows key or clicking on the thumbnail in the lower-left hot corner. Click your account name and picture in the upper-right corner. From the menu, click Sign out.

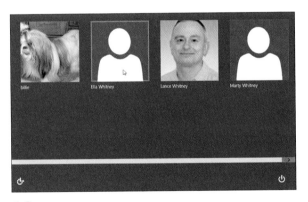

13 Sign in: Press any key to get past the Lock screen. Select your account.

tip After you set up the picture, Windows displays a Sign-in options link at the login screen, letting you use your password or picture.

14 Draw the gestures: The picture you chose appears. Draw the three gestures on the picture in the order in which you created them. If you draw them successfully, Windows displays the Start screen. If you have trouble drawing them, click Start over to try again.

tip You do not have to be precise with the gestures but close enough to match them.

The Windows 8 Start screen replaces the old Windows Start menu as your starting point, so to speak. As such, the Start screen is home to all of your application tiles, both Windows 8 and desktop. You can customize the look of your Start screen, but only to a certain degree. Because the Start screen is already set up with a variety of different color tiles, you cannot use your own personal photos or pictures as a background image. But you can at least change the color and style of the Start screen background to something easy on your eyes. This task explains how to customize the Start screen with a specific color and style.

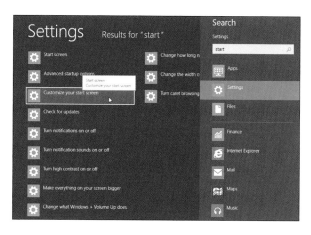

1 Access the Start screen settings: At the Start screen, type the word **start**. Under the search field, click Settings. In the search results displayed in the left pane, click Customize your start screen.

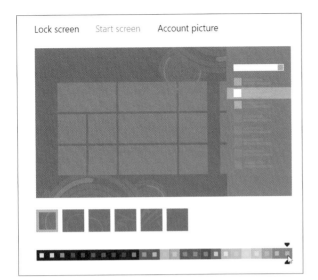

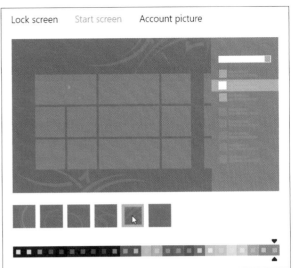

2 Set the color: Click a color on the horizontal palette bar. The Start screen preview window appears in the new color.

3 Set the style: Click a style from the one of the six boxes above the horizontal palette bar. The Start screen preview window displays the new style.

4 View the changes: Return to the Start screen by pressing the Windows key or by clicking on the thumbnail in the lower-left hot corner.

5 Tweak your changes: If you are not happy with the color or style, press the Windows key to return to the PC settings screen. You can try other colors and styles and switch back and forth between the Start screen and the PC settings screen until you are happy with your choices.

tip You may have to experiment with different colors. Some colors might be too bright or too dark, while others may contrast with the tiles.

Personalizing the Windows Lock Screen

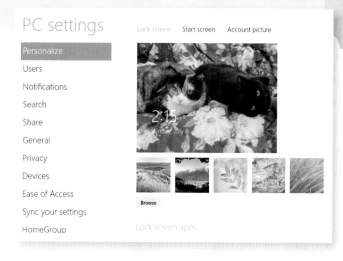

The Windows 8 Lock screen appears just before the login screen after you boot up your PC. Pressing any key at the Lock screen immediately brings you to the login screen. At first glance, the Lock screen seems unnecessary, especially on a PC. But the screen displays useful information in the foreground, including the date and time, battery charge on a laptop, wireless signal, and notifications. You can personalize the Lock screen by displaying your own image in the background. But more importantly, you can customize the notifications that appear so you know if new e-mail, instant messages, or calendar appointments await you. This task explains how to personalize the Windows Lock screen.

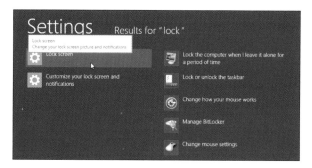

1 Access the Lock screen settings: At the Start screen, type **lock**. Under the search field, click Settings. In the search results displayed in the left pane, click Customize your lock screen and notifications.

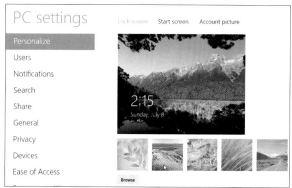

2 Change background image: At the Personalize page for the Lock screen, click on one of the thumbnail images displayed under the current image. That image immediately becomes the new Lock screen background.

4 Choose a new image: You can now view any existing pictures stored in your Pictures folder or drill down to any subfolders that may contain additional pictures. You can also click the Files link to view pictures in other locations. Click on an existing picture. From the app bar, click Choose picture.

3 Browse other images: If none of the existing images excites you, click Browse to choose an image from your Pictures folder.

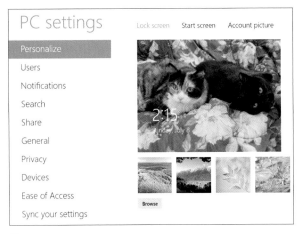

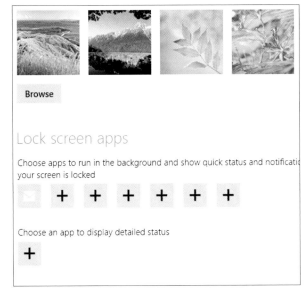

5 View new picture: The new picture replaces the older picture as your Lock screen image.

6 Choose Lock screen apps: Scroll to the bottom of the Lock screen personalization page until you see the section for Lock screen apps. Here you can choose which apps continue to run when the screen is locked and display a status and notification on the Lock screen.

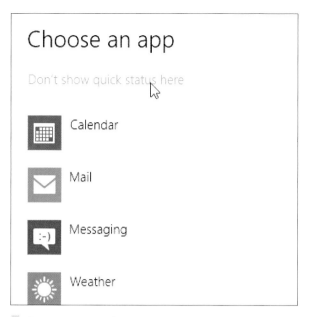

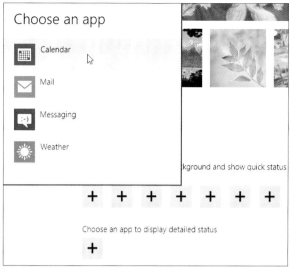

7 Remove a Lock screen app: The apps already set up for the Lock screen display their icons. To remove that app from the Lock screen, click its icon. In the Choose an app window, click Don't show quick status here.

8 Add a Lock screen app: The apps not set up for the Lock screen display a plus symbol. Click one of the plus symbols. Windows displays a Choose an app window where you can pick the app you want to add. Click that app. To add additional apps, click the other plus symbols and add an app from the list.

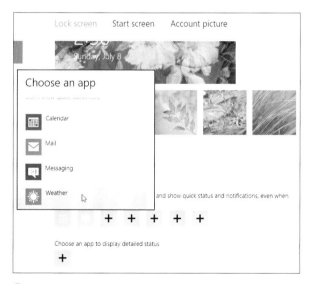

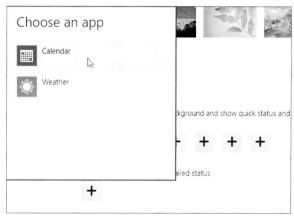

9 Change a Lock screen app: You can also change one app to another. Click the icon for an existing Lock screen app. In the Choose an app window, click a different app. The new app replaces the older one.

10 Display detailed information: Click the icon below the line that says Choose an app to display detailed status. Click the app for which you want to see detailed status on the Lock screen.

11 Access Lock screen: After you make your changes, you can view your new Lock screen. Return to the Start screen by pressing the Windows key or clicking on the thumbnail in the lower-left hot corner. Click your account name and picture in the upper-right corner. Choose Lock from the menu.

12 View new Lock screen: At the Lock screen, your new background image and the notifications that you set up are displayed.

tip You first need to add images to your Windows Pictures folder in order to use them as Lock screen images.

Quick Fix

Managing Your Searches

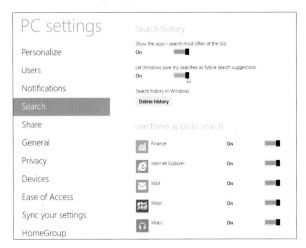

From the Start screen, type the word **search**. Click Settings. In the search results on the left pane, click the Search setting. From the Search screen, choose whether to show the apps you search the most at the top and let Windows save your searches as future suggestions. You can also choose which apps should be included in searches.

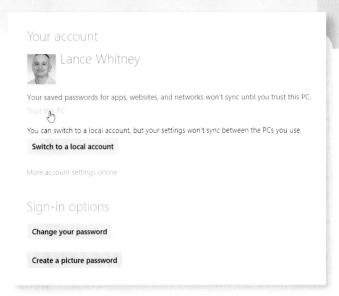

S etting up a PC with a Microsoft account offers several benefits, such as the ability to automatically access SkyDrive and other online services, synchronize certain passwords among multiple PCs, and view a list of apps downloaded from the Windows Store on other PCs. But before you can take advantage of the password synchronization, you have to set up a trust relationship for each new Windows 8 PC. Setting up the trust adds your computer to a list of other trusted PCs and helps confirm you as the user of the computer. This task explains how to trust a Windows 8 computer.

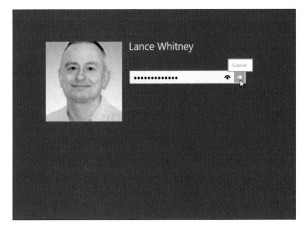

1 Log in: Log in to Windows 8 with a Microsoft account.

2 Access the Users page: Launch the desktop by clicking the Desktop tile on the Start screen. Hover your mouse in the lower-right hot corner to display the Charms bar. Click the Settings charm and then select the Change PC settings option. In the left pane of the PC settings screen, click Users.

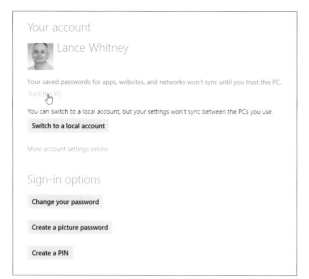

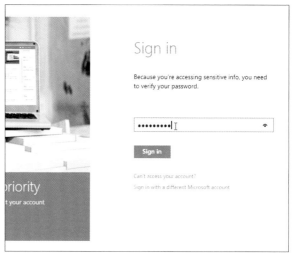

3 Trust the PC: If the PC is not yet trusted, a message appears at the top of the Users pane that "Your saved passwords for apps, websites, and networks won't sync until you trust this PC." Click the Trust this PC link.

4 Add PC: Internet Explorer displays your Microsoft account page and prompts you to log in. Type your Microsoft account password and click Sign in.

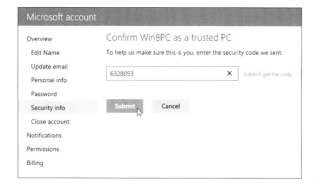

5 Confirm PC as trusted: Microsoft should have sent you a code in an instant message to your mobile phone. If you did not receive the code, click the I didn't get the code link and follow the prompts to have the code resent to your phone or sent by e-mail. Click Next.

6 Receive confirmation: Windows should now confirm that your PC is trusted. Click OK.

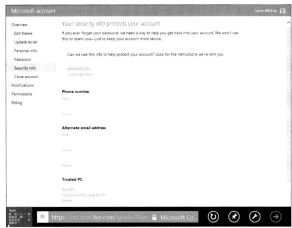

7 View account information: Windows displays your account information page, listing your current PC as a Trusted PC.

8 Return to Start screen: You can now return to the Start screen by clicking on the thumbnail in the lower-left hot corner or pressing the Windows key.

tip From your Microsoft Account page, you can also trust other Windows 8 PCs that you have set up beyond your current one.

Setting the Default Version of Internet Explorer

Open the desktop version of Internet Explorer. Click the Tools icon. From the pop-up menu, click Internet options. Click the Programs tab. In the Opening Internet Explorer section, select the Always in Internet Explorer setting if you want the Windows 8 version to be the default. Select the Always in Internet Explorer on the desktop setting if you want the desktop version to be the default. Leave the setting as is to let IE decide.

Syncing Your Windows Settings

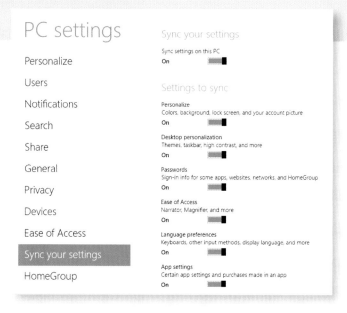

PC settings

Personalize
Users
Notifications
Search
Share
General
Privacy
Devices
Ease of Access
Sync your settings
HomeGroup

Sync your settings

Sync settings on this PC
On

Settings to sync

Personalize
Colors, background, lock screen, and your account picture
On

Desktop personalization
Themes, taskbar, high contrast, and more
On

Passwords
Sign-in info for some apps, websites, networks, and HomeGroup
On

Ease of Access
Narrator, Magnifier, and more
On

Language preferences
Keyboards, other input methods, display language, and more
On

App settings
Certain app settings and purchases made in an app
On

Logging in to Windows 8 with a Microsoft account lets you synchronize key settings across your different Windows 8 computers. This option ensures that you maintain a consistent environment and settings across all of your PCs without having to configure and customize each one separately. But you do not have to use this option. You can turn off synchronization completely to give each PC its own unique environment. If you choose to maintain synchronization, you can control which items are included, such as backgrounds and colors, desktop personalization, passwords, language preferences, and app settings. This task explains how to sync your settings.

1 Search for sync: From the Start screen, type the word **sync**. Click the Settings category. In the search results on the left pane, click Sync your settings.

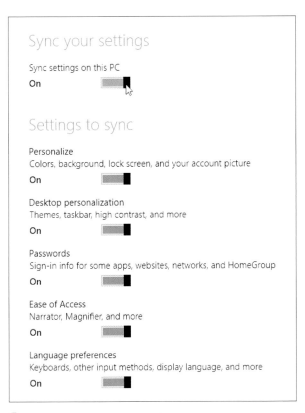

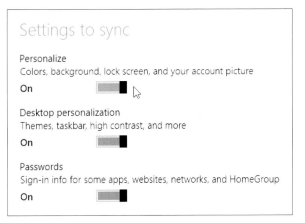

Settings to sync

2 **Turn syncing on or off:** Under Sync your settings, set the Sync settings on this PC option to On or Off. If you set the option to Off, then all the settings below it are automatically set to Off. If you set or keep the setting to On, then you can proceed to the next steps.

3 **Set personalization:** If you want to sync the colors, background images, Lock screen, and account screen settings, leave the Personalize option at On. Otherwise, set it to Off.

4 **Set desktop personalization:** If you wish to sync your desktop themes, taskbar, and contrast, leave the Desktop Personalization option at On. Otherwise, set it to Off.

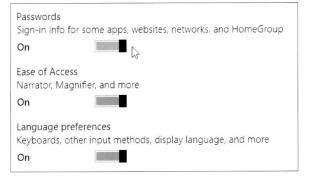

5 **Set passwords:** If you want to sync the passwords for certain apps, websites, and your homegroup network, leave the Passwords option at On. Otherwise, set it to Off.

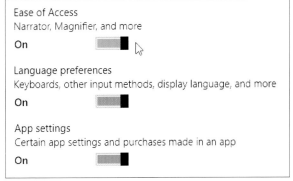

6 **Set Ease of Access:** If you want to sync the Narrator, Magnifier, and other Ease of Access settings, leave this option at On. Otherwise, set it to Off.

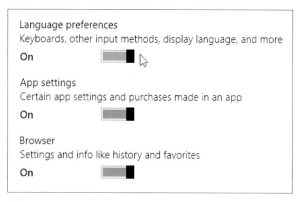

7 Set language preferences: If you want to sync your language preferences, leave this option at On. Otherwise, set it to Off.

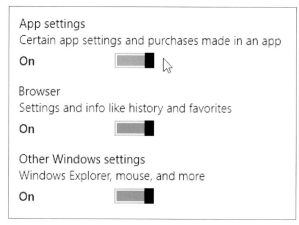

8 Set app settings: If you want to sync certain apps settings and in-app purchases, leave the App settings option at On. Otherwise, set it to Off.

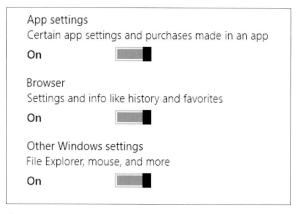

9 Set browser settings: If you want to sync the history and favorites for your default browser, leave this option at On. Otherwise, set it to Off.

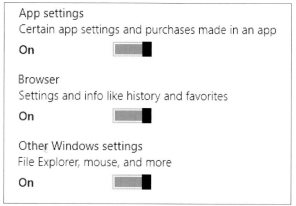

10 Set other settings: If you want to sync certain settings for File Explorer, your mouse, and other items, leave the Other Window settings option at On. Otherwise, set it to Off.

Sync over metered connections

Sync settings over metered connections

On

Sync settings over metered connections even when I'm roaming

Off

Sync over metered connections

Sync settings over metered connections

On

Sync settings over metered connections even when I'm roaming

Off

11 Sync over metered connections: If you want to sync settings over metered connections, leave this option at On. Otherwise, set it to Off, and the settings will sync only over a nonmetered connection, typically a Wi-Fi connection.

12 Sync over metered connections when roaming: If you want to sync settings over metered connections when roaming, turn this option to On. Otherwise, leave it at Off, and the settings will sync only if your mobile PC is not roaming.

tip You may have to experiment with some of the settings to see which ones you want to leave on and which ones to leave off.

Quick Fix

Enabling Protected Mode in Internet Explorer

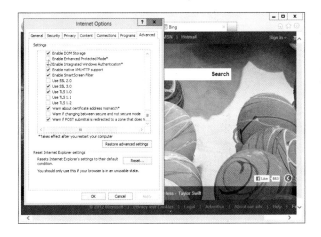

Open the desktop version of Internet Explorer by clicking its taskbar icon. Click the Tools icon in the upper-right corner. From the pop-up menu, click Internet options. Click the Advanced tab. Scroll to the bottom of the list until you see the Enable Enhanced Protected Mode option. Select that option. The next time you reboot your PC, Enhanced Protected Mode will be in effect.

Adding Files to Your SkyDrive Page

A s Microsoft's online storage service, SkyDrive offers several benefits. You can store your documents and other personal files in the cloud so that they are accessible from any SkyDrive-enabled computer anywhere online. You can synchronize documents and other files so that the same versions remain consistent both online and among all your computers. Windows 8 provides a Windows 8 app through which you can access your content on SkyDrive. You can also download and install a SkyDrive desktop application that gives you control over which folders and files to upload and synchronize to SkyDrive. This task explains how to set and use your online SkyDrive account.

1 Log in: Log in to Windows 8 with a Microsoft account.

2 Access the SkyDrive website: Open Internet Explorer by clicking its Start screen tile.

3 Open SkyDrive website: In the address field for Internet Explorer, open your SkyDrive website by typing **www. skydrive.com**.

4 View your SkyDrive page: Internet Explorer displays your SkyDrive web page. Tiles for your three default folders appear — Documents, Pictures, and Public. You can use Documents and Pictures to store your own personal files; you can use Public to store files you want to share with others.

5 Open SkyDrive Pictures folder: Click the tile for the Pictures folder to open it.

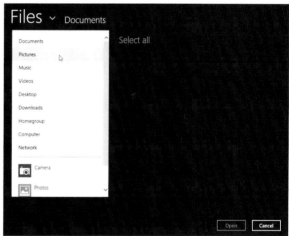

6 Open local Pictures folder: Click the Upload menu. In the Files screen, click the word Files and then select the folder from which you want to upload files (in this case, Pictures). Click the Upload menu. In the File Upload window, navigate to your local Pictures folder.

7 Select files: Select the pictures you want to upload to SkyDrive. Click Open.

8 View files in SkyDrive: Your selected files are uploaded to the Pictures folder on SkyDrive.

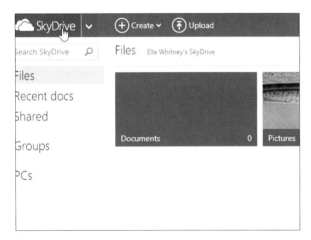

9 Move back to SkyDrive page: Click the SkyDrive icon in the upper-left corner to move back to the root of your SkyDrive page.

10 Move to the Documents folder: Click the Documents folder tile.

tip SkyDrive users who originally had 25GB of free storage were allowed to keep that amount by choosing the option in early 2012.

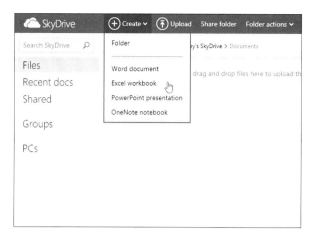

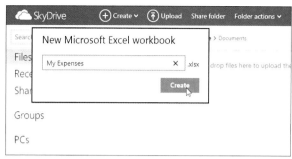

11 Create a new document: Click the Create menu and select the Excel workbook option.

12 Name the document: In the New Microsoft Excel workbook window, type a name for the workbook and click Create.

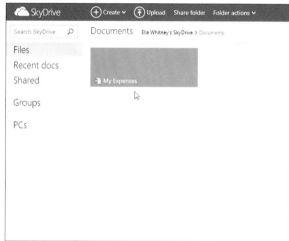

13 Fill in the document: Microsoft's Excel Web App opens for you to create the spreadsheet. Type some information in a few of the cells.

14 Return to SkyDrive: When you are finished, click the SkyDrive link at the top of the screen to return to SkyDrive. Open the Documents folder. A tile for the new Excel file appears.

tip SkyDrive offers 7GB of free storage for new users. Click the Manage storage link to view your options if you need more space.

Using the Windows 8 SkyDrive App

Ella's SkyDrive ⌄ 3 items

W indows 8 comes with an app in which you can access your online SkyDrive files. As explained in the task "Adding Files to your SkyDrive Page," SkyDrive lets you store your documents and personal files online so that they are accessible from any computer via your Microsoft account. Through the Windows 8 Sky-Drive app, you can view and navigate through your online folders. You can view and open certain types of files, such as photos and songs. You can also open and edit certain Word documents, Excel spreadsheets, and other types of files using Microsoft's Web Apps. This task explains how to use the Windows 8 SkyDrive app.

1 Log in: Log in to Windows with a Microsoft account that already has files stored in SkyDrive. The process for uploading files to SkyDrive is explained in the task "Adding Files to your SkyDrive Page." Follow the steps in that task to create the necessary folders and files.

2 Open SkyDrive: Launch the Windows 8 SkyDrive app by clicking its Start screen tile.

3 View folders: Tiles for your SkyDrive folders appear.

5 Open a document: Click the tile for a specific file, such as an Excel spreadsheet, to open it.

4 Open a folder: Click a specific tile to open that folder, such as Documents.

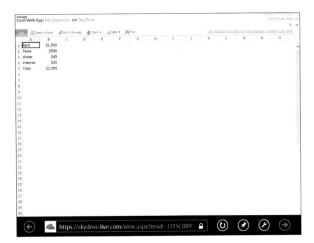

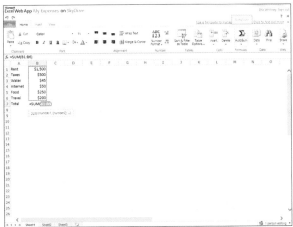

6 View file: Internet Explorer opens to display your file in the Excel Web App window.

7 Edit the file: Click the Edit in Browser button on the toolbar if you want to edit the document. The document opens in the Word Web App editor where you can modify it.

9 Return to SkyDrive: Move your mouse to the upper-left hot corner of the Start screen until you see the thumbnail for SkyDrive. Click on that thumbnail. Click the name of your current folder. From the menu, click the name of your SkyDrive account.

8 Close Internet Explorer: Move your mouse to the top of the screen until the cursor turns into a hand. Drag the cursor to the bottom of the screen to close the file and Internet Explorer.

11 Open a picture: Click on a specific image. The image displays full screen.

10 View pictures: Click on another folder, such as Pictures.

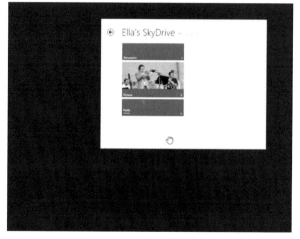

12 Return to your SkyDrive folders: Click on the screen until you see the Back button in the upper-left corner. Click that button to return to your Pictures folder.

13 Close Sky-Drive: Move your mouse to the top of the screen until the cursor turns into a hand. Drag the cursor to the bottom of the screen to close SkyDrive.

tip You can also download a desktop SkyDrive app, which is covered in the task "Setting Up the SkyDrive for Windows App."

Setting Up the SkyDrive for Windows App

You can set up your SkyDrive account through the web, as described in the task "Adding Files to Your SkyDrive Page." You can access and view your SkyDrive files using the Windows 8 SkyDrive app, as described in the task "Setting Up the Windows 8 SkyDrive App." In addition, you can download and install a desktop SkyDrive application for Windows that lets you set up and synchronize specific folders for SkyDrive. This application gives you the ability to access your SkyDrive files directly from File Explorer, add new files to SkyDrive from your desktop, and organize your SkyDrive folders and files as if they were local to your PC. This task explains how to set up and use the SkyDrive for Windows application.

1 Log in: Log in to Windows with a Microsoft account.

2 Open SkyDrive website: Open Internet Explorer by clicking its Start screen tile. In the address field for IE, open the SkyDrive website by typing **www.skydrive.com**. Log in with your Microsoft account if needed. On your SkyDrive page, click the Get SkyDrive apps link in the lower left corner.

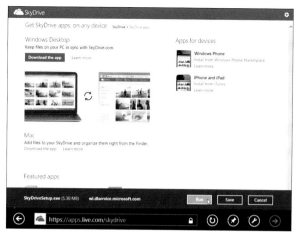

3 Get the SkyDrive apps: On the SkyDrive apps page, click the Download the app button for SkyDrive for Windows Desktop.

4 Install the SkyDrive app: Choose the option to Run the file SkyDriveSetup.exe. Click Yes if a User Account Control window asks if you want to allow the following program to make changes to this computer.

5 Wait for app to install: The SkyDrive application installs.

tip You can download a SkyDrive app for the Mac, the iPhone, the iPad, and Windows Phone devices.

6 Set up the application: At the Welcome to SkyDrive window, click Get started. If the Sign in page appears, type your Microsoft account ID and password and click Sign in.

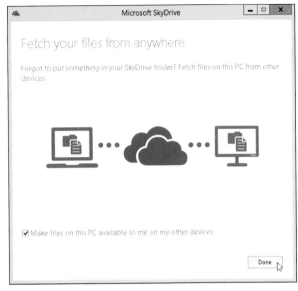

7 Confirm the SkyDrive folder: The Introducing your SkyDrive folder window shows that your SkyDrive folder will be created under your personal folder. Click Change if you want the folder to be created elsewhere. Otherwise, click Next.

8 Sync files from other devices: The Fetch your files from anywhere window shows that any files synced to Sky-Drive from your current computer will be synced to other computers. If you do not want to do this, deselect the check box. Otherwise, click Done.

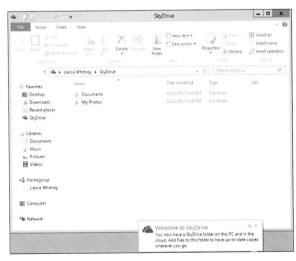

9 View your SkyDrive folder: A File Explorer window appears showing you your new SkyDrive folder. Your local Sky-Drive folder synchronizes with your online SkyDrive folders to dowload all the existing content.

tip You can also copy files from your local folders to your SkyDrive folders by dragging and dropping them.

tip To manage the SkyDrive application, click the Show hidden icons arrow on the Windows system tray and then click the SkyDrive icon.

Opening Files with Specific Applications

Certain types of files can be opened by different applications in Windows 8, both Windows 8 apps and desktop apps. As some examples, JPEG and other image files can be opened by the Windows 8 Photos app, by Paint, or by Windows Photo Viewer. MP3 and other audio files can be opened by the Windows 8 Music app or by Windows Media Player. PDF files can be opened by Microsoft Reader or by Adobe Reader. And text files can be opened by Notepad or WordPad. You can choose which application should open a particular file each time, or you can set up a permanent file association so that the same application opens a particular file type every time. This task explains how to open files with specific applications.

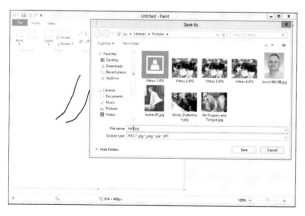

1 Create an image file: From the Start screen, type **paint**. In the search results on the left pane, click the Paint icon. In Paint, draw a line or two. Choose File ➔ Save As. In Paint, choose the option to save as a JPEG picture. Change the name to test.jpg and save the file in the default location of your Pictures folder. Close Paint. Press the Windows key to return to the Start menu.

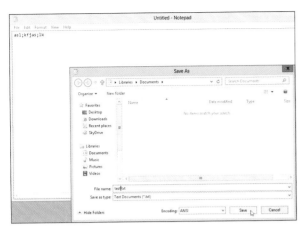

2 Create a text file: From the Start screen, type **notepad**. From the search results on the left pane, click the Notepad icon. In Notepad, type a few characters. Choose File ➔ Save. Change the name to test.txt and save the file in the default location of your Documents folder. Close Notepad.

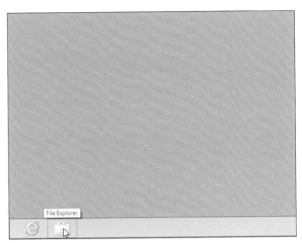

3 Open File Explorer: From the desktop, open File Explorer by clicking its taskbar shortcut.

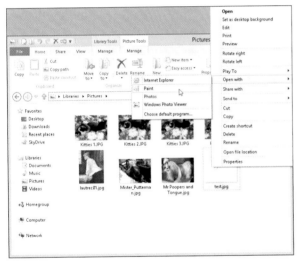

4 Open image in Paint: Open your Pictures folder. Right-click on the test.jpg file. From the pop-up menu, choose Open with ➔ Paint.

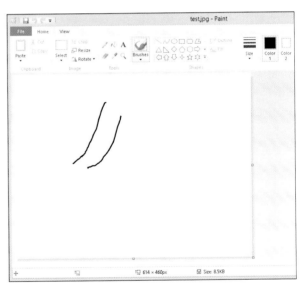

5 View image in Paint: The image opens in Paint. Close Paint.

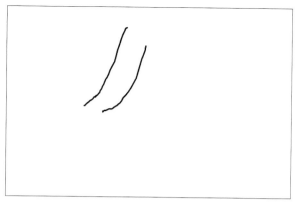

6 Open image file in Photos app: From your Pictures folder, right-click on the test.jpg file. From the pop-up menu, choose Open with → Photos.

7 View image in Photos app: The image opens in the Photos app. Hold down the Windows key and press D to return to the desktop.

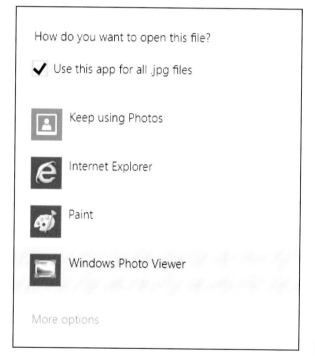

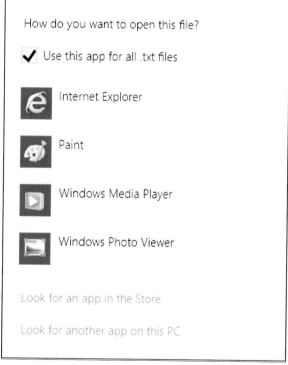

8 Change default program: From your Pictures folder, right-click on the test.jpg file. From the pop-up menu, choose Open with → Choose default program. A How do you want to open this file? window appears. You can open the file with a program other than its default by selecting the Use this app for all .jpg files check box and clicking the app. Close the window by clicking on any empty area of the desktop.

9 Explore more options: Move to your Documents folder. Right-click on the test.txt file. From the pop-up menu, choose Open with → Choose default program. The How do you want to open this file? window appears. Click the More options link. Other applications appear that could potentially open this file. Click Cancel to close the Open with window.

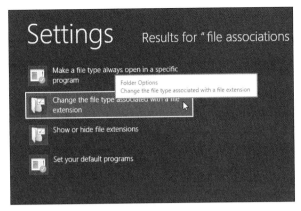

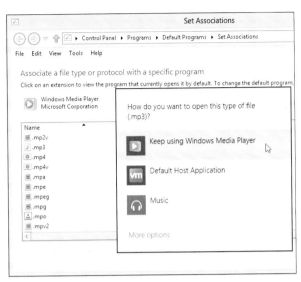

10 View list of associations: Return to the Start screen by pressing the Windows key. From the Start screen, type **file associations**. Click Settings. In the search results on the left pane, click Change the file type associated with a file extension.

11 Set a file association: The Set Associations window opens. Scroll down the list of extensions until you see one for .mp3. Double-click the .mp3 association. The How do you want to open this type of file window appears. You can choose the Music app or Windows Media Player, or click More options for other choices. Click the app you want to use. That app becomes the default for MP3 files. Close the Set Associations window.

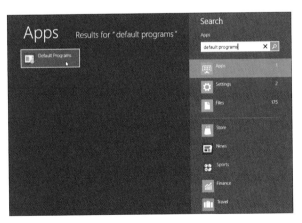

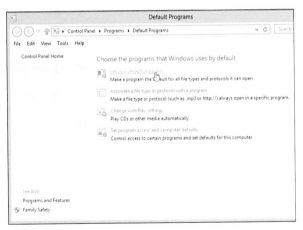

12 Use the Default Programs program: Press the Windows key to return to the Start screen. Type **default programs**. In the search results on the left pane, click the Default Programs app.

13 Set your default programs: In the Default Programs window, click the Set your default programs link.

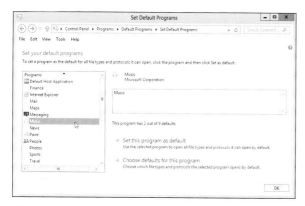

14 Choose file types for specific programs: In the Set Default Programs window, click a specific application, such as Music.

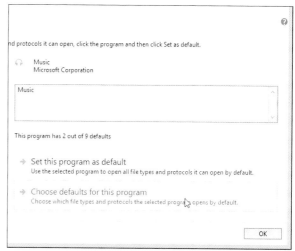

15 Choose defaults for this program: To associate only certain audio files with the Music app, click Choose defaults for this program.

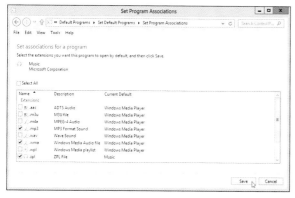

16 Select file extensions: At the next screen, select the audio files that you want associated with the Music app, and deselect the files that you do not want associated with the app. For example, you can select .mp3 and .wma and leave the rest deselected. Click Save when done.

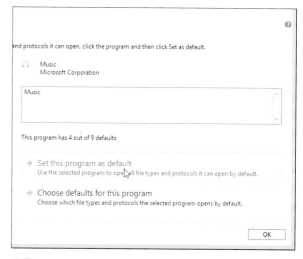

17 Set this program as default: To set the Music app as the default player for all types of audio files, select the app again and click Set this program as default. When done, click OK. Close the Set Default Programs window.

tip As you install more applications, such as image editors and music players, you can always change the default to those new apps.

Printing Content from a Windows 8 App

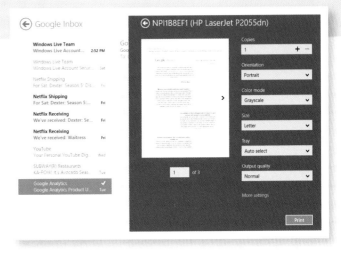

Printing content from a standard desktop application works the same in Windows 8 as in previous versions of Windows. You simply choose File → Print. But printing a file from a Windows 8 app works differently. Instead of choosing a print command from the app itself, you print using the Charms bar. Selecting the Devices charm provides access to your printer and allows you to configure the various settings to determine the format, quality, and other attributes for your printed document. You can print from a variety of Windows 8 apps, including Mail, Photos, Maps, and Internet Explorer. Mail is used for this example, but the process is the same across all Windows 8 apps. This task explains how to print from a Windows 8 app.

1 **Open Mail:** Make sure your printer is turned on. This example uses Mail. Open Mail by clicking its Start screen tile.

2 **Select a message:** Click an e-mail message to print.

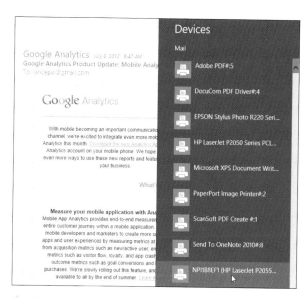

3 Access the Charms bar: Move your mouse to the lower right-hot corner to display the Charms bar. Click the Devices charm.

4 Click the printer: Your printer appears on the list of your devices. Click the name of your printer.

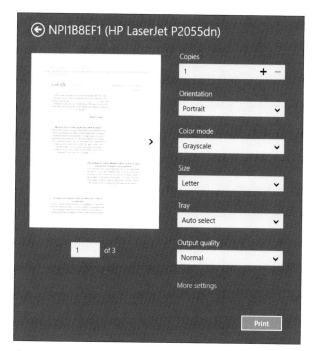

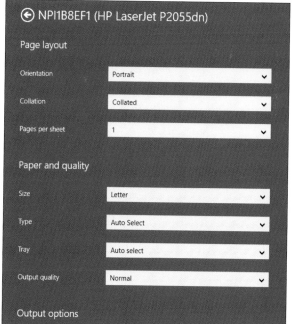

5 Configure basic settings: At the first screen, set the number of copies, the orientation, the color mode, the size, the tray, and the output quality if needed.

6 Configure more settings: Click the More settings link, which is located to the upper left of the Print button. Here you can configure additional settings depending on what your printer supports, such as the collation, pages per sheet, and type of paper. When done, click the Back button to return to the previous screen.

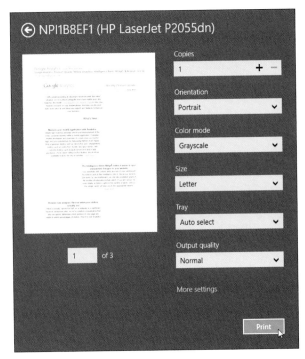

NPI1B8EF1 (HP LaserJet P2055dn)

Copies
1

Orientation
Portrait

Color mode
Grayscale

Size
Letter

Tray
Auto select

Output quality
Normal

More settings

1 of 3

Print

tip Printing from every Windows 8 app offers the same settings and configuration options.

tip You can also press Ctrl+P to access your printer list directly.

7 Print e-mail: Click Print to print your e-mail.

Quick Fix

Choosing Which Apps to Share

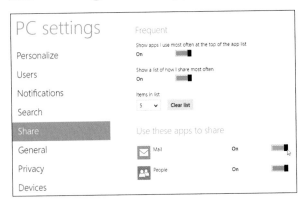

PC settings

Personalize
Users
Notifications
Search
Share
General
Privacy
Devices

Frequent

Show apps I use most often at the top of the app list
On

Show a list of how I share most often
On

Items in list
5   Clear list

Use these apps to share

Mail   On

People   On

From the Start screen, type the word **share**. Click Settings. In the search results on the left pane, click Share setting. From the Share screen, choose whether to show the apps you use the most for sharing at the top and to show a list of how you share most often. You can also determine how many items should appear in the list and which apps should be used for sharing.

Sharing Content from a Windows 8 App

E-mailing files or content within a desktop application works the same in Windows 8 as it does in previous versions of Windows. But e-mailing or sharing files or content from a Windows 8 app uses the Charms bar. So rather than running a command within the application, you trigger the Share charm from the Charms bar to share a photo, a web page, or another piece of content. Using the Share charm ensures that the process of sharing remains consistent across all Windows 8 applications. This task explains how to share content through e-mail or instant messaging from various Windows 8 apps.

1 Share from the Photos app: This example uses the Photos app. Open the Photos app by clicking its Start screen tile.

2 Open a photo: Click on the thumbnail for your local Pictures library. Drill down through the library and click on a specific picture to view it full screen.

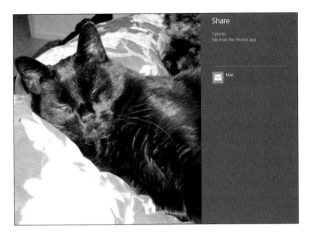

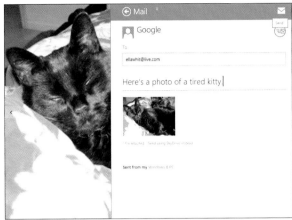

3 Share the picture: Move your mouse to the lower-right hot corner to display the Charms bar. Move your mouse up the bar and click the Share charm. Icons for Mail and perhaps for other programs, such as social networking apps, appear.

4 Share the picture via Mail: Click the Mail icon. The Mail app opens in the right pane of the screen. Type the name of the recipient in the To field. Add a subject in the Subject field. Type any text for the body of the message below the photo. Click the Send button. Mail sends the photo as an attachment and then shuts down. Return to the Start screen by pressing the Windows key.

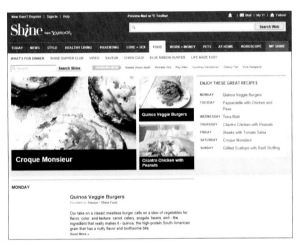

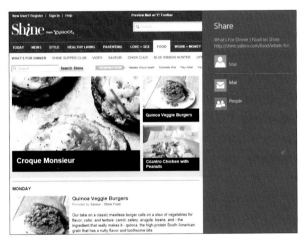

5 Share a web page: This task requires that you have already set up the People app. If you have not, please refer to the task "Adding Accounts to the People App." Open the Internet Explorer Windows 8 app by clicking its Start screen tile. Open a web page by typing its URL in the address bar at the bottom. For this example, you can use www.yahoo.com. At Yahoo, click a specific news story.

6 Share the story: Move your mouse to the lower-right hot corner to display the Charms bar. Move your mouse up the bar and click the Share charm. You should see an icon for Mail, People, and possibly other programs.

7 Choose the People app: Click the People icon.

8 Share the story via a social network: The People app opens in the right pane of the screen. Click the drop-down menu to choose which social network you want to use to share this story — Facebook, Twitter, or LinkedIn. Type your message above the photo. Click the Send button.

tip You can also share content from the Maps app, SkyDrive, Windows Store, and certain third-party Windows 8 apps.

Searching for Content in a Windows 8 App

Searching for content within a desktop application varies from app to app in Windows 8 just as it does in previous versions of Windows. But searching for content within a Windows 8 app uses the Search charm from the Charms bar, thereby offering a consistent approach across all Windows 8 applications. You can search within Mail, Music, Photos, Maps, Weather, and Internet Explorer using the same process. Just open the app, launch the Search charm, and type your search term. Windows displays the search results on the left pane of the screen. This task explains how to search for content within a Windows 8 app.

1 Open the Mail app: This example uses Mail. Open the Mail app by clicking its Start screen tile.

2 Search in Mail: Move your mouse to the lower-right hot corner to display the Charms bar. Move your mouse up the bar and click the Search charm. The Search bar opens with Mail selected.

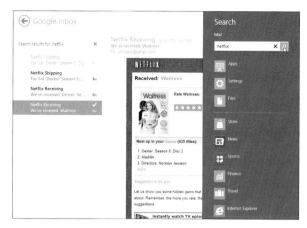

3 Search for content: In the search field, type any text contained in the body of one of your e-mail messages. Click the Search icon. Mail displays any messages containing your search term. Return to the Start screen by pressing the Windows key.

4 Open the Photos app: Open the Photos app by clicking its Start screen tile.

5 Search in Photos: Move your mouse to the lower-right hot corner to display the Charms bar. Move your mouse up the bar and click the Search charm. The Search bar opens with Photos selected as the app and your local Pictures library as the default location in which to search.

6 Search for content: In the search field, type any part of the name of the photo or any tags that have been added to the photo. Any photos matching your search term appear in the left pane. Click on a photo to view it full screen. Return to the Start screen by pressing the Windows key.

> *tip* You can search in a variety of other apps, including Maps, Music, People, News, Sports, Weather, and many third-party Windows 8 apps.

Surfing the Web with Windows 8 Internet Explorer

With Windows 8, Microsoft offers two versions, or views, of Internet Explorer 10 — one that runs in the Windows 8 UI and one that runs in the standard desktop environment. The desktop version of IE is similar to the previous edition of the browser and offers more features than does the Windows 8 version. But the Windows 8 version is designed for quick and simple web surfing, offering a minimal set of controls and options, and instead putting the focus on the web page itself. With the Windows 8 version of IE, you can move back and forth between different websites, open new tabbed pages, and pin pages to the Start screen. This task explains how to surf the web using the Windows 8 version of IE.

1 Open Internet Explorer: Open the Windows 8 version of Internet Explorer by clicking its Start screen tile.

2 View your home page: Internet Explorer opens to display the default home page.

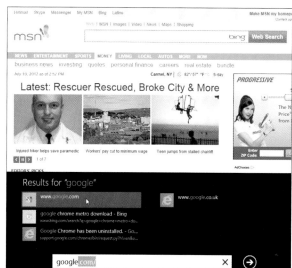

3 Enter a new address: Click in the address bar on the app bar and type the name for a new website, such as Google. Internet Explorer displays a list of suggested sites based on your entry. Click the suggestion that best matches the website you want.

4 View new website: Internet Explorer displays the Google page.

5 Go back: Move your mouse to the left of the screen. A Back button appears in the left middle part of the screen. Click the Back button to go back to the previous page.

6 Go forward: Move your mouse to the right of the screen. A Forward button appears in the right middle part of the screen. Click the Forward button to return to the Google page.

7 Open a page in a new tab: Right-click on the screen to display the top bar if it no longer appears. Click the plus sign in the upper-right corner. In the address field, type the name for a new website, such as Microsoft. Internet Explorer displays a list of suggested sites based on your entry. Click the suggestion that best matches the website you want.

8 View new page: Microsoft's site opens in a new tab.

9 Open another page in a new tab: Right-click on the screen to display the top bar if it no longer appears. Click the plus sign in the upper-right corner. In the address field, type a new web page, such as Yahoo. Internet Explorer displays a list of suggested sites based on your entry. Click the suggestion that best matches the website you want.

10 View new page: Yahoo's site opens in a new tab.

11 Switch between tabbed pages: Right-click on the screen to display the top bar if it no longer appears. Internet Explorer displays thumbnails for all open sites. Click on the Google thumbnail to return to the Google page. Right-click on the screen again. Click on the Microsoft thumbnail to return to Microsoft. Right-click on the screen once more. Click the Yahoo page to return to Yahoo.

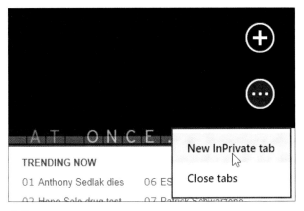

12 Open page using InPrivate browsing: Right-click on the screen to display the top bar again. Click the icon with the three dots. Select the New InPrivate tab option.

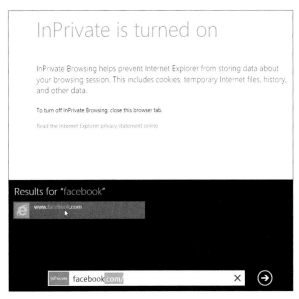

13 View InPrivate page: A page opens to explain the purpose of InPrivate browsing. In the address field, type the name of another website, such as Facebook.

14 View Facebook: The Facebook site opens in an InPrivate tab.

15 Pin a site to the Start screen: Right-click on the screen to display the app bar. From the app bar, click Pin to Start. Change the name of the tile to just Facebook and click Pin to Start. Facebook now appears as a tile on your Start screen and as a Pinned site when you click in the address bar in IE.

16 Return to Yahoo: Right-click anywhere on the screen to display the top bar. Click the tab for Yahoo.

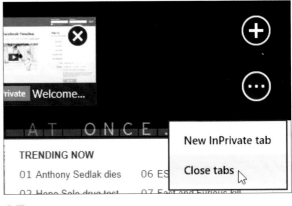

17 Close all pages: Right-click again. Click the icon with the three dots. Select the Close tabs option. All pages are closed except your current one.

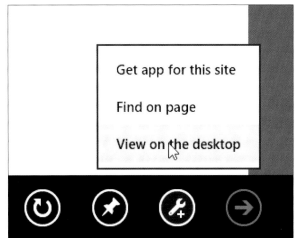

18 Open a pinned site: Click in the address bar. Click the Pinned entry for Facebook to return to Facebook.

19 View page in Desktop version of IE: Right-click to display the app bar. From the app bar, click the wrench icon. Select the View on the desktop option. The page opens in the desktop version of Internet Explorer.

tip To delete your browsing history and set other options, open the Charms bar, click the Settings charm, and select the link for Internet options.

tip You can sort the website tiles on the Start screen but not in Internet Explorer itself.

tip To print your current web page, open the Charms bar, click the Share charm, and select your printer.

tip To share your current web page by e-mail or instant messaging, open the Charms bar and click the Share charm.

Adding Accounts to the Mail App

Mail is a basic e-mail app that lets you send and receive messages for your various online accounts. At the time of this writing, the app supports Windows Live/Hotmail, Outlook, and Google. It also support IMAP for incoming mail. Microsoft may provide support for more accounts, such as POP3, in the final release of Windows 8. If you have accounts at multiple services, you can set up access to all of them and then choose the account you want to use after launching Mail. If you log in with a Microsoft account, then you may already have access to Windows Live/Hotmail by default, but you do have to manually add your other e-mail accounts. This task explains how to set up Mail with your various online accounts.

1 Log in: Log in with your Microsoft account.

2 Open Mail: Open the Mail app from its Start screen tile.

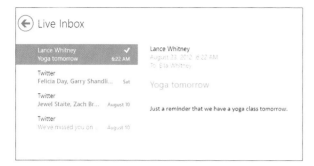

3 View existing mail: You should already see e-mail from your Live account if you logged in with your Microsoft account.

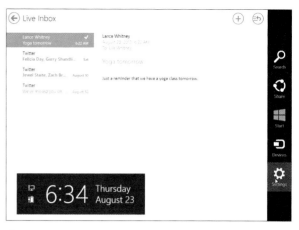

4 Open Settings charm: Move your mouse to the lower-right hot corner to display the Charms bar. Click the Settings charm.

5 Open accounts: In the Settings pane, click Accounts.

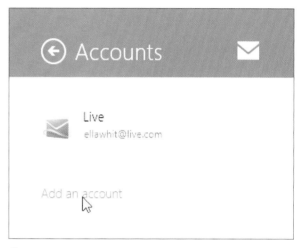

6 Add an account: From the Accounts bar, click the Add an account link.

tip The Mail, People, and Calendar apps are connected, so if you add an account in one, it is automatically added to the other two.

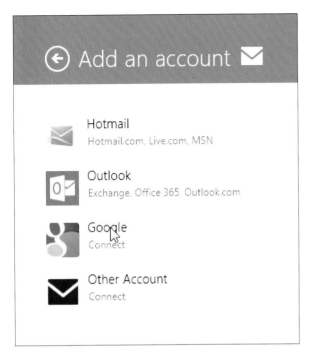

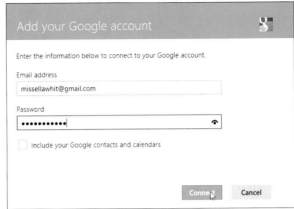

7 Add new account: A list of e-mail services appears, including Hotmail, Outlook, Google, and an option for other accounts. This example uses Google. If you have a Google (Gmail) account, click the entry for Google.

8 Add your Google account: Type the e-mail address and password for your Google account. You can also select the option to include your Google contacts and calendars. Click Connect.

tip You can add an IMAP account by choosing the Other Account option in the Add an account pane.

9 View your Google account: Your Google (Gmail) messages appear.

tip At the time of this writing, Mail does not support POP3 accounts.

10 View all your mailboxes: Click the back button in front of Gmail Inbox to move back to a view of all your mailboxes. Click the folder for Live to see the e-mail for your Live account.

tip At the time of this writing, Microsoft plans to to phase out Hotmail in favor of Outlook.com.

Adding Accounts to the People App

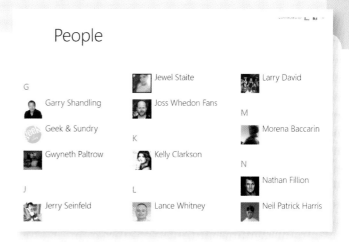

The People app lets you connect to various social networks and display the accounts of your friends and followers. Though this app, you can connect to Facebook, Twitter, LinkedIn, Outlook, and Google. After you set up access to your various accounts, you can view the individual profiles of all your friends and other contacts. You can also contact them via the various social networks, view their locations, and access their full profiles on Facebook, LinkedIn, and other networks. The People app essentially acts as a one-stop shop for viewing and communicating with all of your social network contacts. This task explains how to set up various accounts in the People app.

1 Open People app: Open the People app by clicking its Start screen tile.

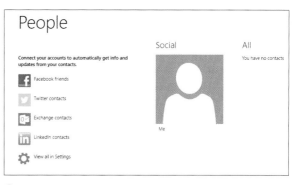

2 View app: The People app opens, displaying options to connect to your Facebook friends, Twitter contacts, Exchange contacts, and LinkedIn contacts.

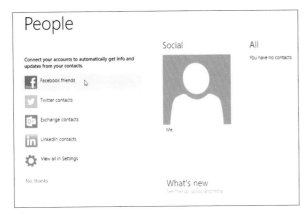

3 Add your Facebook account: Click Facebook friends to connect to your Facebook account.

4 Connect to Facebook: A Stay in touch with your Facebook friends screen appears. Click Connect.

5 Connect to service: At the Connecting to a service screen, type the e-mail address and password for your Facebook account. Click Log In.

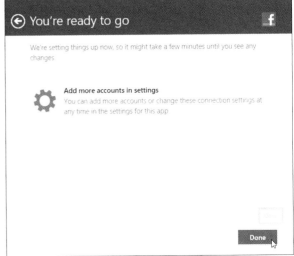

6 Ready to go: At the next screen, click Done.

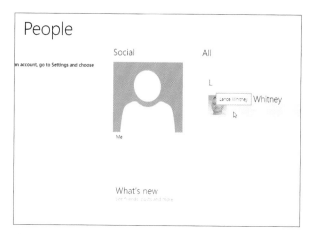

7 View Facebook friends: Under the All section, your Facebook friends appear.

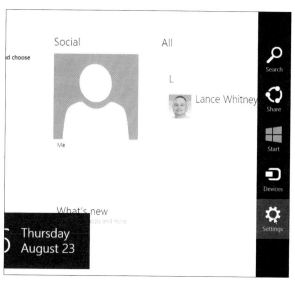

8 Add another account: Hover your mouse in the lower-right hot corner to display the Charms bar and click the Settings charm.

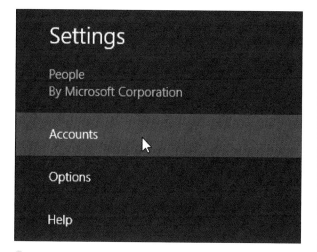

9 Access the Accounts page: From the Settings pane, click the Accounts link.

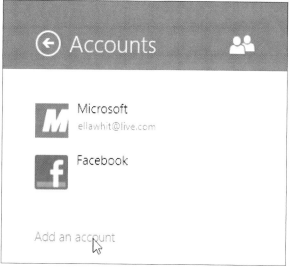

10 Add the account: From the Accounts page, click the Add an account link.

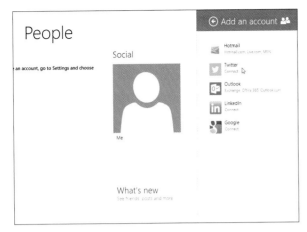

11 Add Twitter: From the Add an account pane, click Twitter, assuming you have a Twitter account.

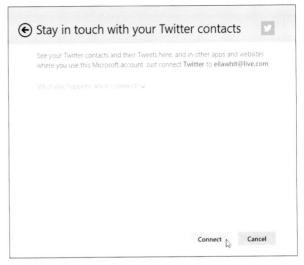

12 Connect to Twitter: A Stay in touch with your Twitter contacts screen appears. Click Connect.

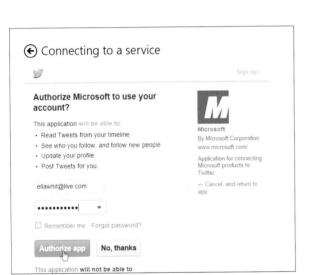

13 Connect to service: At the Connecting to a service screen, type the username or e-mail address and password for your Twitter account. Click Authorize app.

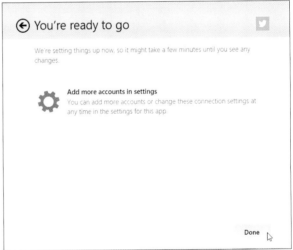

14 Ready to go: At the You're ready to go screen, click Done.

15 View people: The People section now displays all of the Facebook friends and Twitter accounts that you follow. You can click a specific account to view the account details and see a list of recent messages or tweets.

tip At the time of this writing, Microsoft plans to to phase out Hotmail in favor of Outlook.com.

tip The Mail, People, and Calendar apps are connected, so if you add an account in one, it is automatically added to the other two.

Customizing Your Notifications

From the Start screen, type the word **notifications**. Click Settings. From the search results on the left pane, click Notifications setting. From the Notifications screen, choose whether to turn app notifications on or off, turn app notifications on the lock screen on or off, and turn notification sounds on or off. You can also choose which apps should display notifications.

Controlling Your Privacy Options

From the Start screen, type the word **privacy**. Click Settings. In the search results on the left pane, click Privacy. In the Privacy screen, you can turn the following options on or off: Let apps use my location, Let apps use my name and account picture, and Help improve Windows Store by sending URLs for the web content that apps use.

Contacting People via the People App

The People app lets you connect to various social networks and display the accounts of your friends and followers. You can connect with people on Facebook, Twitter, LinkedIn, Google, Hotmail, and Microsoft Exchange. After you set up access to your various accounts, you can view the individual profiles of all your friends and other contacts. You can also contact them through the People app, either through e-mail or through instant messaging, by tapping into the Mail and the Messaging apps that come with Windows 8. If you have not already set up some accounts through the People app, you do so by following the steps in the task "Adding Accounts to the People App." This task explains how to send someone a message and chat with that person through the People app.

1 Open the People app: Open the People app by clicking its Start screen tile.

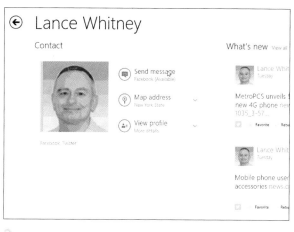

3 IM the acccount: Using the same account, click Send message. You can tell if the person is online because the word Available is listed in parentheses.

2 Select a Facebook account: Click a specific Facebook account.

tip The Messaging app keeps track of people whom you have recently tried to contact.

tip You can open the Messaging app directly to try to IM people whom you recently tried to contact.

4 Send the message: The Messaging app opens for you to type your message. You can send a instant message only if the person is logged in to Facebook. If the person is available, type your message and press Enter. If the person replies, you can then initiate a back-and-forth chat.

tip A Facebook friend must be logged in to Facebook for you to send that person an instant message.

Viewing Appointments with the Calendar App

The Calendar app serves as your appointment book, displaying your schedule daily, weekly, or monthly. You can add a new appointment and fill in all the details, including date, time, location, reminder, and frequency. Though you can manually create appointments in the app, you may find it easier to simply add an existing account to the app, such as Google. Any appointments you record in your existing Google account then automatically synchronize to and appear in your Calendar app. Daily appointments can display on your Start screen through the Calendar's app live tile. This task explains how to view appointments with the Calendar app.

1 Open the Calendar app: Open the Calendar app by clicking its Start screen tile.

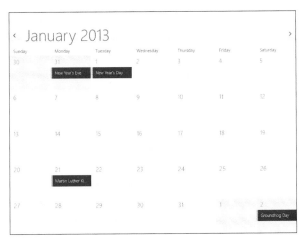

2 View month: The Calendar opens to display the current month with any holidays automatically recorded through your Microsoft account.

3 Access the Settings charm: Move your mouse to the lower-right hot corner to display the Charms bar. Click the Settings charm. From the Settings bar, click Accounts.

4 Add an account: From the Accounts pane, click Add an account.

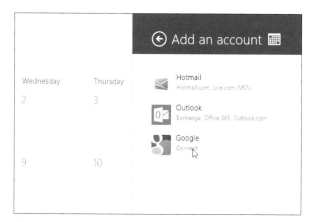

5 Add your Google account: This example uses a Google account, but you can use a Hotmail or Outlook account as well. If you have already set up your Google account for the Mail or People app, then it is automatically added to the Calendar because all three apps are connected. If you have not already added Google to your Mail or People app, click Google.

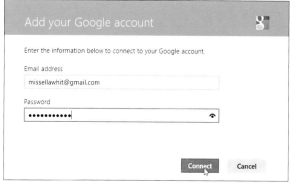

6 Enter your Google credentials: Type the e-mail address and password for your Google account. Click Connect.

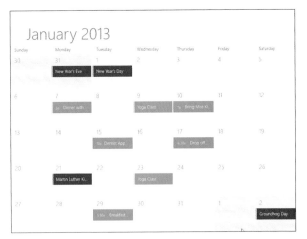

7 View your calendar: The current month's calendar is displayed, while the app syncs with any appointments you have already set up through Google. After a few seconds, you should see any appointments from Google appear in the calendar. Appointments from different accounts appear in different colors.

8 View an appointment: Click on a specific appointment. A Details screen appears showing you the location, date, start time, duration, frequency, reminder, and status. Click the Close button (X) in the upper-right corner to close the Details screen.

tip To change the colors used for the appointments, access the Charms bar, click the Settings charm, and then click the Options link.

9 View other months: Press Page Down or move your mouse's scroll wheel down to move ahead to the next few months. Press Page Up or move your mouse's scroll wheel up to move back to the previous few months.

tip You can add multiple accounts to your Calendar, though it is probably less confusing to keep all your appointments in one account.

Adding Online Accounts to the Photos App

W indows 8 offers a Windows 8 Photos app that lets you view and manage all the photos stored in your Pictures folder. But you can also add and view pictures from SkyDrive, Facebook, and Flickr. If you log in with a Microsoft account and have already uploaded photos to SkyDrive, then your SkyDrive account should automatically display your pictures. But you do need to manually add the accounts for Facebook and Flickr. After you add your Facebook and Flickr accounts, you can view your online photos one by one or launch a slide show to view one after the other. This task explains how to configure the Photos app with your online accounts.

1 Open the Photos app: Open the Photos app by clicking its Start screen tile.

2 View the Photos app: Thumbnails are displayed for your local Pictures library, your SkyDrive account, your Facebook photos, your Flickr photos, and an option to add another device with photos.

3 Connect to Facebook: Click on the Facebook photos thumbnail. At the next screen, click Connect to access your Facebook account.

4 Log in with your Facebook credentials: At the next screen, type your Facebook e-mail address and password. Click Log In.

5 Name New Device: At the next screen, type the name of your computer. Click Save Device.

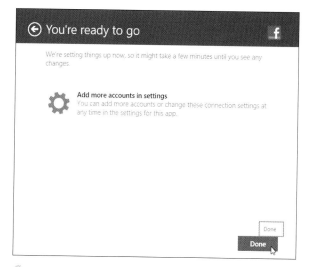

6 Ready to go: At the next screen, click Done.

7 View Facebook photos: After a few seconds, a photo appears in the Facebook thumbnail. Click on the Facebook thumbnail to view your Facebook photos.

8 View a photo: In your Facebook photos, click on an album and then click on a specific photo to view it full screen.

9 View a slide show: Right-click on a photo to display the app bar. From the app bar, click the Slide show button to view a slide show of all the photos in your current folder.

10 Exit slide show: Click on any photo to stop the slide show. Click on the photo again to display the Back button in the upper-left corner. Keep clicking the Back button to return to the Photos app.

11 Add Flickr photos: This step assumes that you have photos stored in Flickr. If so, click on the Flickr photos thumbnail.

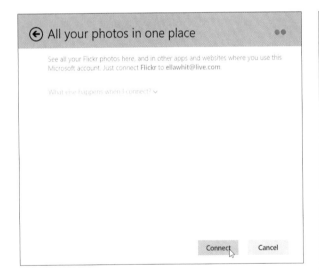

12 Connect to Flickr: At the next screen, click Connect to access your Flickr account.

13 Log in with your Flickr credentials: Your Flickr credentials are actually your Yahoo credentials. At the next screen, type your Yahoo ID and password. Click Sign In.

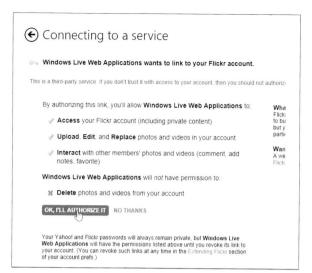

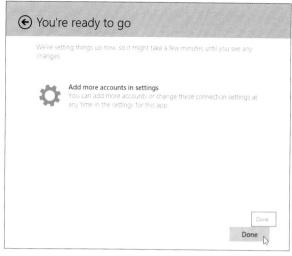

14 Authorize access: At the next screen, click OK, I'll authorize It to authorize access to your Flickr account.

15 Ready to go: At the next screen, click Done.

17 View a photo: From your Flickr photos, click on a specific photo to view it full screen.

16 View Flickr photos: After a few seconds, a photo appears in the Flickr thumbnail. Click on the Flickr thumbnail to view your Flickr photos.

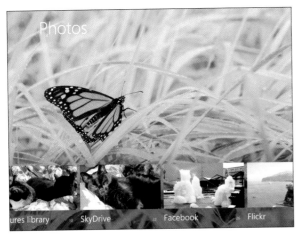

18 Return to library: Keep clicking the Back button to return to the Photos app.

tip Zoom in or out of a photo by moving your mouse cursor and clicking the plus and minus signs in the lower-right corner.

Quick Fixes

Managing Your Security with Windows Defender

At the Start screen, type the phrase **Windows Defender**. In the search results, click the Windows Defender app. If the Virus and spyware definitions are not up to date, click the Update tab and click Update. To run a manual scan, click the Home tab. Choose the type of scan to run — Quick, Full, or Custom. Click Scan now.

Checking Your Firewall Settings

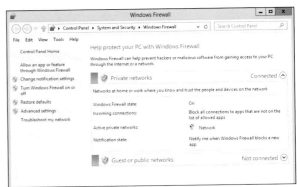

At the Start screen, type the word **firewall**. Under the search field, click Settings. In the search results, click Windows Firewall. In the Windows Firewall window, make sure Windows Firewall is turned on (assuming you are not using a third-party firewall). If Windows Firewall is turned off, click the option in the left pane to Turn Windows Firewall on or off. In the Customize settings for each type of network, turn on Windows Firewall.

Playing Music with the Music App

The Windows 8 Music app lets you play music from your local Music library. It also serves as an online music marketplace, promoting different artists and albums. In addition to playing your own music, you can hop online to preview and purchase other songs and albums. You can also search for music by album, artist, or title to find profiles of various artists along with their albums and songs. Though the traditional Window Media Player offers additional options, such as the ability to rip CDs and burn music onto a CD, the Music app comes in handy if you simply want to play music. This task explains how to play music in the Music app.

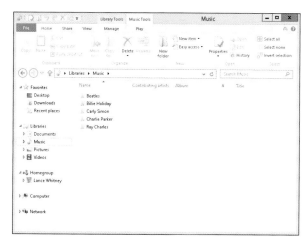

1 Add music: Add music to Windows 8 by burning CDs through Windows Media Player.

2 Open Music app: From the Start screen, open the Music app by clicking its Start screen tile.

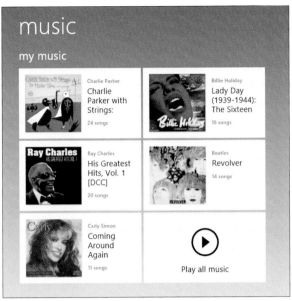

3 View your music: Scroll to the left. The albums and songs that you have added to your Music library appear on the left side.

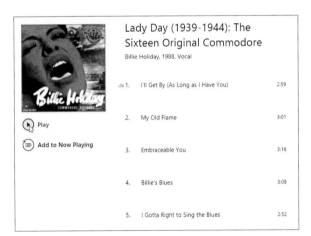

4 Play an album: Click a specific album to open it. Click a specific track and then click the Play button to play it. Otherwise, click the Play button under the album's cover art to play the album starting with the first track.

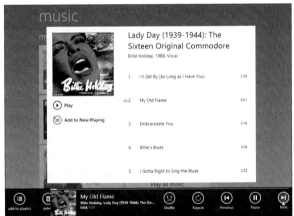

5 Control your music: Right-click any empty area of the screen to display the app bar. Click the Pause button to pause the track. Click the Next or Previous buttons to move to the next or previous tracks. Click the Repeat button to repeat the current track. Click the Shuffle button to shuffle the order of the tracks. If the app bar disappears, right-click anywhere in the Music app to display it again.

6 View player full screen: Right-click on the Music app to display the app bar if it is not already visible. Click on the small album art in the middle of app bar. The Music app changes to full-screen mode.

7 Control track: Click the Pause button to pause the track. Click the Play button to resume the track. Click the Next or Previous buttons to move to the next or previous track. Drag the green circle along the slider bar to move forward or backward in the track. If the controls disappear, simply move your mouse to display them again.

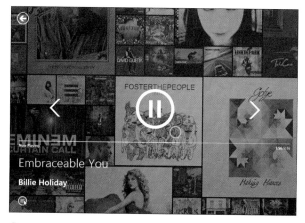

8 Access all tracks: Click the Now Playing icon in the lower-left corner of the screen.

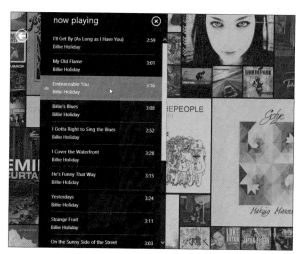

9 View all tracks: A list of all tracks from the current album appears. Click a particular track to play it. Click the X in the upper-right corner of the now playing list to turn off the list.

10 Return to Music app: Click the Back button in the upper-left corner to return to the Music app.

11 View current track: Scroll to the right to view a large image displaying the song currently playing. Click on the image to switch back to the music player.

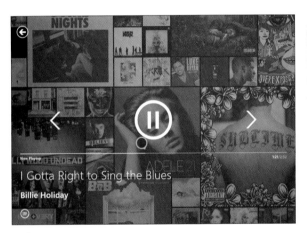

12 Access music player: The music player opens again. Click the Back button to return to the main screen.

tip You can play music either through the Music app or through the traditional Windows Media Player.

tip The Music app can play music in different formats, including WMA, MP3, and AAC (iTunes), but it may have trouble playing protected files.

Adding Album Art to Your Music

After you download an album or rip a CD via Windows Music Player, album art should automatically be found and downloaded as well. You can see the album or cover art in Windows Media Player next to the album and in the Windows 8 Music app next to each track. But sometimes the wrong album art is downloaded, while other times no album art can be found at all. Fortunately, you can correct this problem by finding or manually downloading the right album art yourself directly in Windows Media Player. This task explains how to add or change album art to your music through Windows Media Player.

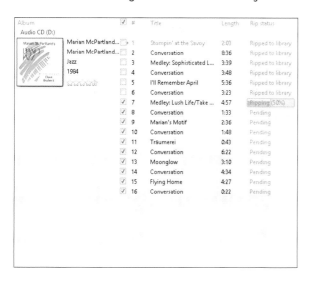

1 Add Music: Open Windows Media Player to rip some music to Windows 8 by burning a few CDs if you have not already done so.

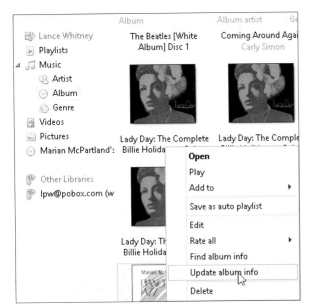

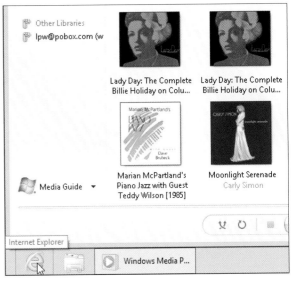

2 Find album info: Right-click on an album whose album art you want to add or change. From the pop-up menu, click Update album info. Wait to see if the correct album art is located and applied. If not, move to the next step.

3 Search for album art: Open Internet Explorer by clicking its taskbar icon.

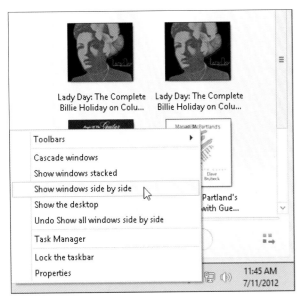

4 Position IE and Media Player: Right-click on the taskbar and select Show windows side by side so that both applications display next to each other.

5 Enter your search query: In Internet Explorer, open the home page for Bing. In the Bing search field, type the full name of the album. You can also add the name of the artist to your search query if needed.

6 Find album art: Bing should deliver search results matching the album name. In Bing, click on the Images category. Find an image that you want to apply to your album.

7 Copy image: Right-click on the image displayed in Bing and click Copy from the pop-up menu.

8 Paste image to album: Right-click on the album in Windows Media Player and click Paste album art from the pop-up menu. The image appears as the album's new art.

tip You can also right-click on an album and select Find album info, but that typically looks for alternate albums, not just album art.

tip The new album art also appears when you view the album's tracks in the Windows 8 Music app.

Finding Places Using the Maps App

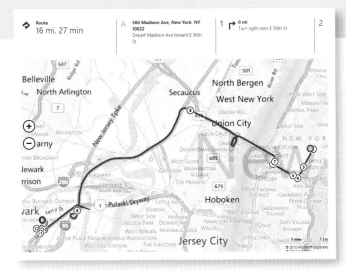

The Maps app starts off by displaying a map of your country and then quickly zooms in to your current location if you allowed the app to do so. You can drag the map to view other nearby areas. You can zoom out to see the entire country or the world or zoom in to see a specific state, city, or address. You can change the view of the map between a road view and an aerial view. You can map out directions between any two locations. And using the Search charm, you can search not just for states and cities but also restaurants, stores, and other businesses. This task explains how to find places using the Maps app.

1 Open the Maps app: Open the Maps app by clicking its Start screen tile.

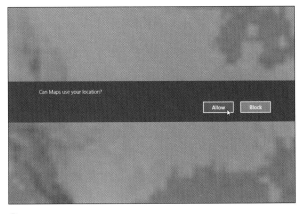

2 Allow Maps to use your location: The first time you open the app, it asks if it can use your location. If you click Block, you will have to type your address any time you want to map out directions from your current location. If you are comfortable having the app find your location, click Allow.

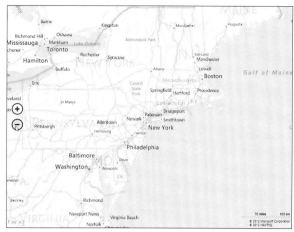

3 View your location: The map zeros in on your current location and displays a gold diamond pinpointing your specific address.

4 Zoom in or out: Click the Zoom in button (+) to zoom in. Click the Zoom out button (–) to zoom out. Move your cursor around the map if the Zoom in and Zoom out buttons do not appear.

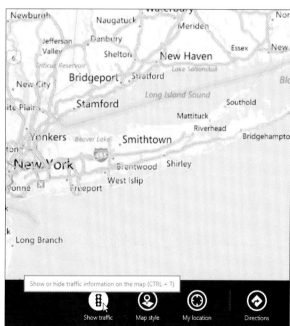

5 Change map style: Right-click anywhere on the map to display the app bar. Click the Map style icon and select Aerial view. You now have a top-down aerial view of your location. Right-click anywhere on the map to display the app bar again. Click the Map style icon and select Road view to return to the road view.

6 Show traffic: Right-click anywhere on the map to display the app bar. Click the Show traffic icon. The map displays the major highways and roads indicating traffic conditions. Right-click anywhere on the map to display the app bar again. Click the Show traffic icon again to turn off traffic display.

7 Open the Search charm: Move your mouse to the lower-right hot corner to display the Charms bar. Click the Search charm.

8 Search for a state: In the search field, type the name of a state, such as California. Click the Search icon. The map displays California.

9 Search for a city: In the search field, erase the name California and type the name of a city, such as Paris. Click the Search icon. The map displays Paris, France.

10 Get directions: Right-click on the map to display the app bar. Click the Directions icon. If you allowed Maps to use your current location, the A field displays My Location. If not, then you need to manually type the address for your current location. In the B field, type the address, city, and state of your destination. Click the right arrow next to the destination.

tip You may need to add the state or country to your search term to find a specific city. When you search for a city without listing state or country, Maps assumes the most obvious city — Rome, Italy, instead of Rome, New York.

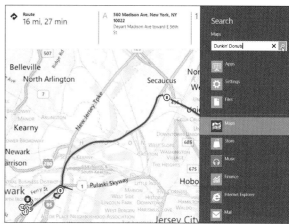

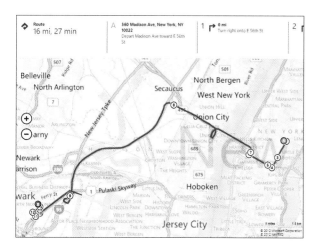

11 View directions to destination: The map displays the route in the bottom pane and the mileage, time, and turn-by-turn directions in the top pane.

12 Search for a business: In the search field, type the name of a business, such as Dunkin' Donuts. Click the Search icon.

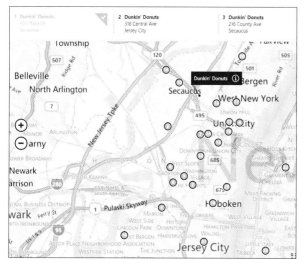

13 View results: The map displays a list of local Dunkin' Donuts shops in and around your destination. Use your mouse to scroll through the list of Dunkin' Donuts shops.

14 View a specific location: Click on a particular shop, and the map shows its location. Click the circled letter i icon on the map to view the address, a link to the website for the store or company, and a link for directions.

15 Clear map: Right-click on the map to display the app bar. Click the Clear map icon to return to the normal map view.

Quick Fix

Ripping a CD in Windows 8

At the Start screen, type **Windows Media Player**. In the search results, click on the app for Windows Media Player. Insert your CD. If Windows Media Player starts playing the CD, click the Stop button. To customize the options for ripping a CD, click Rip settings and choose the various options for format, audio quality, and more. When finished, click Rip CD. The CD's tracks are added to your Windows Music library.

T rue to its name, the News app fills you in on the latest news. Starting with the top story of the day and then displaying the new items across a variety of categories, the app covers stories focusing on your own country, the world, technology, business, entertainment, politics, sports, and health. You can view the latest trending news stories and look at stories from a specific source, such as the Associated Press, the *New York Times,* the *Wall Street Journal, National Geographic,* and many others. You can also search for different people, events, and other items in the news and add the topics that most interest you to your own news page. This task explains how to get the news with the News app.

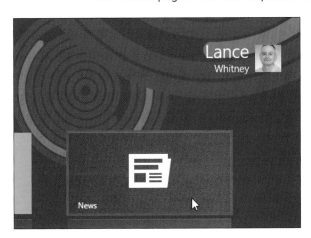

1 Open the News app: Open the News app by clicking its Start screen tile.

2 View app: The News app opens to reveal a featured photo and link to the top news story.

3 View more information: Scroll to the right to see headlines for news stories across other categories, such as the U.S., the world, technology, business, entertainment, politics, sports, and health.

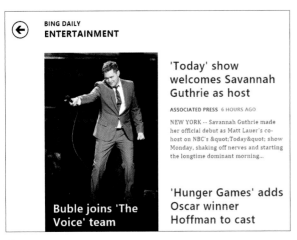

4 View stories for a specific category: Click on a specific category, such as entertainment, to view its headlines.

5 View a specific story: Click a specific headline to view the full story.

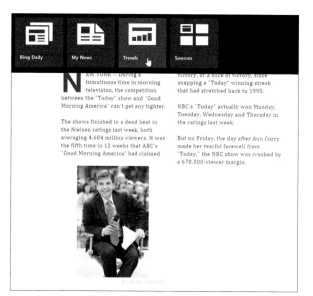

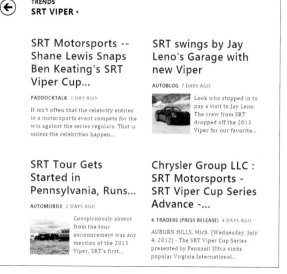

6 Access top trends: Right-click on the screen. From the top bar, click the Trends button to view trending news items.

7 View top trends: Stories from among the top trends appear.

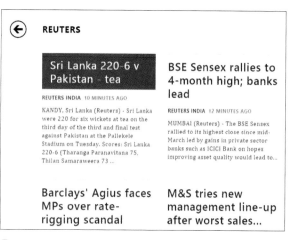

8 Access stories from a specific source: Right-click on the screen. From the top bar, click the Sources button to view a list of all sources supplying the stores for the News app.

9 View stories from a specific source: Click on a specific source to view the latest stories just from that source.

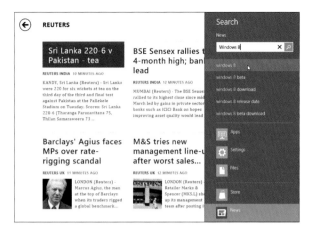

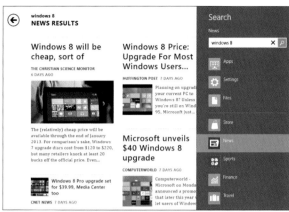

10 Search for a news item: Move your mouse to the lower-right hot corner to display the Charms bar. Click the Search charm. In the search field, type the name of an item that may be in the news, such as **Windows 8**. Suggested topics appear below the search field. Click the one that says Windows 8.

11 View news items on search term: A list of stories on Windows 8 appears in the left pane.

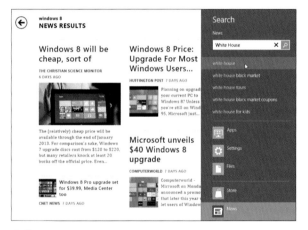

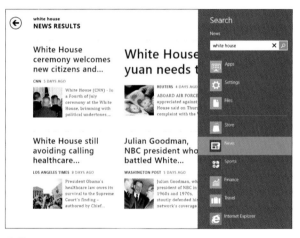

12 Search for another news item: In the search bar's search field, delete Windows 8 as the search term and type another item, such as **White House**. Suggested topics appear below the search field. Click the one that says White House.

13 View news items on search term: A list of stories concerning the White House appears in the left pane.

tip The News app's live tile can display the latest news headlines and photos.

WHITE HOUSE ›

e House threatens veto ealth care repeal

BOSTON GLOBE 11 HOURS AGO

WASHINGTON (AP) — The White House has issued a veto threat for a House bill to overturn President Barack Obama's health care law. The White House says the repeal would cost millions of American families the security of affordable health ...

louse would l Bush tax cut on

12 HOURS AGO

White House press secretary Jay Carney said Monday that President Obama would veto a full....

White House budget chief to testify on defense cuts

POLITICO.COM 11 HOURS AGO

POLITICO's Austin Wright has the full story in On Congress: The acting White House budget director has agreed to testify before the House Armed Services Committee next month on the...

WINDOWS 8 ›

Windows 8 computers to go on sale in October

AP - MSNBC.COM 16 HOURS AGO

Computers running on the next version of Microsoft's Windows operating system will go on sale in October. Microsoft Corp. announced the time frame for Windows 8's mass-market...

New Windows 8-Ready Hybrid Tablet, Convertible Laptop from Fujitsu

PC WORLD 17 HOURS AGO

The Fujitsu Stylistic Q702 joins the growing rank of slate tablets with optional keyboard docks (like the popular Android-based Asus Eee...

14 Access recent items: Right-click on the screen. From the top bar, click the My News button.

15 View recent items: A My News page appears showing the latest headlines for the items you just found — White House and Windows 8.

tip To clear your search history, display the Charms bar and click the Settings charm. Click the Settings links and click Clear history.

Creating a HomeGroup

PC settings

Personalize
Users
Notifications
Search
Share
General
Privacy
Devices
Ease of Access
Sync your settings
HomeGroup

HomeGroup

Create a homegroup

With a homegroup you can share libraries and devices with other people on this network. You can also stream media to devices

Your homegroup is protected with a password, and you'll always be able to choose what you share.

Create

At the Start screen, type the word **homegroup**. Click Settings. In the search results, click HomeGroup. In the HomeGroup section, click Create. After the homegroup is created, choose which files you want to share. Make a note of the membership password.

Following Favorite Teams with the Sports App

Geared for all sports fans, the Sports app provides the latest news, scores, and other information on baseball, football, hockey, tennis, golf, soccer, and racing. You can view the latest news headlines and stories in the world of sports, catch the scores to last night's games, and view upcoming schedules. You can easily switch from one sport to another and remove any sports you do not want to follow. You can also add your favorite teams to get full details on their latest games, news, schedules, player rosters, and team stats. This task explains how to set up the Sports app to get the latest news and follow your favorite teams.

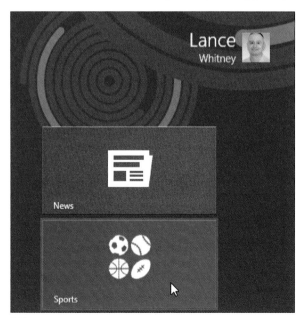

1 Open the Sports app: Open the Sports app by clicking its Start screen tile.

2 View app: The Sports app opens to reveal a featured photo and link to a news story.

3 View information: Scroll to the right to see links to more news stories.

4 View a story: Click one of the stories to read it full screen. Click the Back button to return to the main screen.

5 View more information: Scroll farther to the right to see a schedule of ongoing and upcoming games.

6 View links to all sports and leagues: Right-click anywhere on the screen to display the top bar. The bar displays buttons for different sports and sports leagues, including Major League Baseball, the National Hockey League, the National Basketball Association, and the National Football League.

7 View a specific sport: Click on one of the leagues, such as the National Hockey League, to view the latest news stories, schedules, standings, leading players, and leading teams.

9 View information on team: A page on the Yankees appears with a photo and other details on the latest news. Click on the screen to turn off the search bar.

8 Search for a team or player: Move your mouse to the lower-right hot corner to display the Charms bar. Click the Search charm. In the search field, type the name of a team or player. The Yankees are used for this example. Type **Yankees** in the search field. Suggestions for the Yankees appear below the search bar. Click on the first result for New York Yankees MLB.

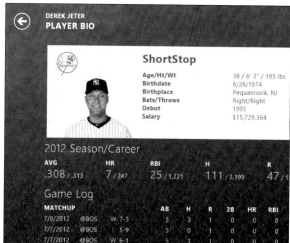

10 View more information on team: Scroll to the right to view more news stories, upcoming schedules, team leaders, stats, and the team roster.

11 View a player: In the team roster section, click on a specific player to view his stats and news items. Click the Back button to return to the previous screen.

12 Add your favorite team: Right-click anywhere on the screen to display the app bar and the top bar. From the app bar, click the Add button. The team is added to your list of favorite teams.

13 Pin your favorite team: Right-click on the screen again. From the app bar, click the Pin button.

14 Pin to Start: Keep the name New York Yankees and click Pin to Start. A tile displaying the team information is added to the Start screen.

15 Access favorite teams: Right-click anywhere on the screen to display the app bar and the top bar. From the top bar, click the Favorite Teams button.

16 View favorite teams: The Favorite Teams page opens to display a selection for the Yankees.

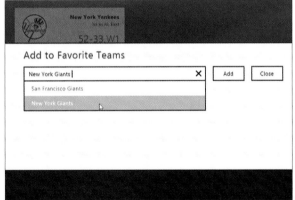

17 Add another team: Under the box for the Yankees, click on the box with the plus sign. Type the name of another team, such as **New York Giants**. Click on the New York Giants from the suggested list under the search box and then click the Close button.

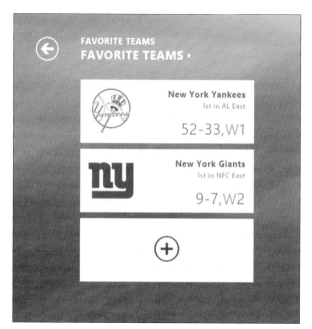

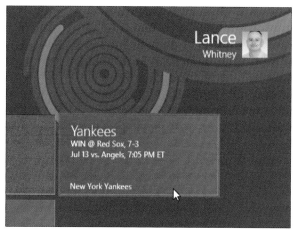

18 View favorite teams: The Favorite Teams page now displays selections for the Yankees and the Giants.

19 Return to Start screen: Press the Windows key to return to the Start screen. Scroll to the end of the screen. A new tile for the Yankees is displayed.

tip You can set up Start screen tiles for your favorite teams when their season starts and remove those tiles when the season ends.

Joining a HomeGroup

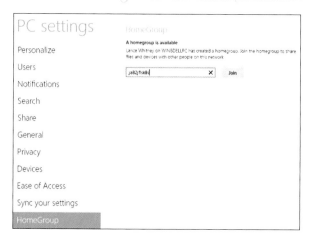

At the Start screen, type the word **homegroup**. Click Settings. In the search results, click HomeGroup. In the HomeGroup section, type the password for the homegroup. Click Join. After you join the homegroup, choose which files you want to share.

Tracking Your Investments with the Finance App

The Finance app provides financial news and stock market information. As such, it is designed to keep you up to date on the latest financial stories along with the latest trends in the stock market, the trading prices of stocks, mortgage rates, mutual fund prices, and other data of interest to investors. You can search for specific stocks, mutual funds, and other investments and add them to your own personal watchlist or even pin them to the Start screen so you can stay abreast of their daily price fluctuations. This task explains how to use the Finance app to view the latest financial news and keep track of your investments.

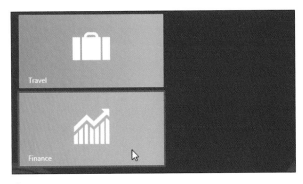

1 Open the Finance app: Open the Finance app by clicking its Start screen tile.

2 View app: The Finance app opens to reveal a featured photo and link to a news story along with the latest figures for various stock market indices, such as the Dow and the NASDAQ.

3 View more information: Scroll to the right to see a detailed graph for the Dow, followed by news headlines, stock market movers, the latest numbers on bonds and commodities, interest rates, and mutual fund picks.

4 Access top bar: Right-click anywhere on the screen to display the top bar.

5 View details on currencies: Click the Currencies button to get more details on that item.

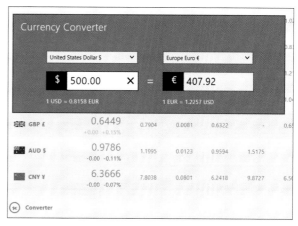

6 Convert currency: Click the Converter button to convert currency from one type to another.

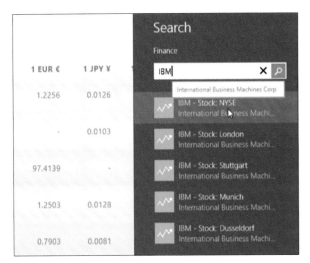

7 Search for a stock or investment: Move your mouse to the lower-right hot corner to display the Charms bar. Click the Search charm. In the search field, type the name or symbol for a stock, such as **IBM**. Suggestions for IBM appear below the search bar, including the stock traded on the New York Stock Exchange. Click that result.

8 View information on stock: A page on IBM appears, with a chart and other details tracking its stock price. Click on the screen to turn off the search bar.

9 View more information on stock: Scroll to the right to view the latest news, statistics, financial information, and fund ownership on IBM.

10 Add stock to watchlist: Right-click on the screen. From the app bar, click the Add button. IBM is added to your watchlist.

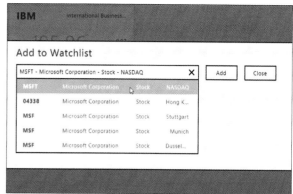

11 View watchlist: Right-click on the screen again. Click the Watchlist button on the top bar. IBM displays as one of your watchlist stocks.

12 Add another stock to watchlist: Under the box for IBM, click on the box with the plus sign. Type the name of another company or ticker symbol, such as Microsoft. Suggestions for Microsoft appear, including one trading on the NASDAQ. Click that result. Microsoft is added to your watchlist.

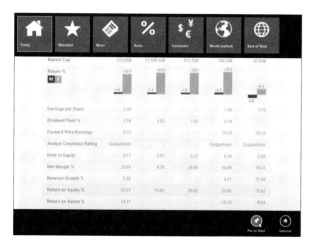

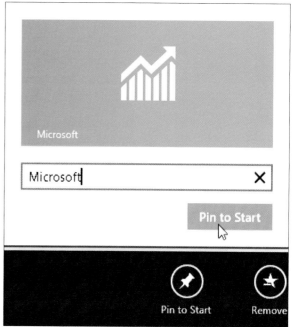

13 Add stock to Start screen: Click the entry for Microsoft. Right-click on the screen. From the app bar, click the Pin button.

14 Pin stock: Name the tile Microsoft and click Pin to Start.

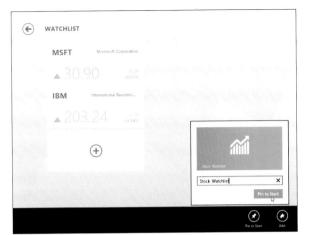

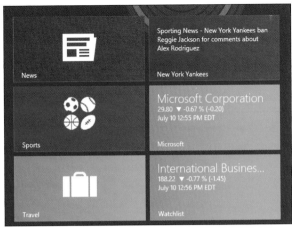

15 Pin watchlist to Start screen: Right-click on the screen. Click the Watchlist button on the top bar. Right-click on the screen again. From the app bar, click the Pin to Start button. Rename the tile Stock Watchlist and click Pin to Start.

16 Return to Start screen: Press the Windows key to return to the Start screen. Scroll to the end of the screen. The new tiles for Microsoft and your watchlist are displayed.

tip The Finance app's live tile can display the latest news headlines, photos, and stock market information.

Quick Fix

Changing HomeGroup Settings

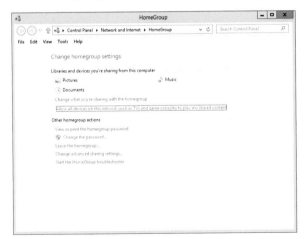

At the Start screen, type the word **homegroup**. Click Settings. In the search results, click on the setting for Change homegroup password. In the HomeGroup window, you can now change what you're sharing with the homegroup, view or print the homegroup password, change the password, leave the homegroup, or change certain advanced sharing settings.

Planning a Trip with the Travel App

The Travel app provides information on different destinations around the world, so you can use it as a travel planner to find information and make arrangements for your next trip. You can read articles and view still and panoramic photos about different cities and other vacation spots around the world. You can also search for a specific location if you already know where you want to go. From there, you can get details on airports, hotels, and restaurants, and even book your air travel and make your hotel reservations with the help of the app. This task explains how to plan your next trip using the Travel app.

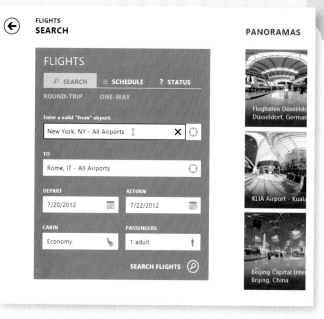

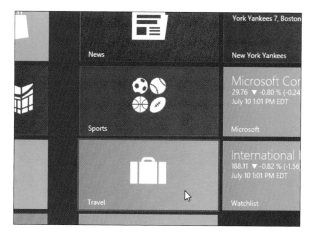

1 Open the Travel app. Open the Travel app by clicking its Start screen tile.

Dubrovnik, Croatia

2 View app: The travel app opens to reveal the featured destination.

3 Search for your destination: Move your mouse to the lower-right hot corner to display the Charms bar. Click the Search charm. In the search field, type the name of your destination, such as **Rome**. Under the search field, Rome, Italy, appears as the suggested destination. Click the result for Rome, Italy.

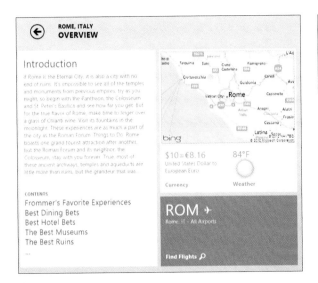

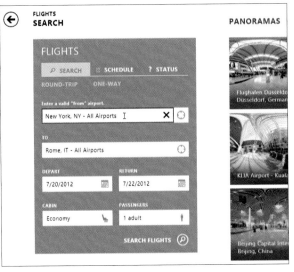

4 View information on destination: The app displays details on Rome. Click anywhere on the screen to turn off the search bar. Scroll to the right to see the introduction, a map, currency information, and a link to book a flight.

5 Find flights: Click Find Flights. In the Flights box, click in the From field. The first time you do this, the app asks if you want to turn on location services and allow Travel to use your location. If you are comfortable turning on location services, click Allow.

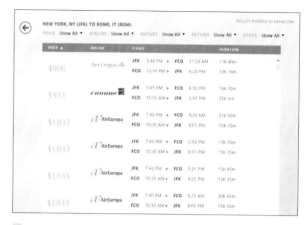

7 View flight information: A flight information screen appears showing you all the flights matching your dates, along with ticket price, airline, departure and arrival times, flight duration, and number of stopovers.

6 Fill out flight information: In the From field, click the round icon to let the app consider all airports in and around your vicinity, or delete the suggestion and type the name or code for your closest airport. Then select the name of the airport that matches your name or code. Type a departure date, return date, cabin type, and number of passengers. Click Search Flights.

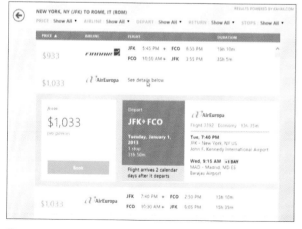

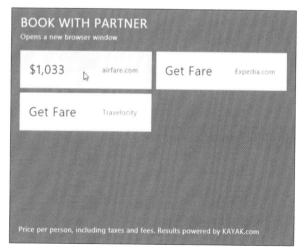

8 Choose a flight: Click on a specific flight to view more details.

9 Book the flight: Click the Book button if you want to book the flight, which you can do online through the website of the airline or a third-party travel partner. Select the airline or travel partner.

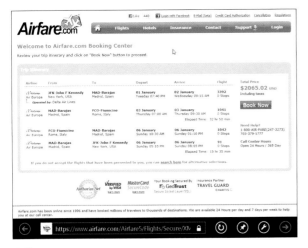

10 Book the flight online: Internet Explorer opens for you to book the flight.

11 Return to the Travel app: Move your mouse to the upper-left hot corner of the screen and click on the thumbnail for the Travel app to return to the app. Click the Back button to return to each previous screen until you reach the information page on Rome.

12 View hotels section: Scroll to the right past the photos, panoramas, and attractions until you see the Hotels section. Click Find Hotels.

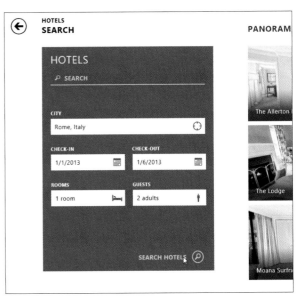

13 Fill out hotel information: Type the check-in and check-out dates, the number of rooms, and the number of guests. Click Search Hotels.

14 View hotel information: A hotel information screen appears showing you all the suggested hotels matching your dates, along with price, rating, and amenities.

15 Choose a hotel: Click on a specific hotel to view more details. Another screen opens to display a description of the hotel, a map of its location, and photos. Click Book if you want to make a reservation, which you can do online through a third-party website. Select the third-party website.

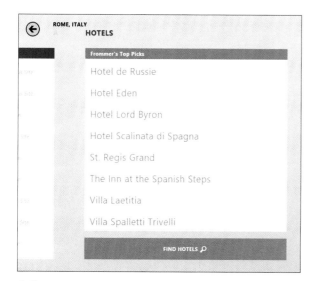

16 Book the hotel room online: Internet Explorer then opens for you to book the hotel room.

tip You can e-mail information on your travel destination to yourself or someone else through the Share charm.

Beat the Clock

Find quicker ways to work in Windows 8 through built-in tools and your own custom shortcuts.

System
Use a restore
PC to restore

System
Recove
Recover Win
system imag

Automa
Fix problems
loading

otions

d on your

Command Prompt
Use the Command Prompt for
advanced troubleshooting

pecific

Startup Settings
Change Windows startup behavior

ir

dows from

Creating a Tile to Restart Windows

Windows 8 no longer provides the traditional desktop Start menu, so there is no Restart command accessible from the Start button. Windows 8 does offer a variety of other ways to restart your computer. You can restart it by clicking the Power button accessible from the Settings charms, by using the Sign out screen, or by pressing Alt+F4 when you are in the desktop. And you can restart it by pressing the Power button or closing the lid if you are using a laptop. But you can save time by creating a tile directly on the Start screen to restart Windows quickly and easily. This task explains how to create a Start screen tile to restart Windows.

1 Access the desktop: Launch the desktop from its Start screen tile.

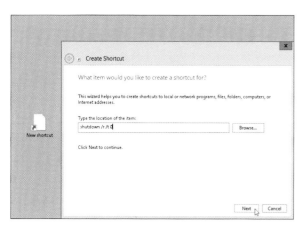

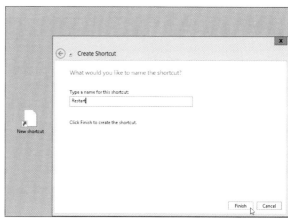

2 Create shortcut: Right-click on the desktop. Select New from the pop-up menu and then select Shortcut. In the Type the location of the item field, type **shutdown /r /t 0**. Click Next.

3 Name it: Name the shortcut Restart. Click Finish.

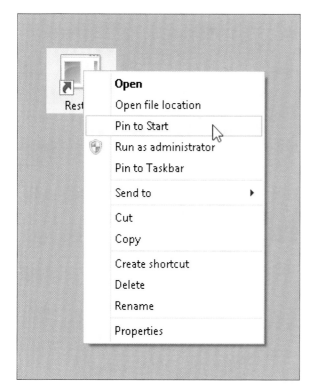

4 Pin shortcut to Start screen: Right-click the shortcut. Select Pin to Start from the pop-up menu.

5 Restart from Start screen: Return to the Start screen by pressing the Windows key or clicking the thumbnail in the lower-left hot corner. Move to the end of the Start screen. Click the tile that says Restart. Windows 8 reboots.

tip You can run your new Restart command from its Start screen tile or from its desktop shortcut.

Creating a Tile to Shut Down Windows

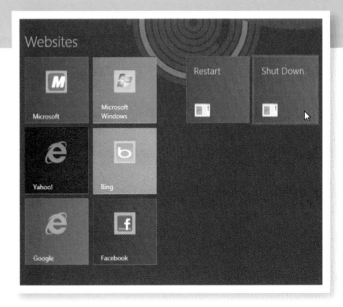

W indows 8 no longer provides the traditional desktop Start menu, so there is no Shut Down command accessible from the Start button. Windows 8 does offer other ways to shut down your computer. You can shut it down by clicking the Power button accessible from the Settings charms, by using the Sign out screen, or by pressing Alt+F4 when you are in the desktop. And you can shut it down by pressing the Power button or closing the lid if you are using a laptop. But you can also create a tile directly on the Start screen to shut down Windows quickly and easily. This task explains how to create a Start screen tile to shut down Windows.

1 Access the desktop: Launch the desktop from its Start screen tile.

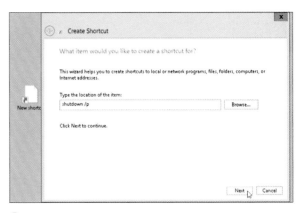

2 Create shortcut: Right-click on the desktop. Select New from the pop-up menu and then select Shortcut. In the Type the location of the item field, type **shutdown /p**. Click Next.

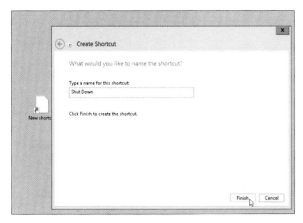

3 Name it: Name the shortcut Shut Down. Click Finish.

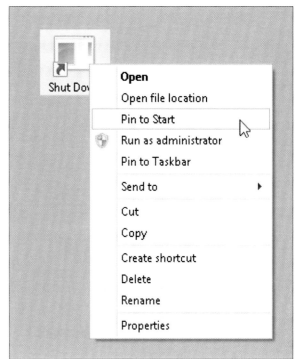

4 Pin shortcut to Start screen: Right-click the shortcut. Select Pin to Start from the pop-up menu.

5 Shut down from Start screen: Return to the Start screen by pressing the Windows key or clicking the thumbnail in the lower-left hot corner. Move to the end of the Start screen. Click the tile that says Shut Down. Windows 8 shuts down.

tip You can run your new Shut Down command from its Start screen tile or from its desktop shortcut.

Creating a Tile to Hibernate Windows

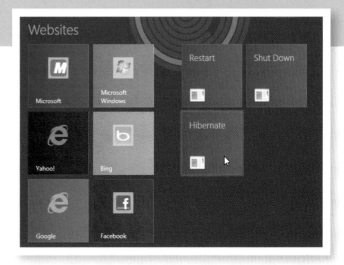

Putting Windows into hibernate mode moves all your current applications, documents, and data from memory onto the hard drive to preserve your current state. When the PC comes out of hibernate mode, everything that was saved is then restored into memory so you can pick up exactly where you left off. You can hibernate the PC by clicking the Power button accessible from the Settings charms, by using the Sign out screen, or by pressing Alt+F4 when you are in the desktop. But the easiest option is to create a Start screen tile to send Windows into hibernate mode. This task explains how to create a Start screen tile to hibernate Windows 8.

1 Access the desktop: Launch the desktop from its Start screen tile.

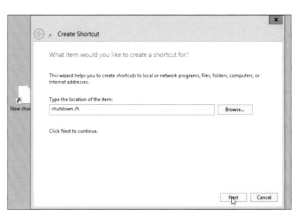

2 Create shortcut: Right-click on the desktop. Select New from the pop-up menu and then select Shortcut. In the Type the location of the item field, type **shutdown /h**. Click Next.

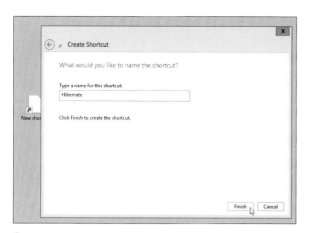

3 Name it: Name the shortcut Hibernate. Click Finish.

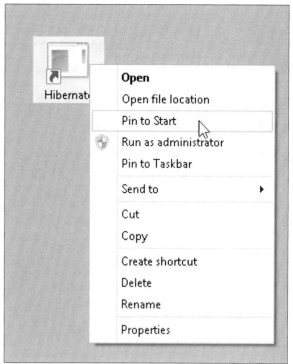

4 Pin shortcut to Start screen: Right-click the shortcut. Select Pin to Start from the pop-up menu.

5 Shut down from Start screen: Return to the Start screen by pressing the Windows key or clicking the thumbnail in the lower-left hot corner. Move to the end of the Start screen. Click the tile that says Hibernate. Windows 8 goes into hibernate mode.

tip You can run your new Hibernate command from its Start screen tile or from its desktop shortcut.

tip You can typically restore Windows from hibernation by pressing the Power button on your PC.

Accessing the Power User Tasks Menu

The Power User Tasks menu offers quick and easy access to a wide variety of Windows features, tools, and commands, many of which were formerly available through the standard Windows Start menu and are still available through Administrative Tools. These include Power Options, Event Viewer, Device Manager, Disk Management, Command Prompt, Task Manager, Control Panel, File Explorer, Search, Run, and Desktop. Instead of hunting for these features on the Start screen, the Apps screen, the desktop, or the Administrative Tools group, you can access them all through the Power User Tasks menu. Microsoft does not officially call this the Power User Tasks menu, but that has become the unofficial name among users. This task explains how to access and run commands from the Power User Tasks menu.

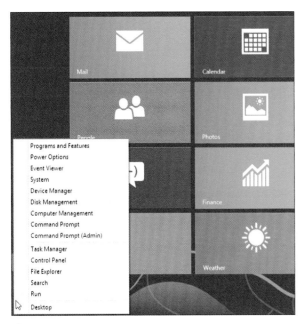

tip You can access the menu by right-clicking in the lower-left hot corner in any screen in Windows 8, not just the Start screen.

tip If a thumbnail of the Start screen or another app appears in the lower-left hot corner, right-click that thumbnail to open the menu.

1 Access the Power User Tasks menu: Move your mouse to the lower-left hot corner from the Start screen. Right-click your mouse in the hot corner. You should see the Power User Tasks menu with several commands.

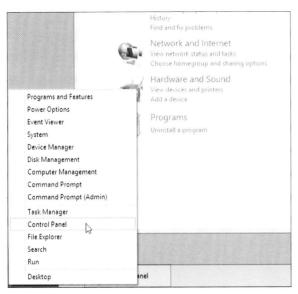

tip You can also hold down the Windows key and press the X key to access the Power User Tasks menu.

2 Select a command: Select any command, such as Event Viewer, Disk Management, Command Prompt, Control Panel, or File Explorer, in order to run it.

Customizing the Power User Tasks Menu

The Power User Tasks menu offers access to a variety of Windows features, tools, and commands, including Power Options, Event Viewer, Device Manager, Command Prompt, Task Manager, Control Panel, File Explorer, Search, and Desktop. You can customize this menu to some degree. Windows 8 limits you to the entries that already appear in the menu, so you cannot add shortcuts for new features, commands, or applications. But you can delete and move commands from one folder or location to another. You an also create a new folder or location for various commands. This task explains how to customize the Power User Tasks menu.

1 Open the folder for Power User Tasks menu: Launch the desktop and open File Explorer. In the address field in File Explorer, type the following path: **%userprofile%\AppData\Local\Microsoft\Windows\WinX**.

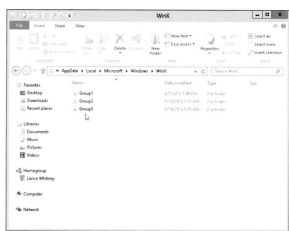

2 View the existing entries: You should see three folders — Group1, Group2, and Group3. These three groups correspond to the three sections displayed on the Power User Tasks menu, going from bottom to top. Each folder contains shortcuts to various commands.

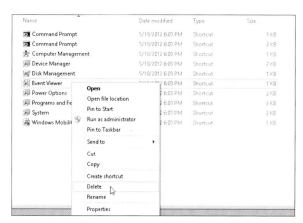

3 Delete a command: For this example, the Event Viewer shortcut in Group3 is deleted. Open the Group3 folder. Right-click the Event Viewer shortcut and select Delete from the pop-up menu.

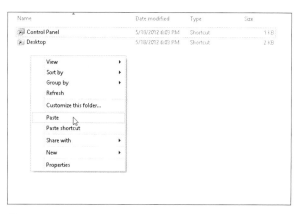

4 Add a command: For this example, a command is moved from Group2 to Group1. Go back one folder and open the Group2 folder. Right-click the shortcut for Control Panel and select Cut from the pop-up menu. Go back one folder and open the Group1 folder. Right-click any empty area of the Group1 window and select Paste from the pop-up menu. The shortcut for Control Panel appears.

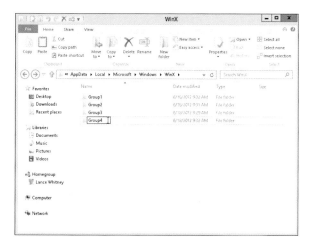

5 Add a folder: Move back one folder to the WinX folder. Click the New Fiolder icon on the Ribbon. Name the new folder Group4.

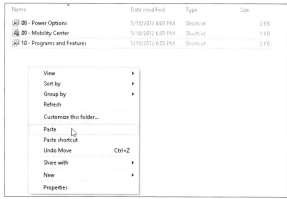

6 Move a command to the new folder: Open Group3. Hold down the Ctrl key and select the shortcuts for Power Options and Programs and Features. Right-click any of the shortcuts and select Cut from the pop-up menu. Move back one folder and open the Group4 folder. Right-click any empty area of the Group4 window and select Paste from the pop-up menu. The shortcuts for Power Options and Programs and Features appear.

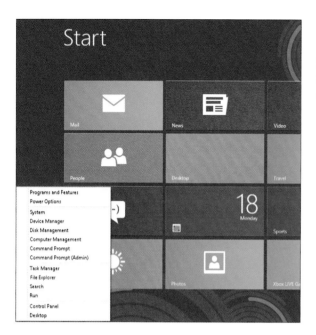

7 View the new menu: Close the File Explorer window. Press Alt+F4 to display the Shut down Windows menu. Choose Sign out from the drop-down menu. Log back in to Windows. Right-click the lower-left hot corner. The redesigned Power User Tasks menu appears.

tip You cannot add new entries to the menu, but you can delete and move commands to organize it to your own preferences.

Quick Fix

Accessing Built-in Help for Windows 8

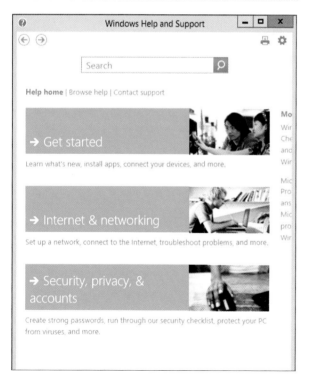

At the Start screen, type **help**. Click the Help and Support app from the search results in the left pane. A Windows Help and Support screen opens with various topics and links that you can click to learn more about Windows 8 and find specific information.

Logging in to Windows Automatically

B y default, Windows 8 requires you to log in with your Microsoft account or a local account to use your computer. This is set up as a security precaution so that other people cannot use Windows and gain access to your applications and personal documents. But if you are using Windows in a safe and secure place, especially at home, having to log in each time can be a hassle. Using the User Accounts Control Panel, you can bypass the Windows Lock screen and login screen to arrive at the Start screen directly. This task explains how to log in to Windows automatically.

1 Open the User Accounts Control Panel: From the Start screen, type **netplwiz**. Netplwiz appears as an app in the search results in the left pane. Click that command.

tip If Windows is set up with more than one account, you can choose any or all of the accounts for automatic login.

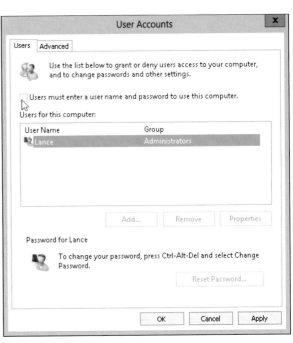

2 Select the account: In the User Accounts Control Panel, select the account that you want to use to log in automatically.

3 Turn off username and password requirement: Deselect the Users must enter a username and password to use this computer check box. Click OK.

5 Restart: Restart Windows. Windows bypasses the Lock screen and login screen to automatically take you to the Start screen.

4 Enter password: Type your password once and then a second time to confirm it. Click OK. Click OK again to close the User Accounts Control Panel.

Changing the Icon for a Desktop Tile

W indows 8 displays specific icons for desktop applications that you have pinned to the Start screen. For example, Calculator displays an icon of a calculator, Notepad displays an icon of a notepad, and File Explorer displays an icon of a folder. Certain folders, such as Documents, Music, and Pictures, also display icons related to their file types. But you may not want to stick with the default choices and instead use different icons. In that case, you can change the icons used for the Start screen tiles and desktop shortcuts for any desktop application or folder. This task explains how to change the Start screen and desktop shortcut icons for desktop applications.

tip You can only change the icon for desktop apps, not for Windows 8 apps.

tip Even after you change the icon for an application, the tile displayed in the Apps screen remains the same.

1 Find the tile for a desktop app: Launch the Apps screen by right-clicking any empty area in the Start screen and selecting All apps from the bottom app bar. Choose the tile for a desktop application whose icon you wish to change, such as Control Panel.

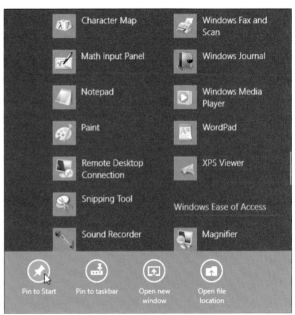

2 Pin the tile to the Start screen: Right-click the tile and select Pin to Start from the app bar.

3 Return to Start screen: Return to the Start screen by pressing the Windows key or clicking the thumbnail in the lower-left hot corner. Move to the end of the Start screen to view the new tile.

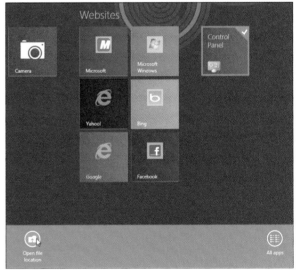

4 Open the file location: Right-click on the tile and select Open file location in the app bar.

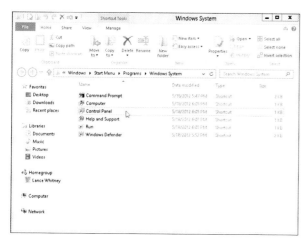

5 View the shortcut: Windows switches to the desktop and displays the application's shortcut in File Explorer.

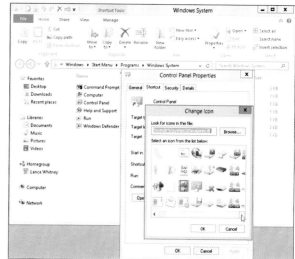

6 View available icons: Right-click the application's shortcut and select Properties from the pop-up menu. From the Properties window, click Change Icon.

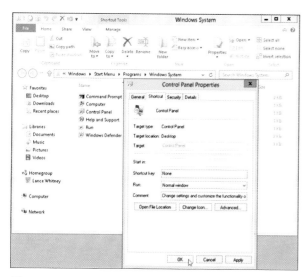

7 Pick the new icon:

The available icons display from the application's executable file or from one of the Windows DLL library files. Browse the icons until you find one you like. Click that icon. Click OK. Click OK again to close the application's properties window.

tip You can find a large number of icons by switching to the C:\Windows\system32\shell32.dll file in the Change Icon screen.

8 View tile's new icon: You should see the application's new icon in File Explorer. Press the Windows key or click the thumbnail in the lower-left hot corner to return to the Start screen. Move to the end of the Start screen to view the application's tile where the new icon appears.

Changing the Number of Start Screen Rows

The Windows 8 Start screen displays a certain number of tile rows based on your screen resolution. For example, a resolution of 800 × 600 displays three rows of tiles, a resolution of 1024 × 768 displays four tile rows, and a resolution of 1280 × 1024 displays five tile rows. But using a Registry tweak, you can increase or decrease the number of tile rows. The minimum number of tile rows is 1, but the maximum number depends on your screen resolution. For example, a resolution of 1024 × 768 can display up to four tile rows, but a resolution of 1280 × 1024 can display up to six tile rows. This task explains how to change the number of tile rows displayed on the Start screen.

1 Open the Registry: Hold down the Windows key and press R to open the Run command. Type **regedit** in the Open field. Click Yes if you receive a User Account Control message asking if you want to allow the following program to make changes to this computer.

tip Back up the Registry key before you modify it. In regedit, choose File → Export, and then name the reg file.

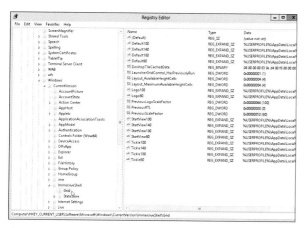

2 Find the right key: Navigate to and click the following Registry key: HKEY_CURRENT_USER\Software\Microsoft\Windows\CurrentVersion\ImmersiveShell\Grid

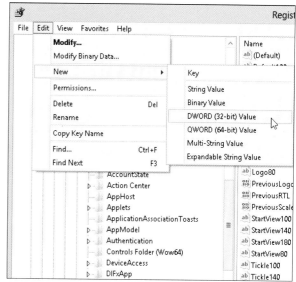

3 Add the value: Choose Edit → New → DWORD (32-bit) Value. Replace the name New Value #1 with the new name Layout_MaximumRowCount. Press Enter.

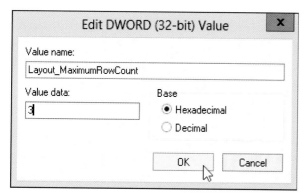

4 Change the value: Double-click the name Layout_MaximumRowCount. Change the value in the Value data field from 0 to the number of rows you want to display. Depending on your screen resolution, the maximum number of rows can vary from 3 to 6, while the minimum is 1. For example, if you want to display three rows on the Start screen, type **3**. Click OK.

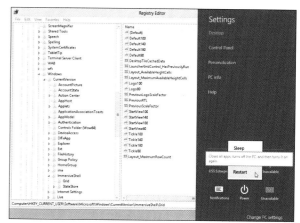

5 Reboot: Restart your computer for the changes to take effect.

6 Check the Start screen: After your computer reboots, log in to Windows. Check the Start screen. The tiles appear in the number of rows you specified.

tip You can restore the Registry key by double-clicking the reg file in File Explorer.

7 Return to the default: To return to the default number of rows for your resolution, open the Registry again. Return to the HKEY_CURRENT_USER\Software\Microsoft\Windows\CurrentVersion\ImmersiveShell\Grid key. Right-click on the Layout_MaximumRowCount subkey and click Delete from the pop-up menu. Restart your computer and log back in to Windows.

Quick Fix

Troubleshooting Computer Problems

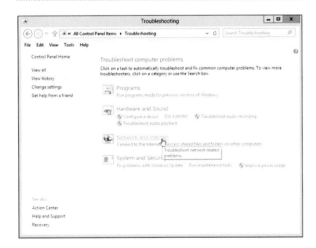

Open Control Panel. Click System and Security. Under Action Center, click Troubleshoot common computer problems. Click the category that best matches the problem you are experiencing. Then click a specific task to allow Windows to detect and try to resolve the problem.

Turning Windows Features On or Off

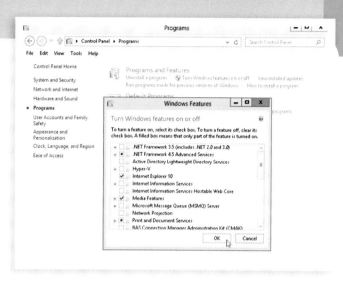

Certain Windows features that you may need are turned on by default, including Internet Explorer, Windows Media Player, Windows Fax and Scan, and Windows Search. But other features, including Hyper-V and Telnet, are not enabled by default. These features are available in Windows 8 but are simply not enabled. You can easily turn certain Windows features on and off depending on whether you need them. For example, you may need the Telnet client to open a telnet session on a remote computer but not need the Windows Gadget Platform if you do not intend to display gadgets on your desktop. This task explains how to turn various Windows features on and off.

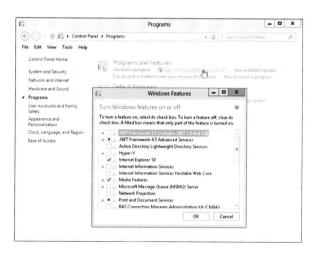

1 Open the Windows Features screen: Launch the desktop by clicking the Desktop tile on the Start screen. Hover your mouse in the lower-right hot corner to display the Charms bar. Click the Settings charm and click the link for Control Panel at the top of the bar. In Control Panel, click the category for Programs. Under Programs and Features, click Turn Windows features on and off.

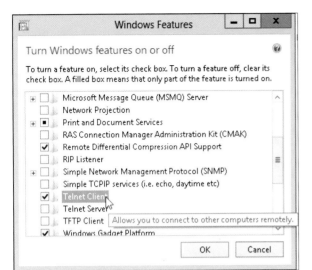

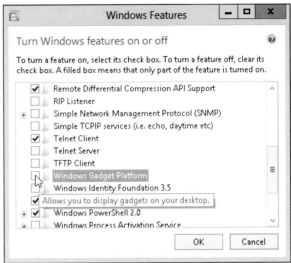

2 Select a feature to turn on: As one example, the Telnet client allows you to open a telnet session onto a remote computer. Select the Telnet Client check box to turn it on.

3 Select a feature to turn off: Most of the features enabled are ones you want to keep. But as one example, the Windows Gadget Platform is needed only if you want to display gadgets on the desktop. Deselect the Windows Gadget Platform check box to turn it off.

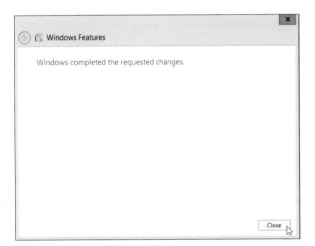

tip You need to turn on the Hyper-V feature if you want to run virtual machines in Windows 8.

4 Enable changes: After you select the features to turn on or off, click OK. Windows searches for required files and then applies the changes. After the selected features have been turned on or off, Windows displays a screen indicating that it has completed the requested changes. Click Close or click Restart now if Windows prompts you to reboot your PC.

Forcing an Application to Shut Down

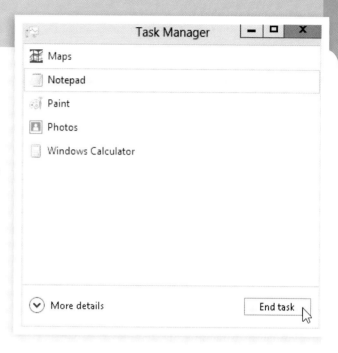

Windows applications can sometimes be stubborn and freeze or lock up, preventing you from closing them the normal way. If an application hangs, you should wait at least a couple of minutes to see if it comes back to life, especially if it is a productivity program with recent work that you have not yet saved. But if it looks like the application will not unfreeze, then it may be time to manually close it. Shutting down a program from Windows Task Manager has been the standard solution. But the Task Manager in Windows 8 offers a simpler design that shows you just the names of open applications, letting you easily select the one you want to close. This task explains how to force an application to shut down using Task Manager.

1 Open Windows 8 UI programs: Open two Windows 8 UI programs from the Start screen. For this example, the Maps and Photos programs are opened.

2 Open desktop programs: Move to the Apps screen by right-clicking any empty area of the Start screen and selecting All apps from the app bar. Open Calculator. Return to the Apps screen. Open Paint. Return to the Apps screen. Open Notepad.

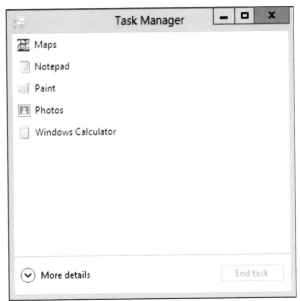

3 View open apps: In the desktop, right-click any empty area of the taskbar and select Task Manager from the pop-up menu. Task Manager opens with a list of all the apps you just opened.

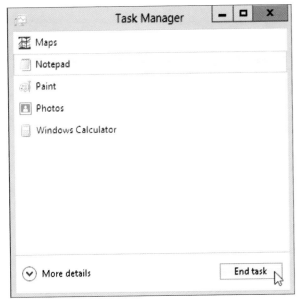

4 Close an application: Select one of the apps, such as Notepad. Click End task. Notepad closes and disappears from the list.

tip You can force both Windows 8 UI and desktop apps to shut down.

tip Typically, you would only close an app this way if it were frozen and not responding.

Managing Open Applications in Task Manager

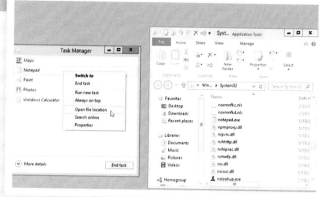

The new Task Manager in Windows 8 offers much more than just the ability to manually shut down a frozen application. It lets you view a list of all open applications and processes. It lets you switch to any open application. It lets you view an application's properties. And it lets you search for an application's executable file online so that you can learn more about it. All of this information can help you troubleshoot a misbehaving application or pick up more details about an unknown application. This task explains how to manage and learn more about open applications through Task Manager.

1 Open Windows 8 programs: Open two Windows 8 apps from the Start screen. For this example, Maps and Photos are opened.

2 Open desktop programs: Move to the Apps screen by right-clicking any empty area of the Start screen and selecting All apps from the app bar. This task uses Calculator, Paint, and Notepad as examples. Open Calculator. Return to the Apps screen. Open Paint. Return to the Apps screen. Open Notepad.

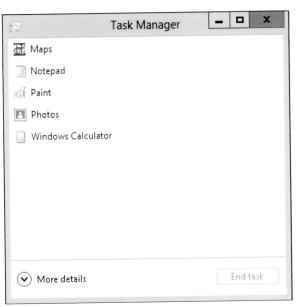

3 View open apps: Hold down the Windows key and press D to launch the desktop. In the desktop, right-click any empty area of the taskbar and select Task Manager from the pop-up menu. Task Manager opens with a list of all the apps you just opened.

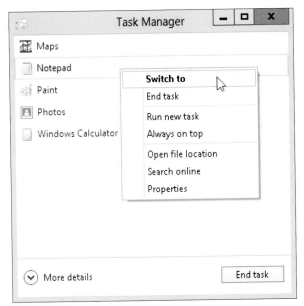

4 Switch to an open app: Right-click on the app you want to display, such as Notepad, and select Switch to from the pop-up menu. That application is displayed.

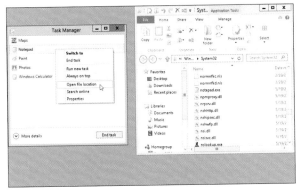

5 View file location: Click the taskbar icon for Task Manager to switch back to it. In Task Manager, right-click any open desktop application, such as Calculator, and select Open file location from the pop-up menu. A File Explorer window appears showing the application's executable file. Knowing the location and name of the file can be handy if you want to create a shortcut to the file.

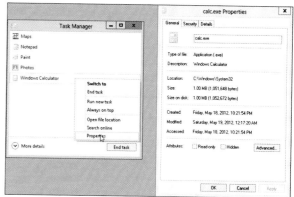

7 View the app's properties: Click the taskbar icon for Task Manager to switch back to it. In Task Manager, right-click any open desktop app, such as Calculator, and select Properties. A window for the application's properties appears, displaying its name, size, version number, and other details.

6 Search for app online: Click the taskbar icon for Task Manager to switch back to it. In Task Manager, right-click any open app, such as Paint, and select Search online from the pop-up menu. Internet Explorer opens with search results on the application you selected. This can be helpful if you spot an unknown application in Task Manager and want to know more about it.

8 Keep Task Manager on top: Click the taskbar icon for Task Manager to switch back to it. In Task Manager, right-click any open app and select Always on top from the pop-up menu. This ensures that Task Manager is always in the foreground, on top of any other open applications or windows.

tip The file locations for Windows 8 apps are in a folder for which you have no permissions, so Windows will not allow you to access them.

Monitoring the Performance of Your Apps

The new Task Manager in Windows 8 simplifies the process of managing and monitoring your open applications. You can manually shut down an application that has locked up. You can learn more about an application by viewing its file properties or searching for it online. The new Task Manager also gives you a clearer and cleaner view of the amount of resources being used by each open application. For each application, you can view how many CPU cycles and how much memory are being used. You can also determine the speed at which the application is accessing the hard drive and network. This can be helpful in finding an application that is hogging too many resources. This task explains how to monitor the performance of open applications.

1 Open Windows 8 programs: Open two Windows 8 programs from the Start screen. For this example, Maps and Photos are opened.

2 Open desktop programs: Move to the Apps screen by right-clicking any empty area of the Start screen and selecting All apps from the app bar. This task uses Calculator, Paint, and Notepad as examples. Open Calculator. Return to the Apps screen. Open Paint. Return to the Apps screen. Open Notepad.

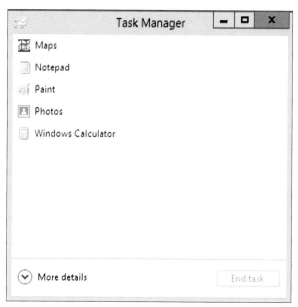

3 View open apps: Hold down the Windows key and press D to launch the desktop. In the desktop, right-click any empty area of the taskbar and select Task Manager from the pop-up menu. A list appears of all the apps you just opened.

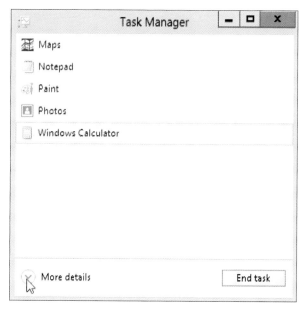

4 View more details: Click the More details button in the lower-left corner of Task Manager.

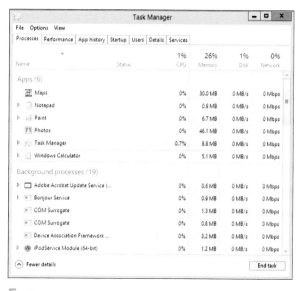

5 View processes: Click the Processes tab. How many CPU cycles and how much memory are being used are displayed as is the access speed of the hard drive and network per application. This tab displays the same information for Windows processes.

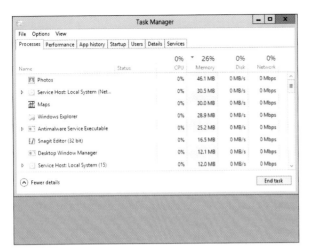

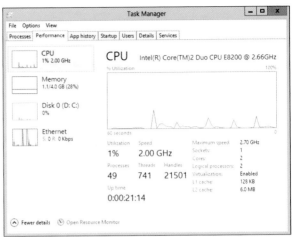

6 Sort the view of processes: By default, the processes are listed alphabetically by group and then by name. But you can change the view. Click the CPU category to see which processes are taking up the most CPU cycles. Click the Memory category to see which ones are taking up the most memory. Click the Disk category to see which ones are accessing the hard drive the most. Click the Network category to see which ones are accessing the network the most.

7 View PC performance: Click the Performance tab. Here you can see the total amount of CPU cycles, memory, hard drive access, and network access being used by all open apps. Click a specific category to view more details and a larger graph of its activity.

tip Double-click any of the categories in the Performance tab, and the Task Manager window shrinks in size to display just the performance information.

Viewing a History of Your Windows 8 Apps

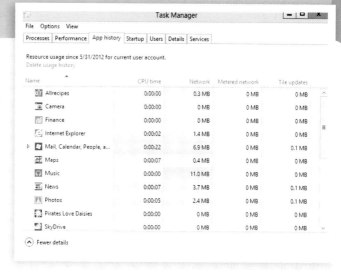

The Windows 8 Task Manager offers a variety of features, including the ability to shut down frozen applications, learn more about your open applications, and monitor the performance and percentage of resources being used by your open applications. But the Task Manager kicks in an additional feature that can help you specifically monitor your Windows 8 apps. The new App history tab displays information on every Windows 8 app installed, specifically the CPU cycles and network bandwidth taken up by each one, as well as the amount of data used by updates to live tiles. This task explains how to view a history of the performance of your Windows 8 apps.

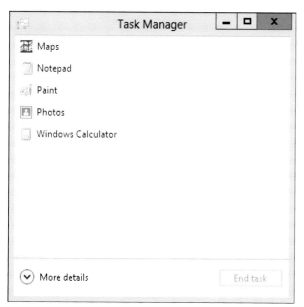

1 Open Task Manager: In the desktop, right-click any empty area of the taskbar and select Task Manager from the pop-up menu. You should see a list of all the open apps.

tip You can view a history of your Windows 8 apps but not your desktop apps.

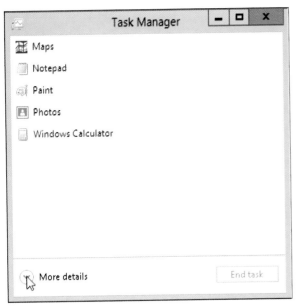

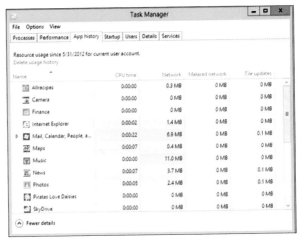

3 View history: Click the App history tab. A history appears of all installed Windows 8 apps, including the CPU cycles, network time (both metered and nonmetered), and the amount of data used by tile updates.

2 View more details: Click the More details button in the lower-left corner of Task Manager.

Quick Fixes

Viewing System Information on Your PC

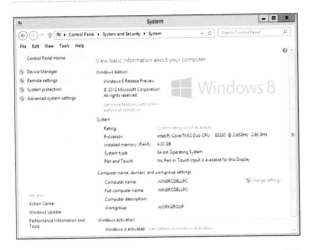

Move your mouse to the lower-left hot corner and right-click to display the Power User menu. Click Control Panel. Click System and Security. Click System. Your PC's name, processor type, memory, and other details display in the right pane.

Running the Windows Experience Index

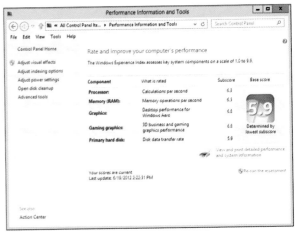

Move your mouse to the lower-left hot corner and right-click to display the Power User Tasks menu. Click Control Panel. Click System and Security. Click System. The link will either say System rating is not available or Windows Experience Index. Select Rate this computer or Re-run the assessment to get the latest performance index on your PC. The Windows Experience Index runs and displays a rating for your PC.

Managing Your Start-up Programs

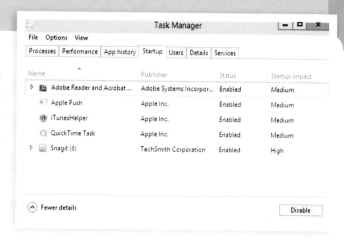

Some Windows applications insist on adding themselves to your Windows start-up routine so they automatically launch after Windows loads. Certain applications, such as security software, need to launch automatically so that they are immediately available. But the majority of applications that force themselves into your start-up routine are simply hogging memory. Install enough applications that insist on loading automatically, and the amount of available memory keeps going down. Previous versions of Windows offered the System Configuration, or msconfig, tool to help you manage your start-up programs. But Windows 8 lets you manage start-up programs through Task Manager. This task explains how to manage your start-up programs.

1 Access the desktop: Launch the desktop from its Start screen tile.

tip Some apps need to start automatically, but many do not. Research an app before you disable it to determine if it needs to start automatically.

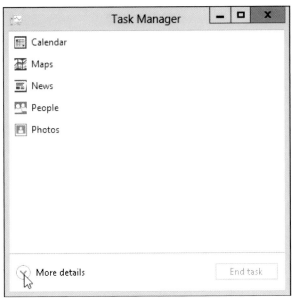

2 Launch Task Manager: In the desktop, right-click any empty area of the taskbar and select Task Manager from the pop-up menu. A list of any open applications appears.

3 View more details: Click the More details button in the lower-left corner of Task Manager.

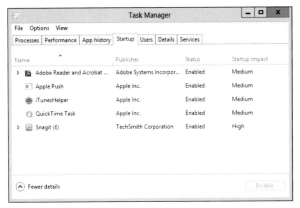

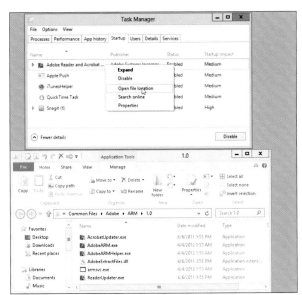

4 View start-up programs: Click the Startup tab to view all the apps that start up automatically.

5 Open file location: Right-click a start-up application and choose Open file location from the pop-up menu. A File Explorer window appears showing the application's executable file.

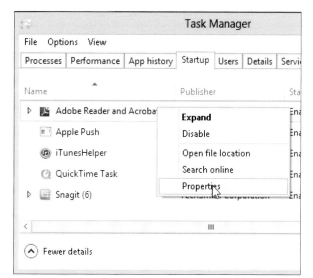

6 View properties: Click the taskbar icon for Task Manager to switch back to it. Right-click any open desktop app and select Properties. A window for the application's properties appears, showing you its name, size, version number, and other details.

7 Search for app online: Click the taskbar icon for Task Manager to switch back to it. Right-click any open desktop app and select Search online. Internet Explorer opens with search results on the application you selected. This can be helpful if you spot an unknown application or file in your start-up routine and want to know more about it, or want to determine whether it is safe to remove the application from your start-up routine.

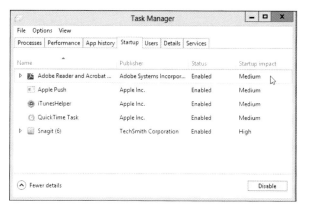

8 View the Startup impact: The Startup impact column indicates the effect an application has on your start-up routine, meaning how severely it slows down your PC's boot sequence. The options include High, Medium, or Not measured.

9 Disable the app from automatic start-up: Click the taskbar icon for Task Manager to switch back to it. If you want to prevent an app from starting up automatically, right-click the app and select Disable from the pop-up menu. The application is prevented from starting up automatically although you can launch it manually. First search for information on any app before you disable it.

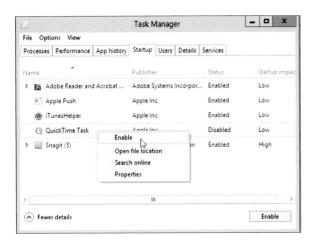

10 Enable the app: Right-click the app and select Enable from the pop-up menu to add it back to your start-up routine.

tip After you install an application, it may take awhile before its start-up impact is measured and displayed.

Quick Fixes

Requiring Ctrl+Alt+Delete at Lock Screen

From the Start screen, type **netplwiz**. Netplwiz appears in the search results in the left pane. Click the netplwiz app. Select the account that you want to press Ctrl+Alt+Delete at the Lock screen. Click the Advanced tab. In the Secure sign-in section, select the Require users to press Ctrl+Alt+Delete check box. Click OK.

Changing User Account Control Settings

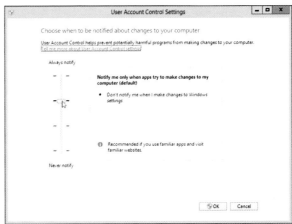

Move your mouse to the lower-left hot corner and right-click to display the Power User Tasks menu. Click Control Panel. Click the User Accounts and Family Safety category. Click User Accounts. Click Change User Account Control settings. Drag the box on the Notify bar to the desired level.

Tracking Down Problems with Event Viewer

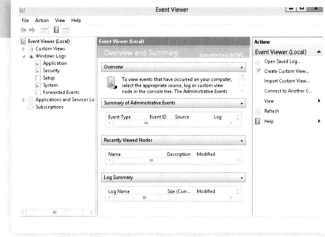

Problems sometimes creep into Windows or Windows applications. A certain application may freeze or crash or stop running properly. Certain Windows features may stop working properly. Tracking down and trouble-shooting problems in Windows can be a difficult and challenging task. But Windows offers a tool that can sometimes lead you in the right direction — Event Viewer. This tool automatically records all events in Windows and labels each event as Information, Warning, or Error. An event with an information label usually provides standard data. But events labeled as warnings or errors can often reveal clues to specific problems. This task explains how to track down problems with Event Viewer.

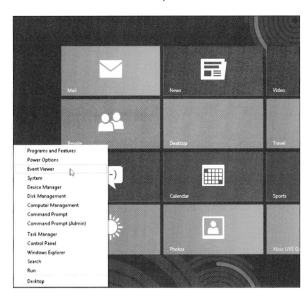

1 Launch Event Viewer: Move your mouse to the lower-left hot corner. Right-click to display the Power User Tasks menu. Choose Event Viewer from the list.

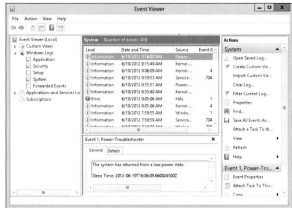

2 View Windows Logs: Click the arrow in front of Windows Logs. At least five folders appear under Windows Logs — Application, Security, Setup, System, and Forwarded Events — each one devoted to a specific type of event.

3 Click a folder: Click the System folder. Each event is labeled one of three levels: Information, Warning, or Error. You can ignore the Information events in troubleshooting a problem. The Warning and Error events are usually more revealing.

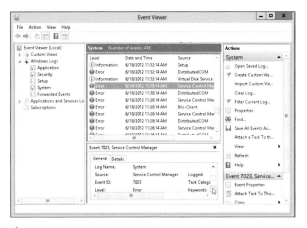

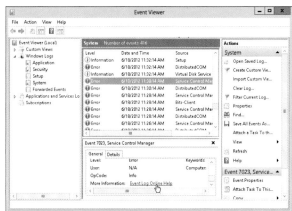

4 Scroll through the folder: Scroll through the Application folder. Select any entry with an Error label. General information and details about the event appear in the lower pane. Scroll to the bottom pane to see all the information and details about the event.

5 View event information online: Click the Event Log Online Help link at the bottom of the bottom pane. An Event Viewer window asks for permission to send the information across the Internet. Click Yes.

tip The Application folder is another folder to check for possible event errors.

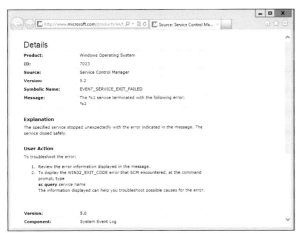

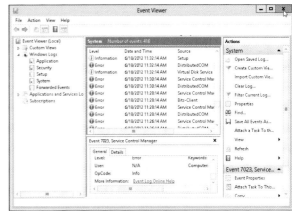

6 View information online: Your default browser opens to display any information on that specific event. If you cannot understand or troubleshoot the information yourself, it may be of use to Microsoft or other technical support representatives who can try to help you resolve the problem.

7 Close Event Viewer: Return to Event Viewer and close the window when you are finished.

Quick Fixes

Installing Microsoft Update

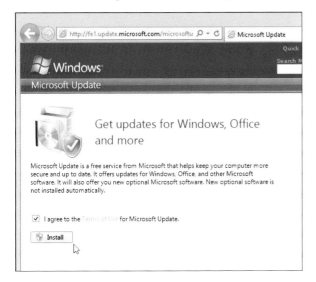

Open Control Panel. Click System and Security. Click Windows Update. Click the Find out more link next to Get updates for other Microsoft products. In your browser, select the I agree to the Terms of Use for Microsoft Update check box. Click Install.

Using Windows SmartScreen

Open Control Panel. Click System and Security. Click Action Center. Select Change Windows SmartScreen settings in the left pane. Choose the option you want among the three. Click OK.

Checking Your Computer for Memory Problems

W indows applications may sometimes freeze or crash unexpectedly without any warning. Other times Windows itself may misbehave by crashing and displaying the familiar blue screen of death, also known as the BSOD. In some cases, the fault may not lie in Windows or in the application itself but rather in your PC's hardware. And one piece of hardware that can potentially develop problems is your computer's memory. Windows offers a Memory Diagnostics tool that can test your PC's RAM to see if any errors occur. If not, you can at least rule out memory problems as the cause of any freezes or crashes. This task explains how to check your computer for memory problems.

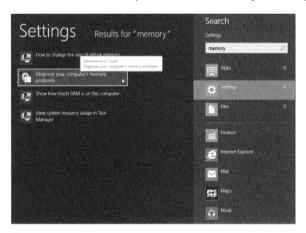

1 Launch Windows Memory Diagnostics: From the Start screen, type **memory**. Click Settings. From the search results on the left, select Diagnose your computer's memory problems.

2 Restart the PC: Windows displays a dialog box asking if you want to restart now and check for problems or check for problems the next time you start your computer. Select the option to restart now.

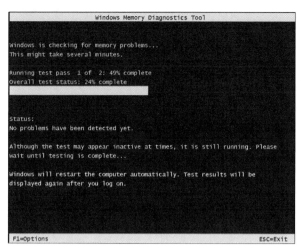

```
                    Windows Memory Diagnostics Tool

Windows is checking for memory problems...
This might take several minutes.

Running test pass  1 of  2: 49% complete
Overall test status: 24% complete
█████████████████████████████

Status:
No problems have been detected yet.

Although the test may appear inactive at times, it is still running. Please
wait until testing is complete...

Windows will restart the computer automatically. Test results will be
displayed again after you log on.



F1=Options                                                      ESC=Exit
```

3 Wait for Memory Diagnostics to run: Windows reboots and starts running the Memory Diagnostics Tool. The test may take several minutes to run, but the screen shows you the percentage of the diagnostic as it is being run. The test makes two passes at scanning your memory.

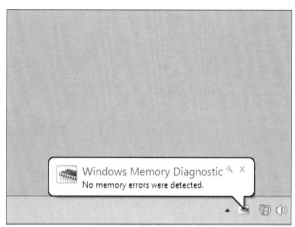

4 Wait for reboot: After the diagnostic completes, Windows reboots. Log back in. Launch the desktop from its Start screen tile. Windows eventually displays a message from the system tray alerting you as to whether any problems were discovered.

tip Pressing F1 lets you choose from among a Basic, Standard, or Extended memory diagnostic, each one more intensive than the previous one.

Quick Fix

Preserving Battery Life on Your Laptop

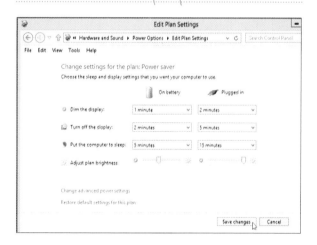

Run your laptop on battery power. Open Control Panel. Click System and Security. Under Power Options, click Change battery settings. Click the Power Saver plan. Click Change plan settings to alter when to dim and turn off the display and adjust the screen brightness. Click Save changes.

Creating a Windows 8 Restore Point

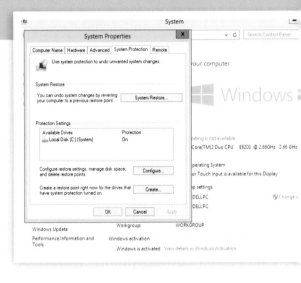

A Windows restore point is a snapshot of your entire Windows environment at a specific point in time. These snapshots can record your Windows environment before you install new software or make other major changes. If you experience problems with Windows or a certain application or just need to revert to an earlier state of Windows, you can do that through a previous restore point. Windows 8 devotes a certain amount of hard drive space to save restore points. You can create as many restore points as you want. Once the available hard drive space is used up, Windows starts deleting the earliest restore points. This task explains how to create a Windows 8 restore point.

1 Open Control Panel: Launch the desktop by clicking its Start screen tile. Hover your mouse in the lower-right hot corner to display the Charms bar. Click the Settings charm. Click Control Panel at the top of the panel.

tip Restore points are automatically created at certain times, but you can always create one manually.

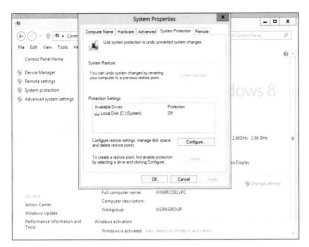

2 Open System Protection: From Control Panel, click the System and Security category, and then click System. In the left pane, click System protection.

3 Check for system protection: Make sure that protection is turned on for your local drive. If it is not, select the drive and click Configure. In the System Protection for Local Disk window, select the Turn on system protection radio button. Click OK.

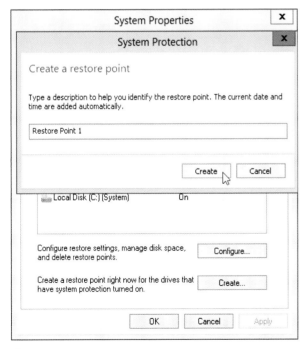

tip Restoring Windows from a restore point is covered in the next task.

4 Create restore point: At the bottom of the System Protection tab, click Create. Type a name for the restore point. Click Create.

5 Close System Protection: After the process has completed, a message that the restore point was created successfully appears. Click Close to shut down that message. Click OK to close the System Properties window and then close the System window.

Deleting a File Permanently

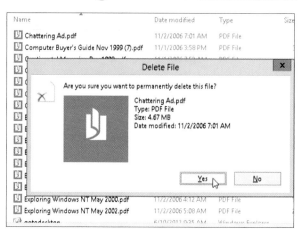

Open File Explorer. Select the file you want to delete. Hold down the Shift key and click the Delete button from the Ribbon. The file is deleted from the hard drive instead of being moved to the Recycle Bin.

Restoring Windows from a Restore Point

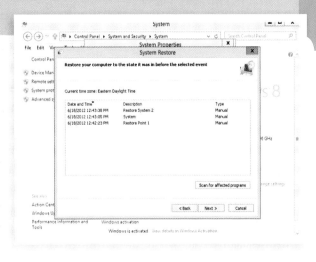

A Windows restore point is a snapshot of your entire Windows environment at a specific point in time. You can use restore points to record your Windows environment before you install new applications or make other changes to your system. If you experience problems with Windows or need to undo recent changes, you can restore your environment to a previous point. Windows 8 devotes a certain amount of hard drive space to save restore points. You can create as many restore points as you want. Once the available hard drive space is used up, Windows starts deleting the earliest restore points. This task explains how to restore Windows 8 from a restore point.

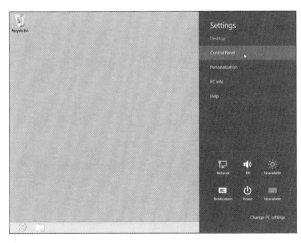

1 Open Control Panel: Launch the desktop by clicking its Start screen tile. Hover your mouse in the lower-right hot corner to display the Charms bar. Click the Settings charm. Click Control Panel at the top of the pane.

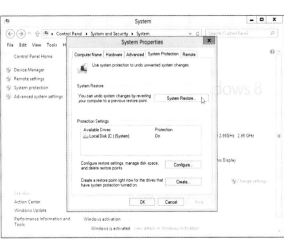

2 Open System Protection: From Control Panel, click the System and Security category and then click System. In the left pane, click System protection.

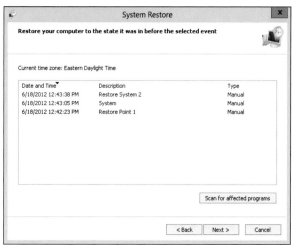

3 Restore Windows: Click System Restore in the System Properties window. The System Restore window may recommend a recent restore point. If you want to use this restore point, click Next. Otherwise, click the Choose a different restore point option and then click Next. If this recommendation does not appear, then just click Next.

4 View restore points: Windows displays a list of all your restore points with their dates and times.

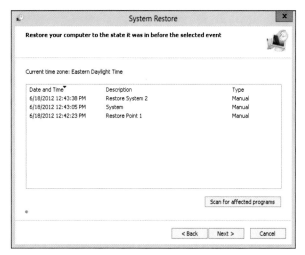

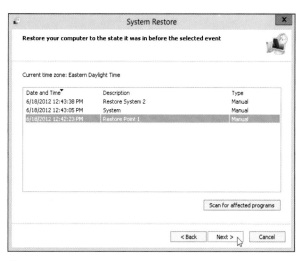

5 Scan for affected programs: Click a particular restore point and then click Scan for affected programs. Windows runs a scan for any applications or drivers that may need to be reinstalled if you choose this specific restore point. If none is detected, then you will not lose any software or drivers if you choose this restore point. If any software or drivers are found, then you may want to try a different restore point or note the programs that need to be reinstalled if you choose this restore point. Click Close.

6 Choose the restore point: Select the restore point you want to use. Click Next.

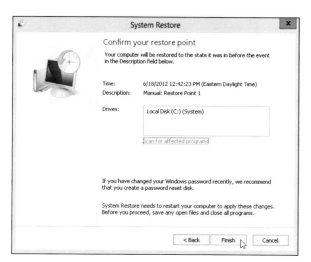

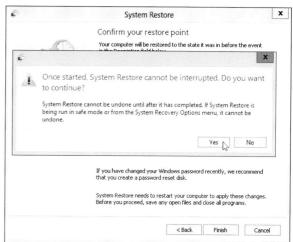

7 Confirm the restore point: Confirm the restore point you want to use. Click Finish.

8 Confirm that you want to continue: Windows asks if you want to continue. Click Yes. You see a message that Windows is preparing to restore your system. After the restore completes, Windows reboots your computer and restores your files and settings. After the restoration, Windows may again reboot your computer.

9 Log back in: Press any key to get past the Lock screen and then log in to Windows.

10 View System Restore message: Open the desktop by clicking its Start screen tile.
A System Restore message appears explaining the outcome of the process.

tip Creating a restore point is covered in the previous task.

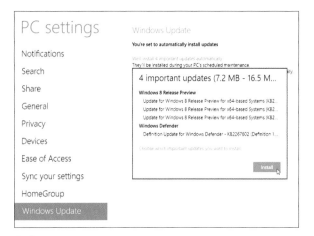

11 Reinstall programs, drivers, and updates: Reinstall any software, hardware drivers, and software updates that were not restored.

Quick Fixes

Changing Your Computer Name

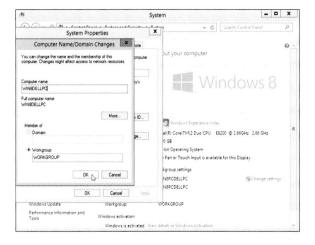

Launch Control Panel. Click the System and Security category. Under System, select the See the name of this computer option. In the View basic information about your computer dialog box, select the Change settings option. In the System Properties dialog box, click Change. In the Computer name field, type a new name for your computer. Click OK. Click OK again. Close the System Properties dialog box. Click Restart Now.

Setting Up Automatic Maintenance

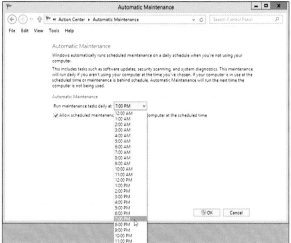

Open Control Panel. Click the System and Security category. Select Action Center. Click the drop-down button next to Maintenance. Under Automatic Maintenance, click Change maintenance settings. In the Run maintenance tasks daily at drop-down menu, select a time. Select the Allow scheduled maintenance to wake up my computer at the scheduled time check box if your computer is in sleep mode at the scheduled time.

Backing Up Your Files through File History

Windows 8 includes a new file history feature that backs up your personal files, including your documents, music, pictures, videos, contacts, browser favorites, and desktop. If one or more of those files are damaged or lost or permanently deleted, you can retrieve the most recent version of the file from history. Once set up, File History runs automatically at specified intervals, though you can also run it manually at any time. You can save your file history on an external drive, such as a USB stick or a network drive, so that the files are recoverable if you cannot access your hard drive due to technical problems. This task explains how to set up the File History feature, first using a USB drive and then using a network drive.

1 Open Control Panel: Open the desktop. Hover your mouse in the lower-right hot corner to display the Charms bar. Click the Settings charm. Click Control Panel at the top of the panel.

tip Save your file history on an external or network drive so you can still recover it if your hard drive is no longer accessible.

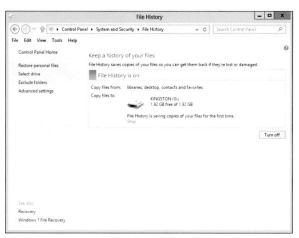

2 Open File History: Plug in a USB drive. From Control Panel, click the System and Security category and then select File History.

3 Choose external drive: File History should detect and display the USB drive. Click Turn on. File History automatically starts saving copies of your files.

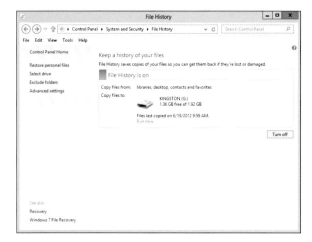

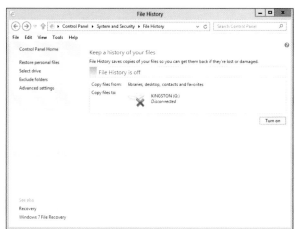

4 Wait for backup to complete: After File History completes its backup, it displays a message telling you when the files were last copied.

5 Change drive: If you want to use a network drive instead of a USB drive, click Turn off. Remove the USB drive.

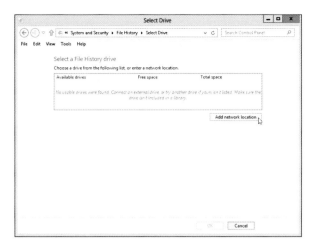

6 Add network location: Click the Select drive option in the left pane. Click Add network location.

7 View network locations: Windows displays the names of other networked PCs and your network drive. Click the network drive you want to use.

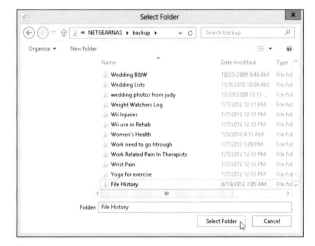

8 Select or create folder: Select a specific folder on the drive in which you want to save the file history. Click the New folder command to create a new folder to store the file history. Click Select Folder.

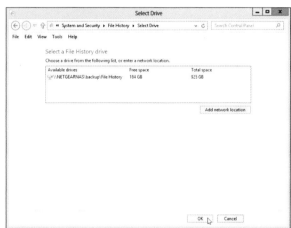

9 Confirm new location: In the Select Drive screen, click OK. Windows asks if you want to move your existing files to the new location. Click No. The network drive now appears as the new location for the file history.

10 Wait for backup to complete: File History copies your files to the network location. After File History completes its backup, a message appears telling you when the files were last copied.

11 Exclude folders: Click the Exclude folders option in the left pane. In the Exclude from File History screen, click Add. Choose any folder that you want to exclude from the history. Click Add again to exclude another folder if you want. To include a folder that you have excluded, select it and click Remove. Click Save changes when you are done.

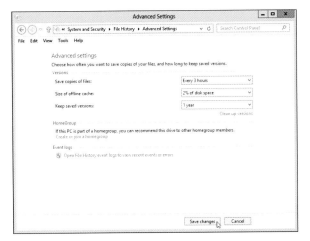

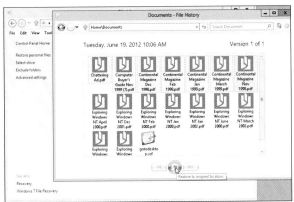

13 Restore files: Click the Restore personal files option in the left pane. Double-click the folder or category of the files you want to restore — for example, Documents. Select the file or files you want to restore. Click the Restore to original location button. A File Explorer window appears showing the restored files in their original location. Close the File History window.

12 Configure Advanced settings: Click the Advanced settings option in the left pane. In the Save copies of files drop-down menu, select how often you want the files to be saved. Every hour is the default. In the size of offline cache drop-down menu, select how much space you want to devote to the file history on the backup location. Five percent is the default. In the Keep saved versions drop-down menu, select how long you want to keep the saved version. Forever is the default. Click Save changes when done.

Refreshing Windows

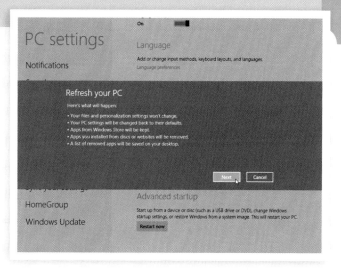

Windows and Windows applications can some-times develop problems, causing the operating system or specific pro-grams themselves to freeze or crash or simply not run properly. Tracking down the specific cause of the problem can be difficult and time-con-suming. Instead of trying to locate the source of the glitch, you may find it easier to simply refresh your PC. Refreshing your PC brings back Windows 8 to an earlier and hope-fully problem-free state. By default, refreshing keeps your Windows 8 apps and your files and documents alive, but it does not retain your desktop apps or your PC settings. This task explains how to refresh Windows.

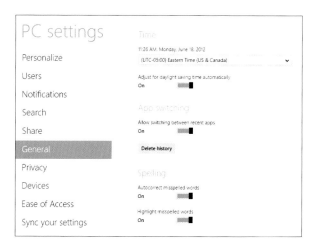

1 Open PC Settings: Hover your mouse over the lower-right hot corner to display the Charms bar. Click the Settings icon. Click Change PC Settings. In the PC Settings screen, click the General category.

tip If you do not have any success refreshing Windows, you may need to reset it, which brings it back to a clean slate.

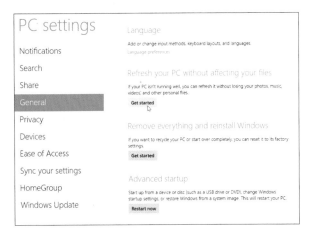

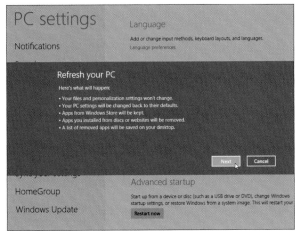

2 Refresh your PC: Scroll down the right page of the General screen until you see the Refresh your PC without affecting your files option. Click Get started.

3 View PC refresh message: A Refresh your PC message appears explaining what will happen. Click Next.

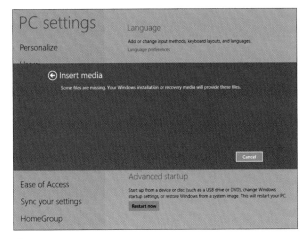

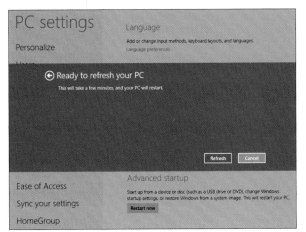

4 Wait: A message appears telling you that Windows is preparing. You may then see a message that says "Insert media: Some files are missing. Your Windows installation or recovery media will provide these files."

5 Insert media: Click Cancel in response to the Insert media message. Insert your Windows installation DVD. Wait a few seconds for the DVD to be read. Click Get started again. Click Next. This time a message appears that Windows is ready to refresh your PC. Click Refresh.

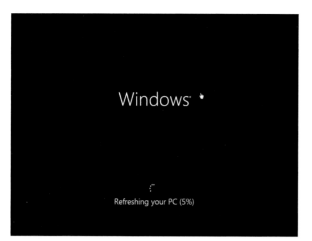

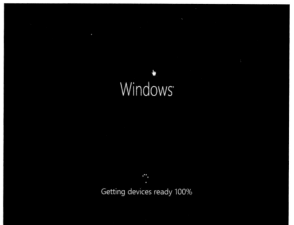

6 Wait for refresh: Windows restarts your PC and displays a message that it is preparing to refresh your PC. A second message appears that Windows is refreshing your PC. A percentage shows the progress of the refresh.

7 Wait for reboot: After the refresh finishes, Windows reboots your PC. A Please Wait message appears followed by various messages that Windows is preparing, getting devices ready, and then getting the system ready.

8 Log back in to Windows: Windows reboots your PC once more and brings you to the Lock screen. Press any key to get past the Lock screen and then log in to Windows.

9 Check your apps and settings: You can now check Windows 8 to make sure that all your Windows 8 apps and customizations are intact.

tip You can retain all your desktop applications and PC settings by refreshing Windows from an image, explained in the next task.

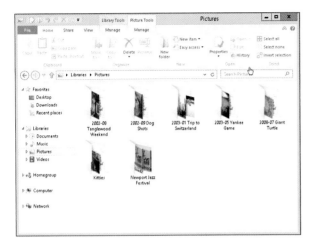

10 Check your files: Open the desktop and view your personal folders to make sure that your documents, pictures, music, and other files are intact.

tip The refresh process can take quite a while, but just be patient. It may be a good time for a long coffee break.

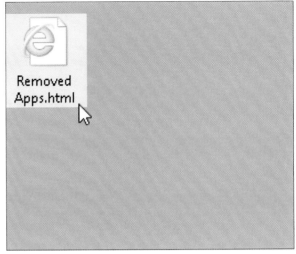

11 Check removed apps: From the desktop, double-click the RemovedApps.html file to view a list of any apps that have been removed. You will typically find that all the desktop apps that you installed have been removed.

tip If you receive Windows 8 with a new PC, be sure to create the installation or recovery media if a physical Windows disc is not included.

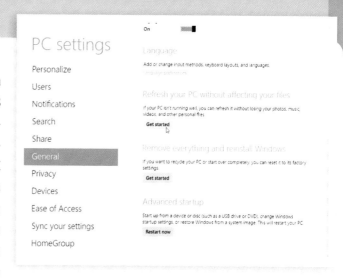

Refreshing your PC is a new feature in Windows 8 that can help resolve system or application problems by restoring your PC to an earlier state. As such, it is an option you can use if Windows or certain applications are not running smoothly or properly. By default, refreshing your PC retains your Windows 8 apps and your files and documents. It also retains your personalization settings. It does not retain your desktop applications or your PC settings. However, by creating an image and refreshing your PC from that image, you can keep your desktop applications and other settings that would normally be lost. This task explains how to refresh your PC from an image.

1 Open command prompt: From the Start screen, type **cmd**. The search results display a Command Prompt tile. Right-click the tile and select Run as administrator from the app bar. Click Yes if a User Account Control dialog box asks if you want to allow the following program to make changes to this computer. A command prompt window opens.

tip The image creation process creates a file called CustomRefresh.wim.

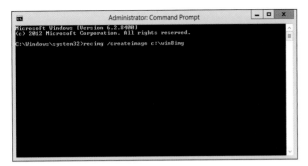

2 Run image command: At the command prompt, type the following string: **recimg /createimage c:\win8img**. For this example, c:\win8img is used as the path and filename for the image file. But you can pick a name other than win8img.

3 View process: On-screen messages appear that Windows is creating the recovery image, creating the snapshot, and then writing the image. The step of writing the image may take a while depending on the size of your Windows 8 environment. After the process is complete, a message appears that says "Recovery image creation and registration completed successfully."

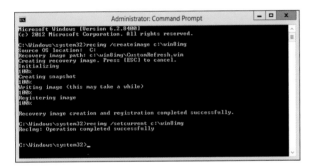

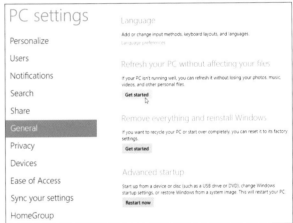

4 Set image as active default: At the command prompt, type the following string: **recimg /setcurrent c:\ win8img**. A message appears that says "Operation completed successfully." Your image is now set as the active and default image. Type exit to close the command prompt.

5 Refresh your PC from the image: At some point, Windows may stop working properly, and you want to refresh it from a recent image. To refresh your PC, hover your mouse over the lower-right hot corner to display the Charms bar. Click the Settings icon. Click Change PC Settings. In the PC Settings screen, click the General category. Scroll down the right page of the General screen until you see the Refresh your PC without affecting your files option.

tip Back up the CustomRefresh.wim file to a USB drive or network location in case the original gets lost.

6 Get started: Click Get started. Click Next. A message appears that Windows is ready to refresh your PC. Click Refresh. Windows 8 automatically refreshes your PC from the image that you set as the current one. Windows restarts. A message appears that Windows is preparing to refresh and then refreshing your PC, accompanied by a percentage showing the status of the refresh.

7 Log back in to Windows: Windows reboots your PC once more and brings you to the Lock screen. Press any key to get past the Lock screen and then log in to Windows.

tip You should periodically create a new image to make sure it holds the latest changes to Windows and your desktop applications.

tip Remember to run the /setcurrent command for each new image that you create.

Resetting Windows

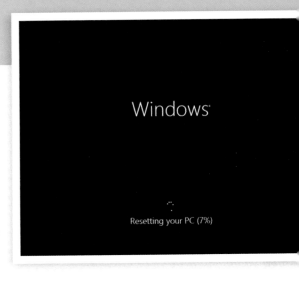

R esetting Windows is a process that essentially brings it back to a clean slate, just as it was when it was first installed. You may want to reset your PC if you are experiencing severe system problems and refreshing your PC does not help. You may want to run a reset if Windows 8 is running slowly or improperly and you just want to start from scratch. You might also decide to run a reset if you plan to give your computer to someone else and you want to remove all traces of your files, applications, and personal settings. This task explains how to reset your PC.

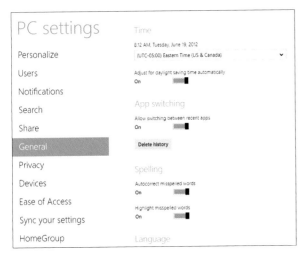

1 Open PC Settings: Hover your mouse over the lower-right hot corner to display the Charms bar. Click the Settings icon. Click Change PC Settings. In the PC Settings screen, click the General category.

2 Reset your PC: Scroll down the right page of the General screen until you see the Remove everything and reinstall Windows option. Click Get started.

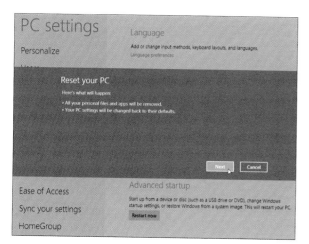

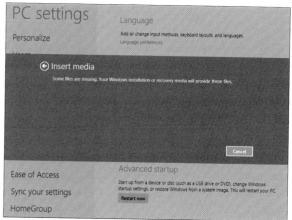

3 View PC reset message: A Reset your PC message appears explaining what will happen. Click Next.

4 Insert media: A message may appear that some files are missing. Your Windows installation or recovery media will provide these files. If you do not have a recovery disc, then insert your Windows 8 installation disc.

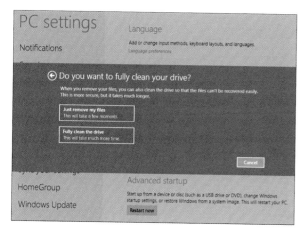

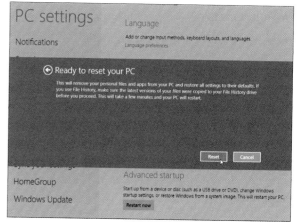

5 Choose to remove files or clean drive: A message then appears asking if you want to just remove your files or clean your drive. If you plan to continue to use Windows, select the Just remove my files option. If you plan to give the PC to someone else, select the Fully clean the drive option to make sure your files cannot easily be recovered.

6 Choose to reset your PC: A message appears that Windows will remove your personal files and apps and restore all settings to their defaults. Click Reset.

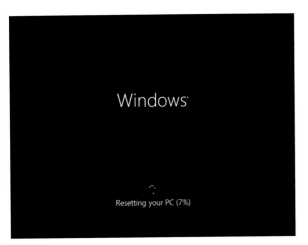

7 Wait for reset: A message appears that Windows is restarting and then preparing your PC. A message then appears that Windows is resetting itself, accompanied by a percentage showing the status of the reset.

8 Enter product key: After the reset has completed, Windows reboots your computer, gets the devices and system ready, and then reboots once more. After the second reboot, Windows prompts you to enter the product key. Type your Windows product key and then click Next.

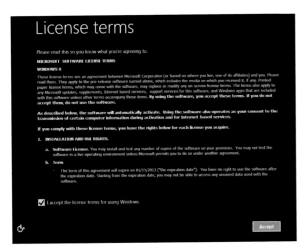

9 Accept license terms: Select the check box to accept the license terms for using Windows, and then click Accept.

10 Personalize Windows: Complete the personalization process to set up Windows per your preferences and account.

tip If you receive Windows 8 with a new PC, be sure to create the installation or recovery media if a physical Windows disc is not included.

Booting into Safe Mode

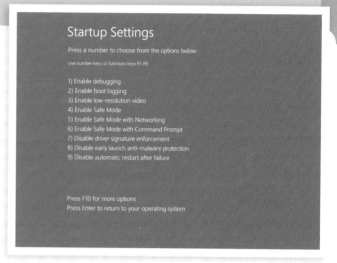

Startup Settings

Press a number to choose from the options below:

Use number keys or functions keys F1-F9

1) Enable debugging
2) Enable boot logging
3) Enable low-resolution video
4) Enable Safe Mode
5) Enable Safe Mode with Networking
6) Enable Safe Mode with Command Prompt
7) Disable driver signature enforcement
8) Disable early launch anti-malware protection
9) Disable automatic restart after failure

Press F10 for more options
Press Enter to return to your operating system

Windows may sometimes be unable to load properly due to a problem with a system file or driver. The problem could be related to the video configuration, the network configuration, or other factors. One way to load Windows in the face of bootup issues is to launch it in Safe Mode. Safe Mode lets Windows boot up in a minimal configuration by bypassing certain drivers that may be causing errors. Booting into Safe Mode is one way to help you narrow down a specific problem. You can boot into Safe Mode in Windows 8 through the traditional System Configuration tool or through the new Advanced Boot Options menu. This task explains how to boot into Safe Mode both ways.

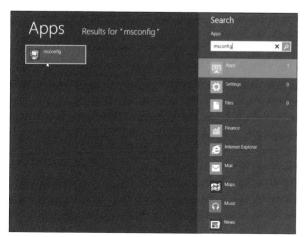

1 Launch the System Configuration tool: From the Start screen, type **msconfig**. Click msconfig from the search results on the left pane.

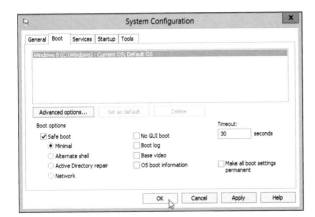

3 Restart PC: Windows asks if you want to Restart or Exit without Restart. Click Restart.

2 Change to Safe boot: From the System Configuration tool, click the Boot tab. Select the Safe boot check box. If you want to see if you can connect to the Internet or your local network, select the Network radio button. Otherwise, leave the Minimal radio button selected. Click OK.

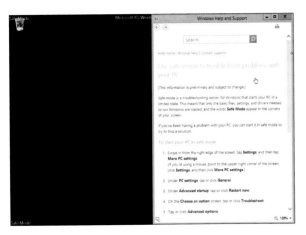

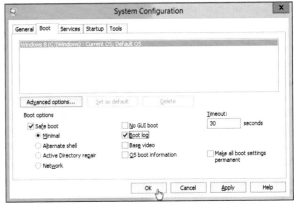

4 Boot into Safe Mode: First see if Windows boots up successfully in Safe Mode. If so, log back into Windows. A minimal environment of Windows appears and loads the desktop. A Windows Help window displays information on using Safe Mode to troubleshoot problems with your PC.

5 Capture a boot log: If you cannot detect the specific problem with your PC, you can enable a boot log to capture bootup information. Open the System Configuration tool again by typing and selecting **msconfig** at the Start screen. Click the Boot tab. Select the Boot log check box. Click OK. Windows asks if you want to Restart or Exit without Restart. Click Restart.

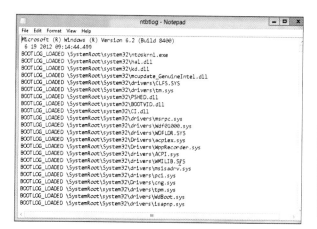

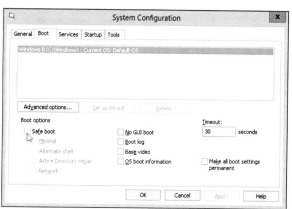

6 Check boot log: Log back in to Windows. Open the desktop and launch File Explorer. Navigate to the c:\Windows folder. Look for and open a file called ntbtlog.txt. This file shows all the Windows system files and drivers that are loading and not loading under Safe Mode.

7 Turn off Safe boot: At the Start screen, type **msconfig**. Click msconfig from the search results on the left page. From the System Configuration tool, click the Boot tab. Deselect the Boot log and Safe boot check boxes. Click OK. Restart Windows.

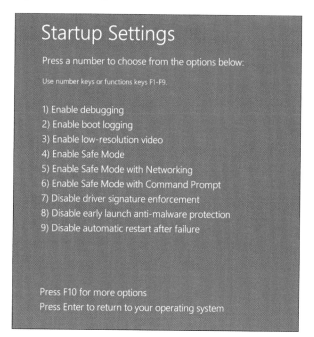

tip Choosing Safe Mode with Command Prompt lets you run specific commands. Type help at the command prompt to see a list of all commands.

8 Reboot into Safe Mode from Options menu: You can also boot into Safe Mode from the Advanced Boot Options menu. Open the Charms bar by holding down the Windows key and pressing C. Click the Settings charm, select PC settings, and then select General. Scroll to Advanced startup and click Restart now to load the options menu. Click the Troubleshoot option. Select Advanced options and then select Startup Settings. Click Restart. Windows reboots. Select the Safe Mode setting you wish to use.

Booting into the Options Menu

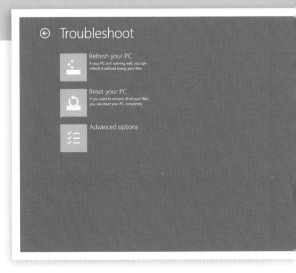

W indows 8 offers an Advanced Boot Options menu that provides options to refresh or reset your PC or perform more advanced tasks, such as restoring Windows from a restore point or system image, running an automatic repair of Windows, booting into a command prompt, and changing the start-up behavior of Windows. You can boot into this menu from the General section in the PC settings screen. But if Windows will not boot up due to a system or driver problem, how can you access the Advanced Boot Options menu? By using your Windows installation media and running a repair, you can access the options menu directly. This task explains how to boot into the Advanced Boot Options menu.

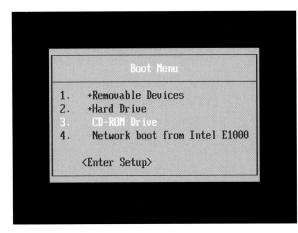

1 Boot from Windows installation media: Start your computer. Press the key to change the order of your boot devices. This key varies from PC to PC but may be Esc or F12, for example. Insert your Windows 8 installation disc into your CD/DVD drive. Choose the option to boot from CD-ROM/DVD drive. Press any key to boot from your CD or DVD.

tip If Windows cannot boot, you sometimes may have to try several recovery options.

2 Accept default options: Windows displays the setup screen. Click Next to accept the default options and move to the next screen.

3 Choose Repair option: At the next Windows Setup screen, click the Repair your computer link.

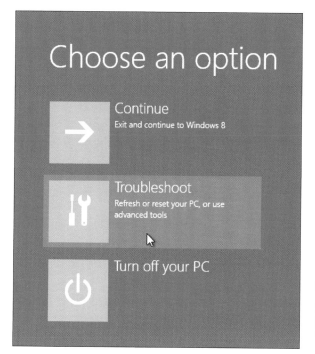

4 Choose option: Windows displays the Advanced Boot Options menu. Click Troubleshoot.

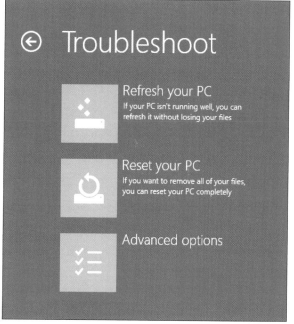

5 Try a refresh: From this menu, you can first try to refresh your PC.

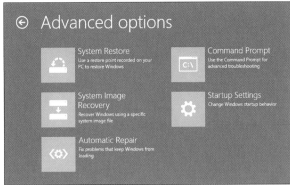

7 Choose an advanced option: From the Advanced options menu, you can attempt a system restore, system image recovery, or an automatic repair.

6 Try advanced options: If you are unable to refresh your PC, click Advanced options.

tip Resetting your PC should be the final option but one that should be able to restore Windows to a bootable state.

8 Try a reset: If none of those options works, boot back into the Options menu if it is not loaded. Select the Reset your PC option to try to reset your computer to a clean state.

Creating a Tile for the Options Menu

Windows 8 offers an Advanced Boot Options menu accessible upon reboot. This menu provides options to refresh or reset your PC or perform more advanced tasks, such as restoring Windows from a restore point or system image, running an automatic repair of Windows, booting into a command prompt, and changing the start-up behavior of Windows. You can boot into this menu from the General section in the PC settings screen. But a quicker option is to create a Start screen tile to reboot Windows directly into the menu. This task explains how to create a Start screen tile to launch the Advanced Boot Options menu.

1 Access the desktop: Launch the desktop from its Start screen tile.

tip You can run your new Restart to Options menu command either from its Start screen tile or from its desktop shortcut.

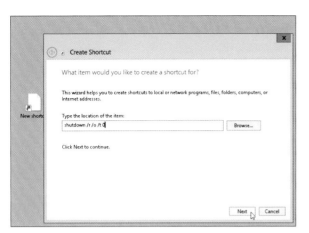

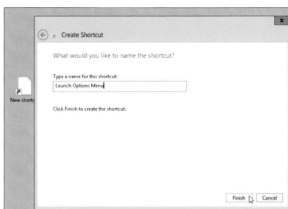

2 Create shortcut: Right-click the desktop. Select New from the pop-up menu and then select Shortcut. Type **shutdown /r /o /t 0** in the Type the location of the item field. Click Next.

3 Name it: Name the shortcut Launch Options menu. Click Finish.

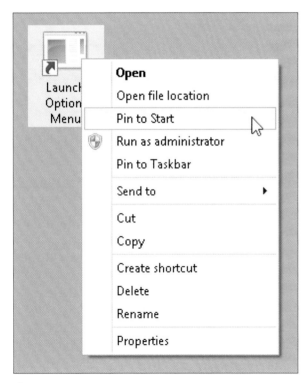

5 Restart Windows from Start screen: Return to the Start screen by pressing the Windows key or clicking the thumbnail in the lower-left hot corner. Move to the end of the Start screen. Click the Launch Options Menu tile.

4 Pin shortcut to Start screen: Right-click the shortcut. Select Pin to Start from the pop-up menu.

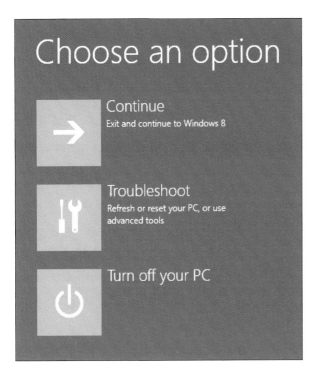

tip You can also access the Options menu by holding down the Shift key while you click Restart from the Power icon in the Settings pane.

6 Launch Advanced Boot Options menu: Windows 8 launches the Advanced Boot Options menu. From here, you can select the Troubleshoot option and then either refresh or reset your PC, or click Advanced options to view more choices to troubleshoot, restore, or recover your PC.

Running an Automatic Repair in Windows

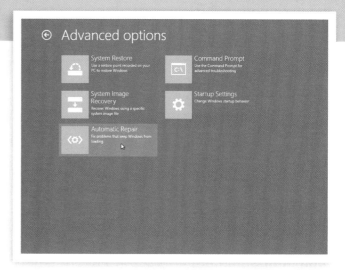

If Windows is having trouble loading, one option is to run an automatic repair. In cases like this, certain Windows start-up or system files may become lost or corrupted. The automatic repair attempts to analyze your Windows environment to determine why the operating system is not loading properly. Automatic repair is an option in the Advanced Boot Options menu. If Windows fails to load, it should automatically attempt a repair, or at least direct you to the Options menu where you can run a repair yourself. If Windows is intermittently not loading properly and you are able to boot up, you can boot into the Options menu from Windows and run the automatic repair manually. This task explains how to run an automatic repair from the Advanced Boot Options menu.

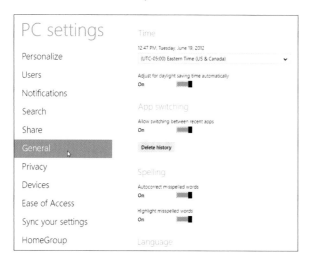

1 Open PC Settings: Hover over the lower-right hot corner to display the Charms bar. Click the Settings charm. Click Change PC Settings. In the PC Settings screen, click the General category.

tip If Windows cannot automatically repair your computer, then you may need to reset it instead.

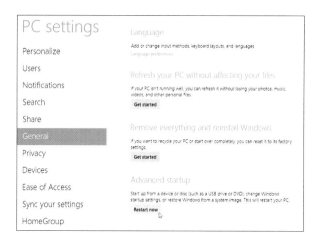

2 Choose Advanced startup: Scroll down the right side of the page of the General screen until you see Advanced startup. Click Restart now.

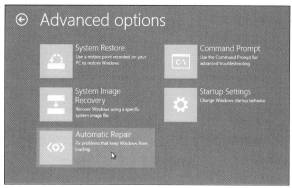

3 Select the Troubleshoot option: Windows quickly restarts and presents the Advanced Boot Options menu. Click the Troubleshoot button. Click the Advanced options button. Click Automatic Repair.

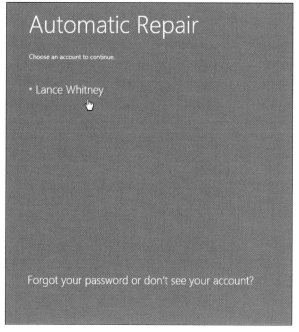

4 Choose account: Windows reboots and displays an Automatic Repair window. Click the name of your account to continue. At the next screen, type the account's password.

5 Wait for diagnosis: Windows displays a message that it is diagnosing your PC. If no problems are found or Windows cannot repair your PC, a message appears that Automatic Repair could not repair your PC. You can click Shut down to turn off your PC, or click Advanced options to return to the Options menu. If Windows is able to repair Windows, a message appears telling you that Windows was repaired.

Adding Another Language to Windows 8

Windows 8 supports a variety of languages beyond English. If you or other people in your home or office are more comfortable using a different language, you can add support for that language. Adding support for a specific language typically displays Windows buttons, menus, dialog boxes, and other objects in that language. It also lets you type characters in that language using a physical or on-screen keyboard. You can add support for more than one language to Windows and simply switch among the different keyboards for each language depending on who is using the PC. This task explains how to add another language to Windows 8.

1 Open Control Panel: Open the desktop. Hover your mouse in the lower-right hot corner to display the Charms bar. Click the Settings charm. Click Control Panel at the top of the pane.

2 Add a language: In the Clock, Language, and Region category, select the Add a language option. In the Change your language preferences window, click the Add a language command. Windows displays a list of languages.

3 Choose the language: Select the language you want to install — for example, Japanese. Click Add. If more than one region is available for a certain language, such as French or Italian, click Open. Choose the specific region and then click Add.

4 Add the language pack: A button for the new language appears. Click the Options link for the new language. If a language pack is available, you see a Download and install language pack link. Click that link. If a User Account Control message appears, click Yes to allow the program to make changes to this computer.

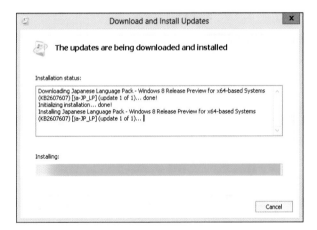

5 Wait for installation: The language pack is downloaded and installed.

6 Close update window: After the language pack is installed, Windows tells you that the installation is complete. Click Close. If a language pack is not available, click Cancel at the Options page.

7 Make the new language the primary one: Click the new language in the Language screen. Click Move up to make it the primary language. You can also click the Options link and select the option to make the new language the primary one. Close the Language window.

8 Log out of Windows: Log out of Windows and then log back in with your account. The Start screen tiles display in the new language. Click an app, such as Mail, Messaging, Weather, or Photos. The text is displayed in the new language. Open Internet Explorer. The web pages display in the new language.

10 Display the on-screen keyboard: Right-click any empty area of the taskbar. Move to the Toolbars command and select Touch Keyboard from the menu. Click the keyboard icon on the taskbar. The on-screen keyboard displays certain characters of the language currently set as the default.

9 Change the keyboard: Open the desktop by clicking its Start screen tile. A language icon appears in the system tray on the desktop. Click the icon to switch among the various language keyboards that have been installed.

11 Switch back to previous language: Open Control Panel. In the Clock, Language, and Region category, select the Add a language option. Click the setting for the previous language and click Move Up. Log out of Windows and then log back in. The previous language now displays.

12 Remove new language: Open Control Panel. In the Clock, Language, and Region category, select the Add a language option. Click the setting for the new language and click Remove to uninstall it.

tip You can also switch from one language keyboard to another by holding down the Windows key and pressing the spacebar.

Pooling Your Hard Drives with Storage Spaces

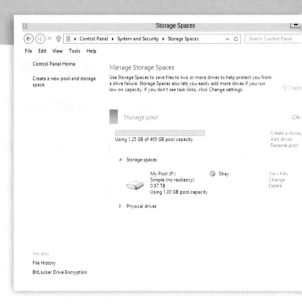

Storage Spaces is a feature new to Windows that lets you combine several physical drives into one pool of storage. For example, you can connect two or three external drives to your computer and use them all as one large virtual storage space. This feature gives you the ability to share your storage to house large groups of files, such as your entire music or video collection. It also lets you mirror your data, so that any content saved on one physical drive is also saved on another drive in the pool, offering you redundancy in case of a problem. If one drive fails, your data is still available on another drive in the pool. Storage Spaces provides different levels of redundancy depending on the number of physical drives that are part of the pool. This task explains how to pool your drives with Storage Spaces.

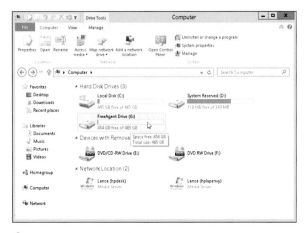

1 Connect a new drive: Connect one or more external drives to your Windows 8 computer.

2 Open Control Panel: Open the desktop. Hover your mouse in the lower-right hot corner to display the Charms bar. Click the Settings charm. Click Control Panel at the top of the pane.

3 Access Storage Spaces: Click the System and Security category and then select Storage Spaces.

4 Create a new pool and storage space: In the Manage Storage Spaces window, click the Create a new pool and storage space option. Click Yes if the User Account Control dialog box asks if you want to allow the following program to make changes to this computer.

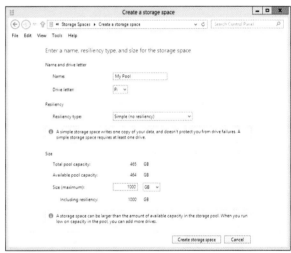

5 Select new drive: In the Select drives to create a storage pool window, you should see your new drive or drives listed. Select the check box in front of the first drive to select it. Click Create pool. A message appears that Windows is preparing drives and creating the pool.

6 Create name, type, and size: In the Enter a name, resiliency type, and size for the storage space window, type a name for your storage space in the Name field. Select a drive letter and then select the type of resiliency you want to use. Selecting each type from the drop-down menu displays a brief explanation. Type the amount of drive space for the pool. A message appears that Windows is creating and then formatting the storage space.

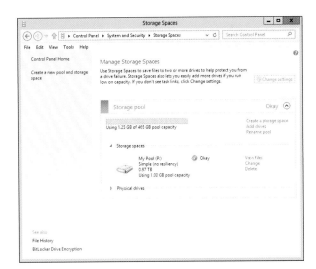

7 View storage space: After the storage space has been created, you can view it in the Manage Storage Spaces window. Depending on the resiliency type you choose, you can now start using the storage spool to directly store files, or use it as a mirror to automatically store multiple copies of your files.

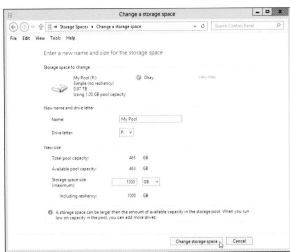

8 Change options: Click the Change link next to the storage space if you want to change any of the options. Then click Change storage space.

9 Add drive: Connect another drive. Click the Add drives link next to the Storage pool.

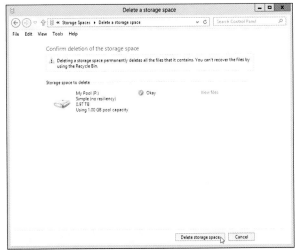

10 Delete storage space: Click the Delete link next to the storage space to delete it. Any files stored on the storage space are also deleted. Click Delete storage space.

tip *You need to use an external drive with ample storage, so a USB stick with only a few gigabytes of space will not suffice.*

11 Delete pool: If you no longer want to use the storage pool, click the Delete pool link to delete it.

Quick Fix

Freeing Up Disk Space

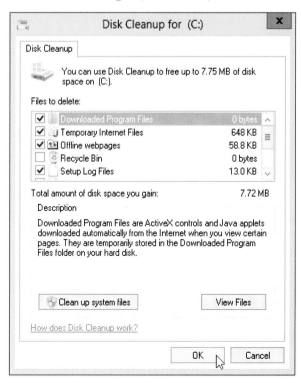

Open Control Panel. Click the System and Security category. In the Administrative Tools group, select the option to free up disk space. Select the drive you want to clean up if more than one drive exists. Windows runs the Disk Cleanup for your hard drive. Choose the types of files you want to remove. Click OK. Click Delete Files to confirm that you want to permanently delete these files.

Using the Windows 8 Remote Desktop App

The Remote Desktop feature in Windows lets you connect to and control a remote PC. This can be helpful if you need to access a computer in another location. You can also use the Remote Desktop feature to troubleshoot and resolve problems on a computer owned by a friend or family member or someone else in need of your expertise. Previous versions of Windows provide a Remote Desktop Connection desktop tool. But Windows 8 also offers a Windows 8 UI-based Remote Desktop app with many of the same features and functions. The computer that you access remotely is known as the host; the computer that you connect with is known as the guest. To serve as a Remote Desktop host, the Windows 8 PC must be running Windows 8 Professional. This task explains how to use the Windows 8 Remote Desktop app.

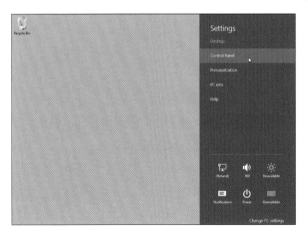

1 Open Control Panel: Boot up your host computer. On this computer, open the desktop. Hover your mouse in the lower-right hot corner to display the Charms bar. Click the Settings charm. Click Control Panel at the top of the pane.

tip To serve as a Remote Desktop host, the PC must be running Windows 8 Professional.

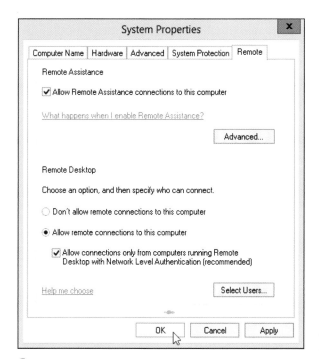

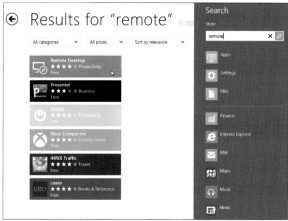

2 Set up access on host: From Control Panel, click the System and Security category. From the System section, select the Allow remote access option. In the System Properties window, select the Allow remote connections to this computer radio button. If you receive a message that the computer is set up to go to sleep or hibernation when not in use, click OK. Leave the Allow connections only from computers running Remote Desktop with Network Level Authentication check box selected. Click OK.

3 Find Remote Desktop app for guest: On the guest computer, open the Windows Store by clicking its Start screen tile. Hold down the Windows key and press Q to launch the search bar. Type the word **remote** and click the magnifying glass search icon. The Remote Desktop app appears among the search results in the left pane and under Recommendations in the right pane.

4 Install Remote Desktop app on guest: Click the app and then click Install to download and install it.

5 Launch Remote Desktop app: Return to the Start screen and move to the end of the screen. Click the Remote Desktop tile.

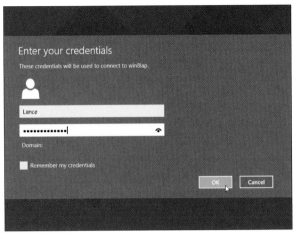

6 Connect to remote PC: In the bottom field of the Remote Desktop app, type the name or IP address of the host computer that you want to connect to. Click Connect.

7 Enter credentials: Type the username and password of the account you want to use on the remote PC. This should be an account with administrative privileges on the host computer.

tip Remember to log in with an account that has administrative privileges on the host computer.

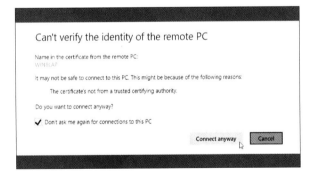

8 Verify PC: You may receive a message saying that Windows cannot verify the identity of the remote PC. Select the Don't ask me again for connections to this PC check box and click Connect anyway.

9 Use the remote PC: You should now be able to use your mouse and keyboard to navigate the remote PC, open applications, run commands, and work with files on the host computer.

10 Use the toolbar: Click the Remote Desktop toolbar at the top of the screen. Click the Home button to return to the Home screen of the Remote Desktop app. Click the Connection button to display the status of your connection. Click the Zoom button to zoom into the screen. Click the Start button to go to the Start screen on the remote PC. Click the App commands button to display the app bar.

11 Disconnect from remote PC: Click the Remote Desktop toolbar at the top middle of the screen. Click the X of the thumbnail for your current remote session to close and disconnect it. Close the Remote Desktop app.

Quick Fixes

Defragmenting Your Hard Drive

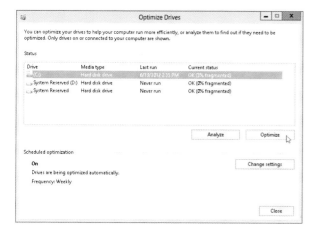

Open Control Panel. Click the System and Security category. Under Administrative Tools, select defragment and optimize your drives. Select the drive you want to defragment if more than one drive exists. Click Analyze. If the drive is severely defragmented, click Optimize.

Compressing a File

In File Explorer, right-click on the file you want to compress. Move your mouse to the Send to option and select Compressed (zipped) folder. The file is then compressed using the Zip format.

Using the Remote Desktop Connection Tool

The Remote Desktop Connection tool in Windows lets you connect to and control a remote PC. This can be helpful if you need to access a computer in another location. You can also use the RDC tool to troubleshoot and resolve problems on a computer owned by a friend or family member or someone else in need of your expertise. Windows 8 offers a Windows 8-based Remote Desktop app with the ability to connect to a remote PC. But the standard Remote Desktop Connection tool is also available if you do not want to use the Windows 8 version. To serve as a Remote Desktop host, the Windows 8 PC must be running Windows 8 Professional. This task explains how to use the standard Remote Desktop tool.

1 Open Control Panel on the host: Boot up the host computer. Open the desktop on the host computer. Hover your mouse in the lower-right hot corner to display the Charms bar. Click the Settings charm. Click Control Panel at the top of the pane.

tip To serve as a remote desktop host, the PC must be running Windows 8 Professional.

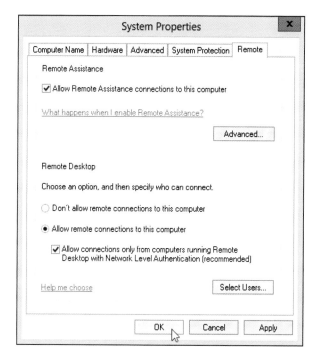

3 Open Remote Desktop Connection app: On the guest computer, open the Apps screen by right-clicking any empty area of the Start screen and clicking the All apps icon on the app bar. In the Windows Accessories category, click the Remote Desktop Connection tile.

2 Set up access on host: From Control Panel, click the System and Security category. From the System section, select the Allow remote access option. In the System Properties window, select the Allow remote connections to this computer radio button. Leave the Allow connections only from computers running Remote Desktop with Network Level Authentication check box selected. Click OK.

4 Connect to the remote computer: In the Remote Desktop Connection window, type the name or IP address of the host computer that you want to access. Click Connect.

5 Enter credentials: Type the username and password of the account you want to use on the remote PC. This should be an account with administrative privileges on the host computer.

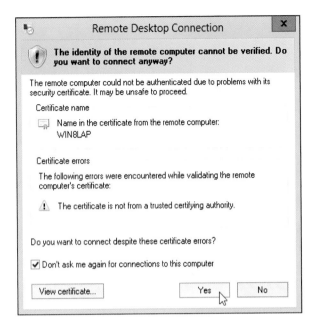

6 Verify PC: You may receive a message saying that Windows can't verify the identity of the remote computer. Select the Don't ask me again for connections to this computer check box and click Yes to connect.

7 Use the remote PC: You should now see the screen of the remote computer on the guest. You can use your mouse and keyboard to move around the screen, launch applications, and open files on the host computer.

tip If the toolbar disappears, hover your mouse at the top of the screen to make it reappear.

8 Open different features: Click the down arrow of the Remote Desktop Connection toolbar at the top. The App commands option displays the app bar, the Charms option displays the Charms bar, the Snap option snaps an application to the left or right, the Switch apps option switches to a different open app, and the Start option switches to the Start screen.

tip Click the pin button on the Remote Desktop Connection toolbar to turn off the display of the toolbar.

9 Close the Remote Desktop Connection: Click the X on the Remote Desktop Connection toolbar to disconnect from the remote computer. Windows displays a dialog box saying that your remote session will be disconnected. Click OK.

tip Double-click any empty area of the Remote Desktop Connection toolbar to switch between a full-screen window and a smaller window.

tip Click the Connection icon on the Remote Desktop Connection toolbar to display the status of your connection.

Quick Fix

Securing Your USB Drives with BitLocker

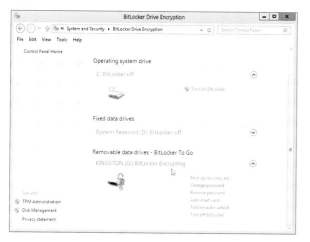

Open Control Panel. Click System and Security. Click BitLocker Drive Encryption. Insert the USB drive you want to encrypt. Click the name of the USB drive. Click Turn on BitLocker. Type a password to unlock the drive, noting the requirements. Type the password again. Click Next. Choose how you want to back up your recovery key. After the key has been backed up, click Next. Choose how much of the drive to encrypt. Click Next. Click the Start encrypting button. Click Close when the encryption is complete. Note that BitLocker is available only in Windows 8 Pro.

Installing Hyper-V to Create Virtual Machines

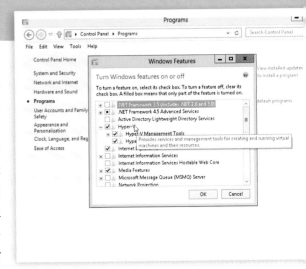

H yper-V is a feature that lets you create virtual machines to run other operating systems within Windows 8. With Hyper-V, you can set up, run, and manage multiple virtual machines for different versions of Windows or other operating systems. You may want to set up virtual machines to test applications and features from other operating systems or run applications that may not be compatible with Windows 8. Unfortunately, Hyper-V requires a certain type of processor and may not be compatible with older computers. It is also available only in Windows 8 Professional. For those of you with computers that can run this virtual machine tool, this task explains how to install Hyper-V.

1 Open Control Panel: Open the desktop. Hover your mouse in the lower-right hot corner to display the Charms bar. Click the Settings charm. Click Control Panel at the top of the pane.

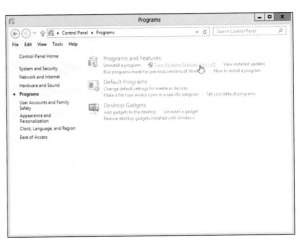

2 Turn Windows features on or off: From Control Panel, click the Programs category. Click the Turn Windows features on or off link under the Programs and Features section.

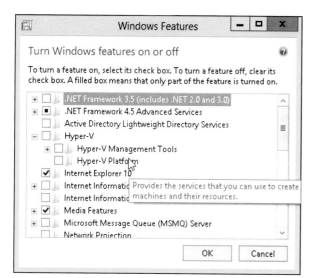

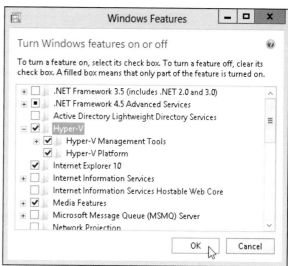

3 See if your PC qualifies for Hyper-V: Click the plus sign in front of Hyper-V. Hover your mouse over the Hyper-V Platform setting. If it is grayed out, a pop-up message appears that says "Hyper-V cannot be installed: The processor does not have the required virtualization capabilities." If this is the case, click OK or Cancel to close the Windows Features screen. If the setting is not grayed out, you can proceed to the next step.

4 Install Hyper-V: Select the Hyper-V check box. The check boxes for Hyper-V Management Tools and Hyper-V Platform are also selected. Click OK to install Hyper-V.

tip The next task explains how to use Hyper-V to create a virtual machine.

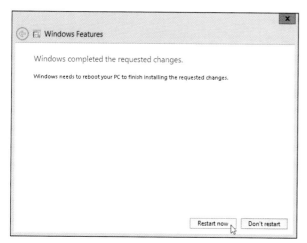

5 Restart PC: After Hyper-V is installed, a message appears that Windows completed the requested changes. Click Restart now to reboot your computer. Windows applies further changes and may reboot once more.

tip Hyper-V is available only in Windows 8 Professional.

6 View Hyper-V tiles: Log back in to Windows. Move to the right end of the Start screen. New tiles for Hyper-V Manager and Hyper-V Virtual Machine Connector appear.

Using Hyper-V to Create Virtual Machines

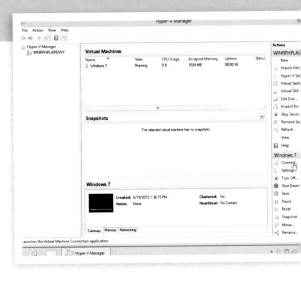

Hyper-V is a feature that lets you create virtual machines to run other operating systems within Windows 8. With Hyper-V, you can set up, run, and manage multiple virtual machines for different versions of Windows or other operating systems. You may want to set up virtual machines to test applications and features from other operating systems or run applications that may not be compatible with Windows 8. The previous task explains how to install Hyper-V, so follow that one if you have not yet installed it. For those who have installed Hyper-V in Windows 8, this task explains how to use the tool to create a virtual machine.

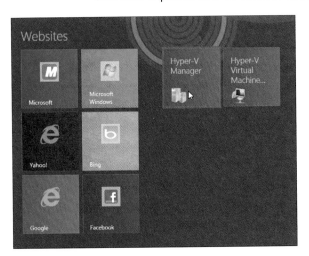

1 Launch Hyper-V: Move to the right end of the Start screen where you see tiles for Hyper-V Manager and Hyper-V Virtual Machine Connector. Click the Hyper-V Manager tile.

2 Create a virtual machine: In the Hyper-V Manager window, the name of your computer should already be highlighted in the left pane and in the Actions pane on the right. If it does not appear in the Actions pane, click the Connect to Server command in the Actions pane, select Local computer, and then click OK. From the Actions pane, click New, and then click Virtual Machine.

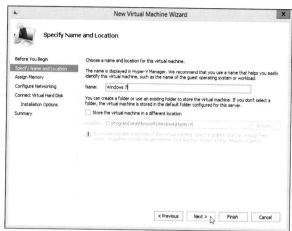

3 Start the New Virtual Machine Wizard: At the Before You Begin screen of the New Virtual Machine Wizard, click Next.

4 Specify name and location: At the Specify Name and Location screen, type a name for your virtual machine. For this example, it is assumed that you are creating a virtual machine for Windows 7. Type **Windows 7** in the Name field. Click Next.

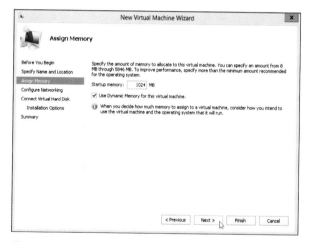

5 Assign memory: At the Assign Memory screen, set the amount of start-up memory to at least 1024MB. You can also select the Use dynamic memory for this virtual machine check box, which allocates available memory to your virtual machines as needed. Click Next.

6 Configure networking: At the Configure Networking screen, leave the Connection option as Not Connected. Click Next.

tip By clicking the Snapshot icon on the toolbar, you can take snapshots of the virtual machine to preserve it at certain states.

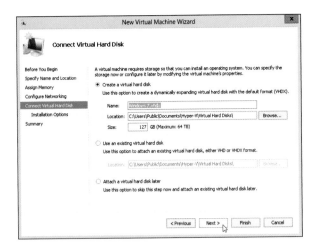

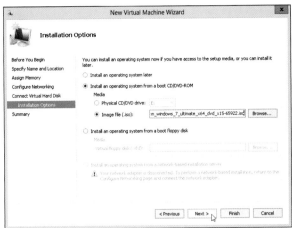

7 Connect virtual hard disk: At the Connect Virtual Hard Disk screen, type **Windows 7** in the Name field for the name of the VHDX file, if it is not already displayed. You do not need to type the vhdx extension; it is automatically added. Leave the other settings alone. Click Next.

8 Choose installation options: At the Installation Options screen, select the Install an operating system from a boot CD/DVD-ROM radio button. You can either select the Physical CD/DVD drive setting and insert your Windows 7 installation disc, or select the Image file (.iso) setting and point to a downloaded ISO file of Windows 7. After you make your choice, click Next.

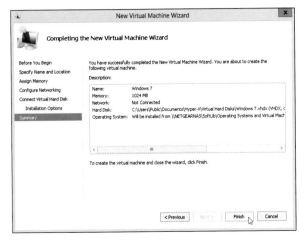

9 Review your options: At the Completing the New Virtual Machine Wizard screen, review your options. You can always click Previous to return to a prior screen and make any changes. If all the settings look correct, click Finish. Windows sets up the virtual disk for your operating system.

10 Start virtual machine: A new section appears in the lower-right pane with the name of your operating system (in this case, Windows 7). From this section, click Start, and then click Connect.

11 Install the operating system: The installation process for the operating system now appears in the virtual machine window. Click the appropriate screens and settings to install the OS.

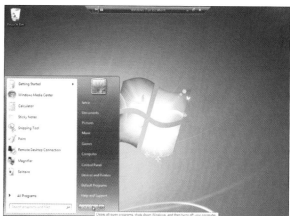

12 Shut down the operating system: After Windows 7 is installed and set up in the virtual machine, shut it down as you would normally; click the Start button and choose Shut down. You can then close the virtual window.

tip Hyper-V is available only in Windows 8 Professional.

13 Launch the operating system: To launch the operating system in the virtual machine again, click Start in the Windows 7 section in the lower-right pane, and then click Connect. Windows 7 launches in its virtual machine.

Inquiring Minds

Find answers to many of the questions and challenges faced by Windows 8 users.

PC settings

Personalize

Users

Notifications

Search

Share

General

Privacy

Devices

E

S

H

Windows Update

Lock screen   Start screen   Account picture

11:09
Thursday, July 26

ursday
26

en apps

Choose apps to run in the background and show quick status and notifications, even
your screen is locked

Search

Share

Start

Devices

Settings

Q & A

Q: How do I get past the Lock screen to access the login screen?

A: You can drag the Lock screen up with your mouse or simply press the spacebar or any other key on your keyboard.

Q: What is the purpose of the Lock screen?

A: The purpose of the Lock screen is to provide key information at a glance, so it displays the date and time as well as notifications for such apps as Mail and Calendar.

Q: I think I am typing the right password. Why is Windows not letting me log in?

A: You can confirm if you are typing the right password by clicking the eye icon to the left of the arrow at the login screen. That temporarily displays the characters of your password after you have typed them.

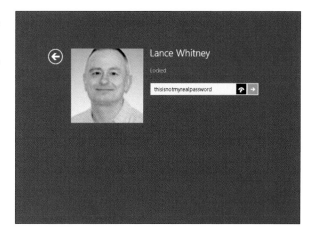

Q: Can I sign in to Windows 8 without being online?

A: Yes. You can sign in to Windows 8 offline with your Microsoft account or a local account. All local applications will work; those that require an Internet connection will obviously not run.

Q: Where is the Start button?

A: Microsoft removed the Start button from the desktop in Windows 8, replacing it with the Start screen, which offers tiles to launch both Windows 8 apps and desktop apps.

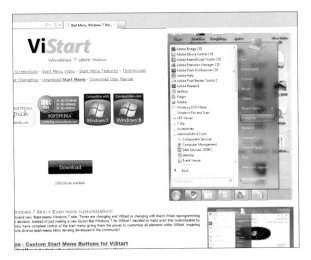

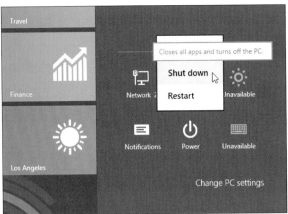

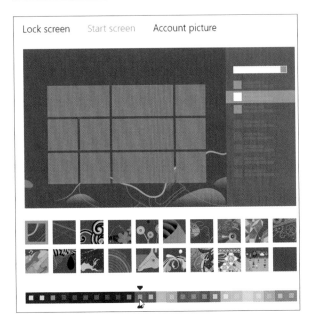

Q: How can I get the Start button back?

A: You cannot get the traditional Start button back. There are a few third-party utilities that replicate the classic Start button and menu, including StartMenu7 (www.startmenu7.com/index.html), ViStart (http://lee-soft.com/vistart), and Classic Shell (http://classicshell.sourceforge.net).

Q: Where is the Shut down option?

A: Because the Start button no longer exists, the Shut down option has been moved. Open the Charms bar from any screen in Windows 8, click the Settings charm, click the Power icon, and then select Shut down from the pop-up menu.

Q: Why can I not find an option to add my own image as background to the Start screen?

A: The Start screen allows you to only choose from a selection of background colors and styles; it does not let you use your own images.

Q: How can I view the date and time? It used to appear in the lower-right corner in Windows 7.

A: You can still see the date and time in the lower-right corner of the Windows 8 desktop. To view the date and time on the Start screen or other screens, hover your mouse over the Charms bar, and the date and time appear in the lower left.

Q: Where can I find the volume control in Windows 8?

A: The volume control icon appears in the system tray on the desktop. To access it in the Windows 8 environment, open the Charms bar from any screen, click the Settings charm, and then click the Volume Control icon. A vertical bar appears that you can use to adjust the volume.

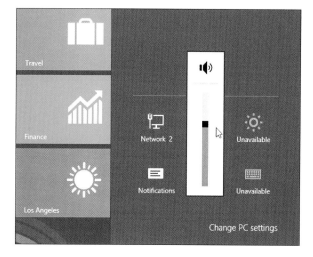

Q: What type of password protection does Windows 8 offer?

A: You can set up a regular text password, a PIN, and/or a picture password. A pin is a four-digit number that you can create. A picture password lets you draw gestures on any image of your choice in order to log in.

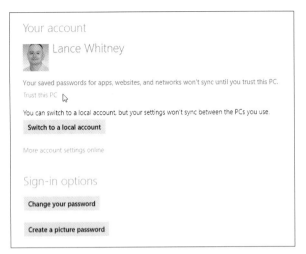

Q: Why does Windows 8 ask me to trust a PC?

A: Trusting a PC allows certain passwords to be synchronized among multiple Windows 8 computers.

Q: Can I resize a Start screen tile?

A: You cannot manually resize a tile as you can a desktop window, but you can change the size of a tile between a smaller square and a larger rectangle.

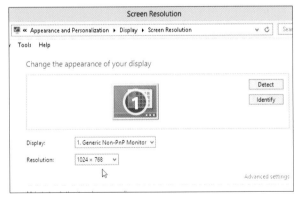

Q: Why does nothing happen when I try to launch a Windows 8 app?

A: The problem could be your screen resolution. Windows 8 apps require a screen resolution of 1024 × 768 or higher. To check your resolution, open the desktop, right-click on any empty area of the screen, and select the Screen resolution option in the pop-up menu.

Q: When I right-click an app from the Task Switcher, why do the Snap left and Snap right commands not appear?

A: The problem could be your screen resolution. Snapping an app requires a resolution of at least 1366 × 768.

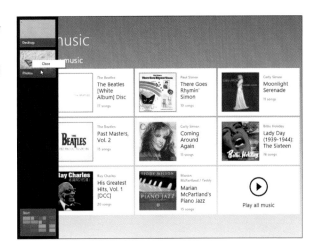

Q: Can desktop applications take advantage of live tiles?

A: No. Only specific Windows 8 apps can work as live tiles. Live tiles display the latest news, information, and content for specific apps, such as Mail, Calendar, Weather, and People.

Q: How do I minimize or close the Apps screen?

A: There is no way to minimize or close the Apps screen directly. You can leave the Apps screen and return to the Start screen by clicking on the Start screen thumbnail in the lower-left hot corner or pressing the Windows key. You can also switch to any open app by moving your mouse to the upper-right hot corner and clicking on the thumbnail for the app.

Q: When I hover over the thumbnail in the lower-left hot corner and move my mouse, why does the thumbnail disappear?

A: If you move your mouse too far diagonally or horizontally, the thumbnail disappears. Try moving your mouse just a small distance or moving it up; the thumbnail should remain on the screen, giving you time to click on it.

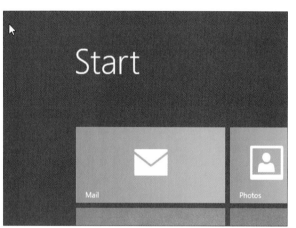

Q: When I move my mouse to the upper-left hot corner and then move it down, why can I not see the thumbnails for the open apps?

A: Keep your mouse cursor as close as possible to the left side of your screen when you move down, and you should be able to see the open apps.

Q: When I snap two Windows 8 apps side by side and try to snap a third, why is one of the existing apps replaced?

A: Windows 8 limits you to viewing only two Windows 8 apps at a time.

Q: Why can I not see individual desktop apps listed in the Task Switcher on the Windows 8 UI screen?

A: The Windows 8 Task Switcher shows your entire desktop with a single thumbnail because the desktop is considered a single app. You can click on the desktop thumbnail to access the entire desktop and then switch to an individual application.

Q: How can I see all the programs currently running?

A: Press Ctrl+Shift+Esc to open the Task Manager, which displays a list of all running programs. You can open the Task Manager either from the desktop or from the Windows 8 environment.

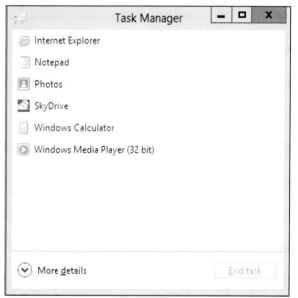

Q: Where is Windows Media Center?

A: Media Center is available only as a separate media pack. You need to be running Windows 8 Pro, and then you can purchase and download the Windows 8 Media Center Pack.

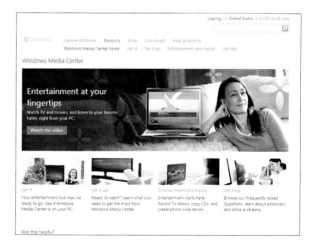

Q: Windows Media Player will not let me play a DVD. Why not?

A: To play a DVD in Media Player, you need to purchase and upgrade to Windows 8 Pro if you do not already have it, and then download the Media Center Pack.

Q: When I open the Windows 8 Music Player and load a CD, why does it want to take me to Windows Media Player?

A: The Windows 8 Music Player only plays digital music stored in your library; it cannot play CDs.

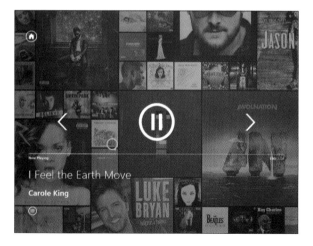

Q: Can I play my iTunes music through the Windows 8 Music app or Windows Media Player?

A: Yes. Both the Windows 8 Music app and Windows Media Player support the M4A or AAC format used by iTunes. However, you will probably run into trouble trying to play protected music.

Q: How do I print from a Windows 8 app? I do not see a print menu or command.

A: You print from Windows 8 apps by selecting the Devices charm from the Charms bar. Choose your printer from the Devices list and then click the Print button.

Q: How do I e-mail or share content from a Windows 8 app?

A: You can e-mail or share content from Windows 8 apps by selecting the Share charm from the Charms bar. From the Share charm, select the app you wish to use for sharing, such as Mail or People. The app opens for you to share your content. You can only share content from certain Windows 8 apps, such as Photos, Music, SkyDrive, and Internet Explorer.

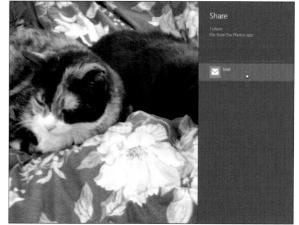

Q: I logged in to Windows 8. Why can I not see any of my SkyDrive photos, Facebook photos, or other online content?

A: Make sure you have logged in with your Microsoft account and not a local account, and make sure that you are online.

Q: Why is the Messaging app not letting me chat with a Facebook friend?

A: The friend must be logged in to Facebook with Facebook chat status set to online for a chat to be possible. If not, you should see a message telling you that you cannot send a message to an offline Facebook friend.

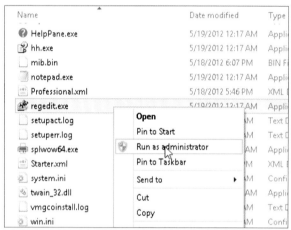

Q: How do I run a file or program as an Administrator?

A: Right-click on the file, and select Run as administrator in the pop-up menu.

Q: Do I need to install antivirus software in Windows 8?

A: No. Windows 8 includes Windows Defender for antivirus security and a firewall to monitor incoming and outgoing traffic. But you can install a third-party antivirus or security program if you want.

Q: When I try to use Remote Desktop Connection to connect to a host PC, why does it refuse to connect?

A: Make sure you have enabled Remote Desktop Connection on the host PC. To do this, open Control Panel and click the System and Security setting. Under the System category, select the Allow Remote Access option and then select the Allow remote connections to this computer setting.

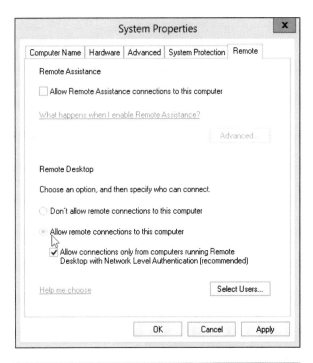

Q: Can I minimize the Ribbon in File Explorer?

A: Yes. Just click the Minimize Ribbon button in the upper-right corner.

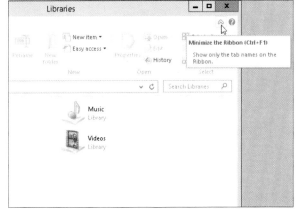

Q: I installed an app but cannot find it. How can I track it down?

A: Open the Apps screen by right-clicking on the Start screen and look for the app. You can also type the name of the app at the Start screen to search for it.

Q: Why can I not reposition a pinned website in Windows 8 IE10?

A: The Windows 8 version of IE10 does not let you reorganize or sort your pinned websites. You can, however, sort your website tiles on the Start screen.

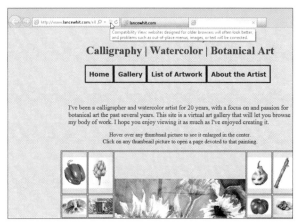

Q: How can I view a website in compatibility mode in Internet Explorer 10?

A: In the desktop version of Internet Explorer 10, click the Compatibility View button in the address bar. You can also press the Alt key to display the browser's menus. Click the Tools menu and then click the option for Compatibility View.

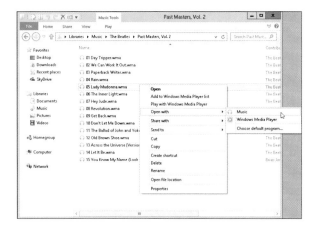

Q: How do I choose the application that I want to use to open a particular type of file?

A: Right-click on the file, choose Open with in the pop-up menu, and then select the application you want to use to open the file.

Q: Can I still manage my start-up programs using msconfig?

A: No. In Windows 8 you manage your start-up programs using the Task Manager.

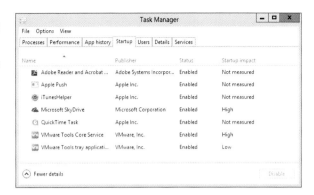

Q: Does Windows 8 offer an XP mode as in Windows 7?

A: No, but Windows 8 does offer a feature called Hyper-V, which lets you run Windows XP and other operating systems in a virtual environment.

Q: What is the difference between refreshing and resetting Windows?

A: Refreshing Windows keeps your Windows 8 apps and your files and documents but does not retain your desktop apps or your PC settings. Resetting Windows brings it back to a clean slate with none of your apps, files, or documents retained.

Q: Will all my Windows 7 applications and hardware run in Windows 8?

A: According to Microsoft, any program or device that runs under Windows 7 should work in Windows 8, though you may need to update or reinstall certain software after you install Windows 8.

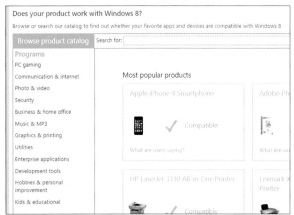

Q: How can I determine if my current software and devices will be compatible with Windows 8?

A: You can check Microsoft's Windows 8 Compatibility Center at www.microsoft.com/en-us/windows/compatibility/en-us/compatcenter/home.

Q: Why does my version of Windows 8 not let me connect to my company's domain?

A: You may be running Windows 8 (standard). Only Windows 8 Professional and Enterprise let you connect to a domain.

Q: I am dual-booting Windows 8 with another version of Windows. Why can I not see the Windows 8 boot menu?

A: You need to make sure Windows 8 is the default option in a dual-boot setup.

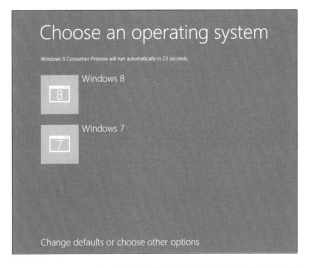

Q: What are the differences between a Microsoft account and a local account?

A: A Microsoft account can automatically synchronize key settings, customizations, passwords, and other content across multiple PCs. It also lets you easily access your online accounts and apps. A local account does not require you to set up a dedicated online account. But it will not let you sync settings across multiple computers, and it does require you to manually log in when accessing SkyDrive and other online services.

Q: Can I switch my Microsoft account to a local account, or vice versa?

A: Yes. You can switch either way.

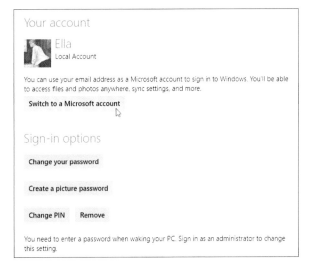

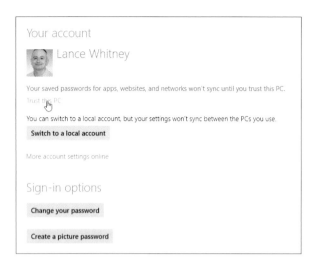

Q: **Will a Microsoft account synchronize my Windows 8 settings and other content with PCs running Windows 7, Vista, or XP?**

A: No. Synchronization only works with PCs running Windows 8.

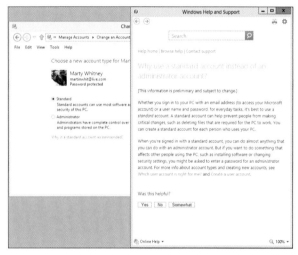

Q: **What is the difference between a Standard account and an Administrator account?**

A: A Standard account limits your access to certain folders and settings and to other accounts on the PC. An Administrator account gives you the ability to manage all accounts on the PC.

Q: **Should I set up an account as Standard or Administrator?**

A: You should set up one account as an Administrator and then you can set up the rest as Standard to limit their access.

Q: How many editions of Windows 8 are available?

A: Windows 8 (standard) and Windows 8 Pro are designed for PCs and tablets powered by Intel chips. Windows 8 Enterprise is available for PCs for companies with enterprise agreements.

Q: What are the differences between Windows 8 Pro and Windows 8 Enterprise?

A: Windows 8 Enterprise includes Windows To Go, DirectAccess, BranchCache, and AppLocker, which Windows 8 Pro does not. Otherwise, the two editions offer virtually the same features.

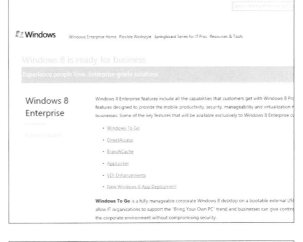

Q: Can I upgrade from Windows 8 to Windows 8 Pro?

A: Yes. You would need to purchase and download the Windows 8 Pro Pack.

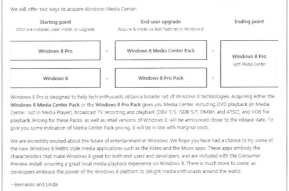

Downloading and installing

⌄ What are the system requirements for Windows 8 Release Preview?

Windows 8 Release Preview works great on the same hardware that powers Windows 7:

- **Processor:** 1 gigahertz (GHz) or faster

- **RAM:** 1 gigabyte (GB) (32-bit) or 2 GB (64-bit)

- **Hard disk space:** 16 GB (32-bit) or 20 GB (64-bit)

- **Graphics card:** Microsoft DirectX 9 graphics device with WDDM driver

  Additional requirements to use certain features:

- To use touch, you need a tablet or a monitor that supports multitouch.

- To access the Windows Store and to download and run apps, you need an active Internet connection and a screen resolution of at least 1024 x 768.

- To snap apps, you need a screen resolution of at least 1366 x 768.

- Internet access (ISP fees might apply)

Q: Can I upgrade directly to Windows 8 from Windows 7, Vista, or XP?

A: You can upgrade from Windows 7, and all your applications, files, and settings are retained. You can upgrade from Windows Vista with Service Pack 1, and your personal files and settings are retained. Without SP1, only your personal files are retained. You can upgrade from Windows XP with SP3, but only your personal files are retained.

Q: What are the system requirements for Windows 8?

A: A 1 GHz or faster processor, at least 1GB of RAM for the 32-bit edition (2GB for the 64bit edition), 16GB of free hard drive space for the 32-bit edition (20GB for the 64-bit edition), and a Microsoft DirectX 9 graphics device are required. A screen resolution of at least 1024 × 768 is needed to run Windows 8 apps, while a resolution of at least 1366 × 768 is needed to snap apps.

Windows 8 Keyboard Shortcuts

Windows 8 offers a variety of keyboard shortcuts to help PC users navigate the new interface and launch different features and commands. Though you can certainly get around using just a mouse, you will probably find it helpful to learn and rely on certain keyboard shortcuts. This section lists the new keyboard shortcuts introduced in Windows 8 along with some of the familiar shortcuts that have long been part of Windows.

Windows 8 UI Shortcuts

Table A.1 details keyboard shortcuts for the Windows 8 UI.

Table A.1 Windows 8 UI Shortcuts

Shortcut	Description
Windows	Go to Start screen, or toggle between Start screen and last app
Right arrow	Move right one tile on Start screen
Left arrow	Move left one tile on Start screen
Down arrow	Move down one tile on Start screen
Up arrow	Move up one tile on Start screen
Home	Move to first tile on Start screen
End	Move to last tile on Start screen
Tab	Switch between Start screen tile and profile name and picture in upper-right corner
Ctrl+-	Zoom out
Ctrl++	Zoom in
Windows+=	Turn on Magnifier
Windows++	Zoom in with Magnifier
Windows+-	Zoom out with Magnifier
Windows+Z	Display app bar in current Windows 8 app
Windows+Tab	Cycle through all open apps on Switch List bar
Alt+Tab	Cycle forward through all open apps in center window
Alt+Shift+Tab	Cycle backward through all open apps in center window
Windows+Q	Search
Ctrl+P	Print from current app
Windows+P	Connect to second screen or projector
Windows+L	Lock PC

Ctrl+Esc	Switch between Start screen and last app
Windows+,	Peek at desktop
Windows+D	Go to the desktop

Charms Bar Shortcuts

Table A.2 details keyboard shortcuts for the Charms bar.

Table A.2 Charms Bar Shortcuts

Shortcut	Description
Windows+C	Display Charms bar
Windows+Q	Display Search charm
Windows+H	Display Share charm
Windows+K	Display Devices charm
Windows+I	Display Settings charm

Search Shortcuts

Table A.3 details keyboard shortcuts for searching.

Table A.3 Search Shortcuts

Shortcut	Description
Windows+W	Search settings
Windows+F	Search files

Windows 8 App Shortcuts

Table A.4 details keyboard shortcuts for Windows 8 apps.

Table A.4 Windows 8 App Shortcuts

Shortcut	Description
Windows+.	Snap current Windows 8 app to the right and then cycle to left and full screen
Windows+Shift+.	Snap current Windows 8 app to the left and then cycle to right and full screen
Alt+F4	Close the current app
Alt+D	Display address bar in Internet Explorer
Ctrl+E	Select search box in Internet Explorer

Desktop Shortcuts

Table A.5 details keyboard shortcuts for the Windows desktop.

Table A.5 Desktop Shortcuts

Shortcut	Description
Windows+M	Minimize all open windows on the desktop
Windows+Shift+M	Restore all minimized windows on desktop
Alt+Esc	Cycle through all open windows
Windows+T	Preview open windows in taskbar
Alt	Show the hidden menu bar in a desktop application
Shift+Delete	Permanently delete a file or other item
Ctrl+N	Open new window in File Explorer
Ctrl+W	Close current window in File Explorer
Ctrl+Shift+N	Create new folder in File Explorer
Alt+F4	Open Shut Down Windows dialog box
F1	Display Help

Miscellaneous Shortcuts

Table A.6 details keyboard shortcuts for miscellaneous features.

Table A.6 Miscellaneous Shortcuts

Shortcut	Description
Ctrl+Shift+Esc	Open Windows Task Manager
Windows+X	Open Power User Tasks menu
Windows+E	Open File Explorer
Windows+R	Open the Run command
Windows+U	Open Ease of Access Center
Windows+Enter	Open Windows Narrator
PrintScrn	Take screenshot of current screen
Alt+PrintScrn	Take screenshot of active window in desktop environment
Windows+PrntScrn	Take screenshot and save to Pictures folders
Ctrl+A	Select all files or other objects in a window
Ctrl+X	Cut selected file
Ctrl+C	Copy selected file
Ctrl+V	Paste copied or cut file
Ctrl+Z	Undo last action
Ctrl+Y	Redo last action

Windows 8 offers certain hidden methods to display key features, such as the Charms bar and the Switch List bar. You can trigger these features by moving your mouse to various hot corners around the screen. This section lists the mouse movements that you can use to launch these features.

Table B.1 details mouse movements to launch certain Windows 8 features.

Table B.1 Mouse Movements

Shortcut	Description
Move to the bottom-left hot corner	Display shortcut to Start screen or previous app
Move to the top- or bottom-right hot corner	Display the Charms bar
Move to the upper-left hot corner	Display shortcut to next active application
Move to the upper-left hot corner and move down	Display the Switch List bar with shortcuts to all open apps
Move to the bottom-left hot corner and right-click mouse	Open the Power User Tasks menu

Resources

T he web provides a wealth of information on Windows 8, from Microsoft's own websites to those of many third parties. You can learn about the latest developments in Windows 8 from informational sites and ask questions and discuss the operating system at a variety of discussion forums.

Informational Websites

Here are several websites where you can find information on Windows 8.

Windows

A Microsoft site with product information on Windows and related programs: http://windows.microsoft.com.

Windows blog

A series of blogs from the folks at Microsoft with the latest news, updates, and stories on Windows. From this page you can access all of the different blogs on Windows and related products: http://blogs.windows.com.

Windows 8

News, downloads, and other resources on Windows 8 from Microsoft: http://technet.microsoft.com/windows-8.aspx.

Windows videos

Various videos from Microsoft's Windows blogs: www.microsoft.com/en-us/showcase/categoryDetails.aspx?catid=products&subcatid=windows.

Microsoft News Center

Microsoft's News Center site with press releases and similar information on Windows and other products: www.microsoft.com/news.

Microsoft support

Microsoft's support website: http://support.microsoft.com.

Microsoft contact support

A Microsoft site where you can ask questions about Windows and other products and receive automated responses: http://support.microsoft.com/contactus.

Windows Facebook page

Microsoft's official Facebook page for Windows: https://www.facebook.com/windows.

Windows Twitter page

Microsoft's official Twitter account for Windows: https://twitter.com/windows.

Microsoft Support Twitter page

Microsoft Support's Twitter page where you can get help on Windows and other Microsoft products: https://twitter.com/microsofthelps.

Windows 8 compatibility center

Search for your current applications and hardware to determine if it is all compatible with Windows 8: www.microsoft.com/en-us/windows/compatibility/en-us/compatcenter/home.

The Windows Club

Stories on Windows 8 and other Microsoft products: www.thewindowsclub.com.

Windows 8 Hacks

Tips, tricks, and tutorials on Windows 8: www.windows8hacks.com.

Discussion Forums

Here are several discussion forums where you can ask questions and get help on Windows 8 issues.

Microsoft Answers

Ask questions about Windows 8 and other Microsoft products: http://answers.microsoft.com.

Windows Eight Forums

A discussion forum broken down into different categories, including Installation & Setup, Network & Sharing, and Software & Apps: www.eightforums.com.

Windows 8 Forums

Another discussion forum with different categories where you can ask and answer questions: www.forumswindows8.com.

Windows 8 Forums

Another Windows 8 discussion forum: http://windows8forums.com.

Windows 8 Forum

A community for discussions about Windows 8: http://eightforum.com.

Windows 8 Forums

A site with articles and forums on Windows 8: www.win8forums.com.

My Digital Life Forums Windows 8 Discussions

A forum page with announcements and conversation threads on Windows 8: http://forums.mydigitallife. info/forums/42-windows-8.

CNET's Windows 8 Forum

A Windows 8 forum run by CNET: http://forums.cnet.com/windows-8-forum.

Utilities

Here are a few websites where you will find certain utilities that can enhance Windows 8.

Windows8 StartMenu

A free gadget that replicates the old Windows Start menu: http://windows8startmenu.codeplex.com.

ViStart

Another utility that replicates and enhances the traditional Windows Start menu: www.lee-soft.com/ vistart.

Stardock's Start8

A utility that provides a Start button to access the Start screen and other features: www. stardock.com/products/start8.

Advanced Boot Options menu A menu that lets you troubleshoot problems, refresh or reset your PC, or restore it from a restore point or image file.

app A shorthand term for a software application.

app bar A bar that appears at the bottom or top of the screen in the Start screen and in Windows 8 apps with icons to launch certain features and options.

app switching A feature that lets you switch from one Windows 8 app to another.

Automatic Repair A feature that tries to fix boot-up problems in Windows by restoring key system and start-up files.

BitLocker A feature that encrypts your hard drive or an external device to protect it from unauthorized access.

charm An icon that appears on the Charms bar providing access to specific features, including Search, Share, Start, Devices, and Settings.

Charms bar A bar that appears on the right side of the Start screen, Apps screen, desktop, and other screens in Windows 8, offering access to various "charms," or icons for searching, sharing, devices, and settings.

contracts A feature used by developers that lets Windows 8 apps and features share certain information and capabilities with each other.

desktop The traditional desktop familiar to Windows users, but now set up as an app within Windows 8.

Devices A charm that lets you send content to printers and other devices.

Ease of Access A series of features designed to enhance the screen or turn on a Narrator for people who may have vision problems.

Family Safety A Windows feature that lets parents set certain limits on the accounts used by their children.

File history A feature in Windows 8 that automatically backs up key files and documents at specific intervals, giving you the opportunity to restore a file that may be lost or corrupted.

flip A way to visually flip through different open apps until you find the one you want to open.

groups A method to organize different Start screen tiles into their own unique sections.

homegroup A local virtual network that you can set up, allowing different Windows PCs to share files and devices among each other.

Hyper-V A Microsoft tool that lets you create and run virtual machines in Windows 8.

live tile A tile that displays new information as it arrives, such as new e-mail messages or news headlines.

local account An account specific to your PC that does not offer direct access to Microsoft's online services or let you sync settings across multiple Windows 8 PCs.

Lock screen The screen that first appears when you boot up Windows, displaying a background picture and notifications.

Microsoft account An account that gives you direct access to various online Windows services and lets you sync key settings and other information across multiple Windows 8 PCs.

notifications Alerts that appear on the Lock screen and Start screen when you have new e-mail, new calendar appointments, or other new information.

PC settings A new Windows 8 UI screen with several categories for various settings to configure and customize Windows 8.

picture password A new type of password that lets you log in by creating and re-creating gestures on an image.

PIN A new feature in Windows 8 that lets you create a four-digit PIN to use as a password.

Power User Tasks menu A menu that appears when you right-click on the lower-right hot corner, offering links to Control Panel, Task Manager, Command Prompt, and other "power user" features. Microsoft has not officially given this menu a name, but unofficially it has been dubbed the Power User Tasks menu.

Refresh A feature that lets you restore Windows 8 without losing your Windows 8 UI files and settings.

Remote Desktop A feature in Windows that lets you connect to and control another computer.

Reset A feature that lets you restore Windows 8 back to a clean slate but does not retain any of your files or settings.

restore point A snapshot of your Windows environment, which you can restore in the event of a problem.

Search A charm that lets you search for apps, files, and settings in Windows 8, and content within certain Windows 8 apps.

Semantic Zoom A feature that lets you zoom in and out of the tiles on your Start screen.

Settings A charm that provides access to various system settings, such as Wi-Fi, audio volume, screen brightness, notifications, and power.

Share A charm that lets you share content from certain Windows 8 apps via e-mail or instant messaging.

SkyDrive Microsoft's cloud-based storage and synchronization service, which lets you store files online and sync them among multiple computers.

Start A charm that returns you to the Start screen.

Start screen The replacement for the traditional Start menu, offering tiles to launch different apps and features.

Startup program An application that automatically launches into memory after Windows loads.

Storage Spaces A new feature in Windows 8 that lets you tie together external hard drives and other devices as pooled storage.

Task Manager A familiar Windows tool that lets you view and shut down open applications and processes, redesigned in Windows 8 to provide more details and options.

Task Switcher A sidebar that appears on the left of a Windows 8 UI, which lets you switch from one open app to another.

tile An icon in the Windows 8 UI that lets you launch an app or Windows feature.

virtual machine A way of running one operating system within another by using virtual machine software, such as Hyper-V.

Windows Defender The antivirus software used by Windows 8.

Windows Experience Index A tool used to determine the performance of your PC in processing power, memory, graphics, and hard drive transfer speed.

Windows to Go A feature in Windows 8 Enterprise that lets you store your Windows 8 environment on a USB stick and run it on another PC.

Windows Media Center An application that lets you view photos and videos, play music, and watch and record live TV, but which is available only as an extra paid option in Windows 8.

Windows Store Microsoft's online store where you can download free and paid Windows 8 apps and connect to third-party websites to download traditional desktop applications.

Windows update A feature that can automatically update Windows with the latest patches and fixes.

Index